THE TALKING FOREST

*Tree Runes
for a New Millennium*

KAY BROOME

Text: Kay Broome
Cover Design: Aaron Davis
Interior Design & Layout: Danielle Smith-Boldt

ISBNs:
978-1-7771170-1-6 (Paperback)
978-1-7771170-0-9 (eBook)

Foreword

Since this is a book introducing a completely new system of divination, this foreword is intended to clarify a few points. The book is written out of a love for the trees of my homeland, Canada. Its intent is to fill a gap in the Pagan lexicon, since there seemingly are no oracles using trees as their exclusive symbols.

The book is organized into three sections: Section I introduces the reader to the system, explaining its development and the various designs. Section II introduces the reader to each individual rune and the history and folklore of the tree it represents. Section III explains various methods of how to read the runes.

Some points of reference on the text. The names of the Talking Forest runes are the same as the trees they represent. The Talking Forest runic names are *always* capitalized, but names of actual tree species are generally not. The first page of each chapter in Section II shows the kenning or the esoteric metaphor for that particular rune in italics and the rune's meaning in regular text.

The reader will also notice that the Talking Forest runes follow a sequence corresponding to the human life cycle. This is not as strange as it may sound. Indeed, one major goal of all divination systems is to examine salient aspects of the human condition. Moreover, trees have had a profound influence on human history and culture. It is therefore appropriate that the Talking Forest array mirrors the human life cycle from cradle to grave. The set is divided into six sections, or *groves,* loosely following the ages of man from childhood to youth and prime of life into the elder years. These groves will be discussed at intervals throughout Section II.

Finally, a note for those readers who are new to paganism. Throughout this book, witches, witchcraft and the horned god are mentioned frequently. As there is still so much misinformation and disfavour surrounding these terms, it is necessary to clarify them.

When I mention witches and their working, I am not referring to Satanists or devil worshippers. The term instead references the practitioners of modern-day Wicca and other Earth-based religions that worship gods of nature, as well as those historical followers of various folk religions of western and northern Europe which contain shamanistic elements.

The horned god references neither the devil nor Satan nor Baphomet (the latter possibly an invention of knights of some obscure Christian sects during the Crusades). Instead, this title alludes to various traditional pagan gods of nature such as Pan, Herne and Cernunnos, who were generally portrayed as having horns or antlers.

THE FOREST FOR THE TREES

INTRODUCTION

A Seed is Planted

Trees are Earth's largest organisms. They neither walk nor talk, nor converse in any palpable way, yet they engage us like no other living thing. Trees connect the only three kingdoms that really matter: branches reach to the distant Sky; roots dig deep into the realm of Earth and trunks draw their sap from the same underground Water that forms the rivers, lakes and oceans which sustain us.

Earth's great boreal and rain forests create our weather; each tree gathering carbon dioxide into its leaves to later release the oxygen animals need to breathe. Further condensation from these leaves results in clouds that provide life-giving rain.

Trees guard the soil, their roots gouging deep into clay and rock, milling it over time into fine, rich tilth. Gale-tossed branches, wind-fallen fruit and autumn leaves all become the humus that nourishes the soil and feeds insects, fungi and other tiny beings crucial to all life.

Forests guard our waterways. The same tree roots that help create soil keep it from eroding further, leaving rivers and lakes clean and lively with fish and other aquatic species. Plants indigenous to the water's edge protect and purify the watershed.

Trees profoundly affect the human psyche. Old trees in particular lend a sense of continuity and a social and historical resonance to their surroundings. Large trees have been found to reduce crime and conflict within communities by giving residents a more secure sense of belonging. Indeed, a street without trees is not a neighbourhood.

Humans and trees share a single trait unique in all of nature: uprightness, or "a vertical perspective" of the world.[1] But while we look most often to the heavens and stars for answers to life's mysteries, the trees find truth not only in the sky, but also in the underworld in which they are rooted. Early peoples knew this and thus sought out trees to disclose these hidden secrets. Shamans of nomadic cultures communicated with the gods by climbing into a tall birch or larch, seeking illumination from the stars in the sky. These shamans also toured the Underworld where dwelt their dead ancestors, using wood from the same revered trees to build a sacred space.

The British Celts were famed for their *nemetons,* huge groves serving as natural outdoor temples. And just about every tree species in Europe appears to have been associated with the witches' sabbat: elder, rowan, hawthorn, ash, walnut. Indeed, the list of trees that witches graced with their dancing and merry-making is long and illustrious.

Now, however, it is possible that the Tree of Life will soon topple. With the reality of unprecedented natural disasters happening every day somewhere on Earth, only a fool still denies the effects of man-made climate change. Religious fanaticism, reckless science and militarism gone mad, coupled with the lack of will to confront the many problems facing us, all this may eventually signal the end of life as we know it.

Yet still there are forests that stand as islands of calm and sanity. Oases of paradise, their silent mysteries hang just out of reach. In a world becoming increasingly hostile and alienating, more people, pagan and otherwise, are seeing trees as treasured heirlooms, gradually awakening to their venerable powers. And renewed contact with local parks and forests are at least a beginning in our quest toward a more purposeful life.

My own woodland sojourns over the last 30 years helped lead me to the creation of a new runic system based on trees of our North American woodlands. This book is the result of my research.

Soil:
A Note on Divining

Divination is one tool that can help us move toward spiritual rebirth and a bonding with Mother Earth. A system of augury based on local tree species can help provide a subconscious link to the entities they represent, unlocking their secrets of wisdom and harmony.

Along with Tarot cards and prayer beads, reading or casting runes is a type of *sortilege* (fittingly from the same root as the French word *sorcièr,* or "witch"). This technique of divination consists of choosing one or more items from among a group of related objects.

With all the mundane worries, tasks and obligations in our lives, it is no wonder that the conscious mind often gets in the way of our quest for enlightenment. By using a deck of Tarot cards, runes or other tools, we are in fact stilling the conscious mind, letting the subconscious take over to answer whatever question we have put forward. Mindful divination can help one deal with life's conflicts, avoid repeating bad habits or simply gain self-knowledge and an understanding of the surrounding world.

Runes, usually fashioned from stones or small pieces of wood, are each inscribed with a simple design that has special significance. Superficially, the symbol may represent an object or concrete reality; but of course, there are many levels and layers of meaning. A note here on *kennings*–these are metaphors attached to the rune's basic meaning, sometimes mimicking its physical shape. On its surface, a kenning's relationship to the rune itself may not be directly apparent. On deeper reflection, it shows hidden truths attached to the rune's meaning. A kenning is much like a riddle.* It helps the reader find understanding and illumination hidden within the enigma.

In the Celtic Ogham, the rune for Coll (or Hazel) is connected to the myth of the Salmon of Knowledge. This creature gained wisdom from eating the hazelnuts of nine trees overlooking a magical pool belonging to the Celtic god of inspiration, Manannan Mac Lir. The rune itself stands for wisdom and knowledge. The Norse rune Gebo (gift, choice), shaped like an X, alludes to the ordeal of the god Odin wherein he attained the mysteries of the runes by lashing himself to the world tree, Yggdrasil.[2] The X shape moreover, is similar to that of the human body with arms and legs outstretched as if tied onto something. These hidden mythic layers are just a few examples of

---

* From the Old English *hriddel,* to sift.

how a divination image can contain various levels of significance. This holds true for the symbols of all divination systems.

The shapes of runic sigils can be of great value in comprehending their meaning. With this in mind, I have designed the Talking Forest runes (*Figure 1,* p. 21) to evoke understanding and facilitate illumination. For example, the rung-like arms of the Larch rune remind us that Siberian shamans used this tree as a ladder, an egress to the spirit world. The kennings for Larch, therefore, are *ladder* and *shaman*. Cherry, the rune of desire, and Linden, that of love, both possess heart-shaped branches. These two runes deal with matters of the heart and thus their shapes imitate this form. Sumac's rune mimics the silhouette of its tree, while simultaneously evoking various horned nature gods such as Pan and Cernunnos.

Each Talking Forest rune has been carefully designed to depict the significance of the salient tree within its physical environment. It may even mirror historical, cultural, ecological and mythical factors surrounding the tree. For truly, the myths and folklore we have created about the natural world say more about us and about the human condition than anything else. By using the Talking Forest as we learn the hidden mysteries of trees, we may also navigate the dark woods within ourselves.

Humus:
Origins of the Talking Forest

From early childhood, I was captivated by the beauty and mystique of the trees of my native Southern Ontario. My five-year sojourn in Vancouver, "the city of forests," only intensified this attraction.

Throughout my life, my personal path to the gods was lined with trees!

For years I examined various systems of divination, searching in vain for the special one whose symbols would readily evoke the grace and majesty of our trees. The Celtic Ogham is not specifically a tree rune set and, in any event, did not appeal to me as such. The Ogham is primarily an excellent system based on Celtic myth and cosmology, just as the Futhark follows Norse mythology.[3]

While seeking a tree Tarot system that would appeal to me, I came upon the Medicine Cards,[4] a deck based on the totems of sacred animals of North America's First Nations people. This wonderful array with its concise and perceptively written guidebook, was not in any way patterned after the standard Tarot. The Medicine Cards got me wondering—if a novel card deck exists based on North American animals, is there one based on trees? Surprisingly, in light of the current popularity of trees, this does not appear to be the case.* I understood that I would have to fashion my own array based on the trees of my native land, and realizing that draftsmanship is not my specialty, I decided to create a system of runes.

I had always admired the simple yet evocative design of the ancient Norse Futhark and was much impressed by Freya Aswynn's excellent study on these runes. Her book, *Leaves of Yggdrasil* cleverly distills the meanings of the Futhark by superimposing each rune upon an illustration of a natural phenomenon or human action which echoes its esoteric significance or *kenning*. Thus Isa—

---

*   There are numerous excellent tree Tarots, but their symbolism generally follows the original Tarot or the Western zodiac. The symbolism is not principally based on trees or their folklore.

the rune of constriction and inertia–is superimposed on an icicle. The Y-shaped Algiz, (protection) is superimposed on a shade tree with a similar silhouette, and so on. Aswynn's simple but effective illustrative tool underlined for me the importance of making each Talking Forest rune encapsulate its tree's *intrinsicness;* its appearance, character and spiritual qualities; even, if possible, its environment. Thus the seeds for a new rune system were planted.

Seed:
How the Talking Forest Was Designed

From the start, I determined that the design for each rune should be simple yet attractive, elegant yet easily rendered. More expressly, it had to immediately evoke the tree it represented.

I felt it would be best if I could devise sigils that were as basic, yet eloquent, as the Norse Futhark (*Figure 2,* p. 22). This ancient array is superbly designed. For example, a cursory examination of the second rune, Uruz, shows a lopsided reversed letter "U." The kenning or iconic meaning of Uruz is *ox* or *aurochs.* The rune indeed does resemble the silhouette of a bison or ox, higher at the shoulders than at the haunches. Its very shape suggests a strong and powerful animal and its meaning denotes strength, primal energy and perseverance.

Uruz   **Isa**

The eleventh rune is Isa and its kenning is *ice*. The figure resembles the lower case "l" and suggests an icicle. Its very shape is a wall or barrier, indicating an immovable object. Beneath this surface meaning lies the concept of constriction or inertia. If Isa appears in a reading, this indicates that the subject can do little about their present situation except wait for it to pass, as one would an ice storm. These are just two examples of how effective the Futhark symbols are—basic yet compelling, immediately evoking the forces they represent.

While devising the Talking Forest array, I felt it essential that each rune be attractive yet simple, while being a distinct avatar of its chosen tree. After about ten years of drafting and revising, I now have the array I wanted and frequently use. Each sigil is simple to draw yet eloquently portrays its particular tree. For example, **Birch** deals with coming of age and the gaining of new experiences. It depicts a slender, light-canopied tree that has *copsed* or developed a second trunk, leaning away from the original as if striking out on its own.

The **Birch** rune depicts a small tree often having two or more trunks.

The Talking Forest **Oak** signals authority and power. This rune indicates a regal, authoritative tree of gaunt frame, who wears his single acorn like a crown.

The **Oak** rune illustrates this tree's imposing size.

The above are just two examples, but a quick perusal of the full Talking Forest array (*Figure 1,* p. 21) suggests an attractive group of symbols that I hope will be embraced by rune users, especially those interested in tree lore. The Talking Forest runes are as easy to draw as the Ogham (*Figure 3,* p. 23). However each, with its own unique character, mirrors the personality, appearance, and sometimes even the habitat of the tree it represents.

While developing the Talking Forest figures, I kept three salient factors in mind. Each rune must mirror:

1. The representative tree's characteristic shape (columnar, steeple-like, vine-like, etc.);
2. The botanical family to which the tree belongs (rose family, birches, pines, etc.); and finally,
3. The tree's function in both the natural environment and human culture (fruit-bearer, ornamental, conifer etc.).

Runes depicting trees such as ash, maple and beech are modeled on a simple vertical centre pole bisecting two horizontal lines. These ample runes represent shade trees with spreading branches and dense foliage. The **Maple** rune, the simplest of these "shade runes," is the only one with straight horizontal lines. These "branches" also mimic the veining pattern readily seen in the individual maple leaf.

The **Maple** rune.

All other shade runes are furnished with wavy branches only because I found this to be more aesthetically pleasing than straight lines. In addition, wavy branches indicate some unique quality in the twigs or foliage of a specific tree species: e.g., the bamboo-like effect of **ash** leaves seen from below, or the tendency for beech leaves to perch horizontally on their twigs.

Ash's *wavy branches allude to the latticed effect of the tree's canopy.*

Talking Forest runes based on a simple "T" shape signify smaller, often delicate-looking trees usually with light, airy foliage. These include birch and other members of its family: **alder,** hazel and the ironwoods.

The **Alder** *rune illustrates a small, delicate member of the birch family.*

A rune with branches ending in spirals denotes a tree with large, showy flowers. These are frequently, but not always, members of the rose family. Spirals ending in a dot indicate the fruit that is the final outcome of the flower. **Apple** and Rowan are examples of such fruit-tree runes.

Large spirals with "fruit dots" suit **Apple,** *our prime orchard tree.*

Dots at the ends of branches without spirals indicate trees with prominent fruit or nuts, but bearing only small or inconspicuous flowers. **Walnut** and Holly are good examples of this type of rune.

Walnut: *nut-bearing tree par excellence.*

An asymmetrical rune shaped somewhat like an "F" indicates a tree possessing a variety of noteworthy features. For example, **Buckeye** is a shade tree that has showy flowers and the large nuts for which it is named. The Talking Forest rune displays one large flower spiral and, below that, a wavy branch with a "nut" falling from it. On the left side of the rune are two branches, one with a "shade bracket." **Catalpa,** another F rune, is Buckeye's mirror image, save that the "fruit dot" is replaced by a squiggly line that represents the pod-shaped fruit.

*The **Buckeye** rune is "male" with nut and flower on the right side.*

I have chosen to use the Aristotelian system of defining "female" trees with their salient features on the left, while "male" trees have them on the right. I perceive the Buckeye as "male" and the Catalpa as "female." Thus the former is a right-handed and the latter a left-handed rune. My attribution of gender, although seemingly arbitrary, has simply grown out of my personal study and communion with the trees.

Catalpa *is a "female" rune with pod and flower on the left side.*

Many Talking Forest runes were designed simply as silhouettes of their representative plant. **Reed** and Sumac are examples of these "iconic" runes. Likewise, two of the conifer runes, Evergreen and Hemlock, are based on the familiar steeple-shaped Christmas tree template, while **Pine** imitates the wind-tossed look of that most emblematic tree of the species, the Scots pine. Willow and Mulberry are "M"-shaped, suggesting their tendency to "weep" or droop.

Reed and *Pine* are examples of iconic runes.

Runes utilizing an "S" shape indicate either creeping plants that are always on the move, or plants that otherwise possess some element of rapid–from a plant's perspective–movement through space. They either crawl or climb, as do ivy and vine, or they are trellised like the rose often is. The Vine rune is shown lying sideways to differentiate it from the upright S shape of Ivy. This also harkens to grapevine's attribute of being cultivated to grow horizontally on fences or pollarded trees, for ease of harvesting. The fourth S rune, **Hedge,** is horizontal as well, for these plants are often cultivated to grow in a row of multiples. The three diagonal lines through the Hedge rune indicate the fence that it virtually becomes.

 *Hedge*

A further note on rune placement as regards the S-shaped runes–due to the symmetricality of these runes, each has a discreet dot underneath, indicating the bottom of the rune. Thus, if the dot is at the top, the rune is upside down.

Similarity of shape between runes is always deliberate and indicates plants with a botanical, structural or symbolic commonality. For example, hawthorn, rowan and bramble are all members of the rose family: the Talking Forest **Rowan** is without thorns and the heavily fruiting **Bramble** appears smaller than **Hawthorn,** with two fruit spirals to the latter's one. Regardless of resemblances between these similar runes, they are still distinctive enough to be easily distinguished.

Hawthorn   **Rowan**   **Bramble**

The *compound* runes, Ironwood, Evergreen and Hazel, each represent two separate, but usually related species.* I felt there were trees with energies so similar, it seemed pointless to allocate separate runes to them; yet each was equally important and cried out to be included in the set. For the sake of simplicity, I composed a sigil melded from two separate runes. For example, the compound rune **Ironwood** is the result of splicing the Hornbeam and Hophornbeam runes together. In all the compound runes, the "feminine" tree is on the left and the "masculine" on the right. Each compound rune is discussed in further detail in its own chapter in Section II.

---

* There is also the compound Oak rune consisting of White and Red Oaks–two types of one species.

Hornbeam + **Hophornbeam** = **Ironwood**

Fruition:
Using the Talking Forest Runes

Divination systems such as the Tarot or the Norse Futhark are generally rectangular or oblong and can only be read as upright or inverted. While creating the Talking Forest, I realized that having round runes would render interpretation of the system problematic. However, an inner voice insisted that these runes must be round and as such I created them. On one occasion, a friend, seeing some of the runes stacked in a pile, noted that they resembled a tree trunk! This pronouncement came as a revelation to me, for we know that a tree's age and virtually all of its history and life experiences can be read in the rings of its trunk. Runic readings are likewise sporadic diary entries of our own life history. And in the same way that a tree's rings are hidden inside its trunk, the Talking Forest runes, or *keys,* reveal truths normally hidden within the subconscious.

With round runes, however, comes the problem of interpreting the way they fall. The upright reading is the most straightforward interpretation, usually auspicious and with qualities active and fully potential. An **upright** rune or key illustrates a tall standing tree or shrub–a healthy plant with all its salient features fully intact and in full strength. For example, a Cedar rune upright would imply healing through purification, an upright Maple a change for the better.

Unlike other systems, a Talking Forest rune's most adverse reading generally occurs not when it is upside down but when the rune is lying on its side. This **toppled** position symbolizes a tree that has fallen and is lying on the ground, indicating a negation or loss of the rune's salient characteristics. For example, a toppled Cedar rune might suggest illness or a need to look after one's health. Maple lying sideways would imply the reader is unable to deal with changes happening in their life. It should be remembered however, that dead trees in nature also provide life to other plants and animals. A felled tree can provide wood for fuel, furniture or a new home. A toppled rune then, can frequently suggest that the rune's energies are still in abundance and useful. However, a sacrifice may have to be made in order to gain a desired result. Hence, a toppled Maple rune might suggest a difficult transition that may eventually work for the best, but something will be lost along the way.

Upside down or **inverted** keys were a complication that stymied me for quite some time. Runes in this position must imply something other than negativity as this attribute is already assigned to sideways or toppled runes. I finally understood inversion as suggesting one of three things.

Firstly, while pondering my impasse, I came to realize that we actually only see trees upside down when they are reflected in a mirrored surface such as a lake or pond. Thus an inverted rune may indicate a *mirroring* of the upright position. Since the trees are reflected in water, they are obviously still rooted in the earth and are presumably healthy. In this way, an inverted rune does not suggest an adverse reading, but rather a reflection or echo of an upright reading. As water often implies the subconscious, so too an inverted rune may suggest that its energies are presently operating on a purely subconscious level. In addition, the mirror world, including that reflected in water, is actually two-dimensional–it has no depth. An inverted rune may therefore suggest that the qualities of the tree represented are somehow attenuated or perhaps even distorted. As an example, Catalpa, the rune of leisure, upside down frequently implies laziness. Inverted Beech often warns of a tendency to dominate others rather than allowing them to make their own decisions.

Inversion can also be interpreted as a seed being planted. Falling from the branches of the mother tree, it has "gone to earth" and is a tree in the making. In this case, the inverted position indicates energy *in embryo,* or in the formative stage. The querent may need to nurture and work on strengths that are offered by the salient rune but are not yet manifest. Depending on surrounding keys, an inverted rune may also suggest that a seed should be planted–the tree's energy is not yet being used but should soon be put into effect. Here the inverted key implies *potential* or outcome resulting from actions indicated by other runes nearby.

Finally, while trying to resolve my issue with runic inversion, I was fascinated to find that in both Hindu and Jewish mythology, the Tree of Knowledge is inverted![5] The roots of the tree are nourished in Heaven, the home of the gods and the branches reach to Earth to endow humans with inspiration and spiritual knowledge. Reading the inverted rune with this theory in mind suggests the voice of deity. Therefore the querent should pay even closer attention. Recall too, that the hanged man of the Tarot (generally perceived as Odin in his struggle to obtain the Futhark runes) is upside down, and therefore sees his tree, Yggdrasil, as inverted!

But what about a rune lying between upright and toppled or between inverted and toppled? In the former case, the tree is leaning–perhaps in danger of being uprooted. This position often indicates energies having trouble establishing themselves and thus there may be friction against the rune's ability to help. A rune landing between toppled and inversion may portend a seed that will not sprout or will die as a sapling. In this case, the rune's powers may not come to fruition or if manifested, may be diminished or short-lived.

The four S runes represent plants that, unlike trees, are easily uprooted and can easily be held upside down by their roots. Under such circumstances, they will die. Therefore, an S rune is **toppled** or given negative circumstance *when it is upside down or inverted*. S runes lying sideways however, are not uprooted. Ivy and grapevine, being creeping plants, grow so well they can crawl over and frequently smother plants in their path! Rose is quite capable of growing sideways along a trellis and the Hedge is a horizontal rune only so as to indicate the *plurality* of the plants making up the hedge. Thus if an S rune is lying on its side, its energies are attenuated but not nullified, and it is read as **inverted,** not toppled. As mentioned previously, there is a small dot at the bottom of each S-rune; the rune is read as toppled when the dot is at the top. When the dot shows on either side of the rune, it is read as inverted. More clarification on reading the S runes can be found in their specific chapters.

When doing a reading, the querent must choose each rune randomly and blindly, from a bag or container large enough to contain and loosely shuffle all forty-two keys. As with other divination systems, interpretation will come from the way each rune lands, as well as its position in relation to adjacent runes. The three layout methods unique to the Talking Forest system–Thicket, Tree and Forest, (*Figure 4, Figure 5,* and *Figure 6*)–are further discussed in Section III: Arboretum.

Trees are not as familiar to us as animals, having very different life cycles. However, the work involved in attempting to communicate with them is uniquely satisfying. When we dig deep into our own roots to converse with the forest, and seek guidance from the trees among us, we may yet spy the Green Man's face in the foliage overhead and hear Dryad voices in the rustling of the leaves.

We have now arrived at the edge of the Talking Forest. I sincerely hope that these forty-two keys will facilitate meditation and spiritual growth for all who use them. I trust that each and every tree depicted in the array will become a familiar friend and guide to the student on the path of illumination.

FIGURE 1
The Talking Forest Runes
© Kay Broome 2009

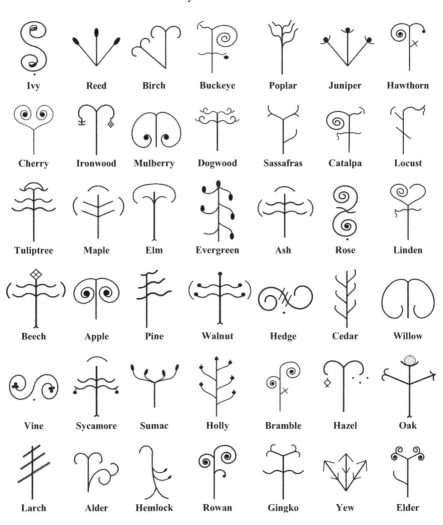

Ivy	Reed	Birch	Buckeye	Poplar	Juniper	Hawthorn
Cherry	Ironwood	Mulberry	Dogwood	Sassafras	Catalpa	Locust
Tuliptree	Maple	Elm	Evergreen	Ash	Rose	Linden
Beech	Apple	Pine	Walnut	Hedge	Cedar	Willow
Vine	Sycamore	Sumac	Holly	Bramble	Hazel	Oak
Larch	Alder	Hemlock	Rowan	Gingko	Yew	Elder

FIGURE 2
The Futhark Runes
(read vertically from top to bottom)

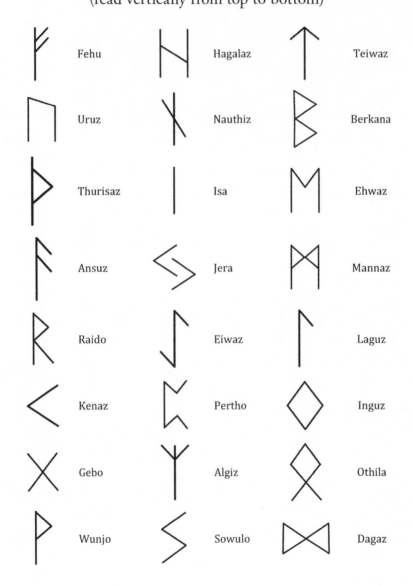

Fehu

Uruz

Thurisaz

Ansuz

Raido

Kenaz

Gebo

Wunjo

Hagalaz

Nauthiz

Isa

Jera

Eiwaz

Pertho

Algiz

Sowulo

Teiwaz

Berkana

Ehwaz

Mannaz

Laguz

Inguz

Othila

Dagaz

FIGURE 3
The Ogham Runes

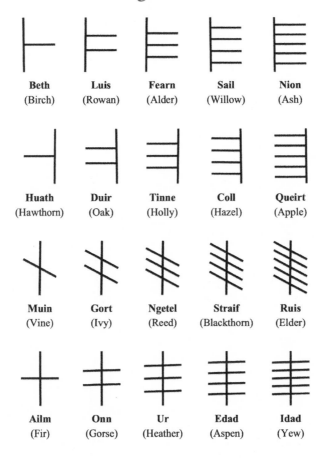

Beth	**Luis**	**Fearn**	**Sail**	**Nion**
(Birch)	(Rowan)	(Alder)	(Willow)	(Ash)

Huath	**Duir**	**Tinne**	**Coll**	**Queirt**
(Hawthorn)	(Oak)	(Holly)	(Hazel)	(Apple)

Muin	**Gort**	**Ngetel**	**Straif**	**Ruis**
(Vine)	(Ivy)	(Reed)	(Blackthorn)	(Elder)

Ailm	**Onn**	**Ur**	**Edad**	**Idad**
(Fir)	(Gorse)	(Heather)	(Aspen)	(Yew)

THE TREES FOR THE FOREST

THE RUNES

Ivy

Kenning: Spiral

Significance: Birth, Inception, Life Force

The spiral, one of the oldest and most sacred symbols in human history, is common in nature. Unlike the circle and the line, however, it is capable of traveling through different dimensions, both inwardly and outwardly, constantly growing, evolving and moving. One could argue that all movement that results in change originated from the spiral. The stalks of growing plants move in a spiral pattern toward sunlight, while their roots, living augers, corkscrew into the ground. Leaves, in their turn, whorl around stems like steps in a spiral staircase. All vertebrate backbones, no matter the species, constantly move and shift in a spiral. The DNA double helix twists around itself. And finally, the mightiest spirals of all are the vast galaxies twirling through the cosmos.

Physical Traits and Environment

Ivy, the first rune in the Talking Forest, references both the true ivies, those familiar houseplants of the *Hedera* genus, as well as the native North American woodbines. All gardeners are familiar with ivy's unsettling ability to set down tendrils that spread and cleave to anything in its path: plants, buildings and fallen logs.

Ivy and woodbine are evergreens; they thrive during mild winters and enter dormancy in freezing weather. North of the Carolinian zone, however, winters are too harsh for these tender plants. Here they only thrive indoors. Although often called American ivy, woodbines are members of the grapevine family. Their Latin name, *Parthenocissus* or "virgin vine," alludes to the plant's trait of springing up as if from nowhere. Most woodbine species have palmate leaves; that is, they are composed of five equally sized leaflets which radiate from the stem. These grow at intervals along the vines. True ivies *(Hedera)* display simple, usually lobed leaves between one and five inches in diameter. They are normally a bright, rich shade of green, although there are forms in variegated green and yellow as well. Woodbine and ivy both display magnificent autumn colour in shades of crimson through to burgundy. In late summer and fall, both yield purple-black berries that are poisonous to humans. All ivies and woodbines need moisture and prefer sun, but can handle shade very well.

Ivy and Woodbine in Folklore

Ivy is inextricably associated with the shepherd god Pan, whose purview is the life force that quickens the mating urge in all living things. It is fitting then that Pan's creature, the goat, is fond of the taste of ivy leaves. Most famously, ivy is linked to the Bacchae, the female worshippers of Bacchus or Dionysus, the Greek god of wine and ecstasy. Also called Maenads, they celebrated this god with orgiastic revels, drinking wine and chewing the leaves of ivy. The toxic substance in the plant would, according to myth, drive these feral women mad enough to tear to pieces any unfortunate creature in their path, human or otherwise.

The well-known Christmas carol, "The Holly and the Ivy" makes much of holly, who "wears the crown," but hardly mentions ivy. There is, however, another very old and obscure English carol "Ivy, Chief of Trees, It Is,"[6] which makes much of this vine, insisting that it is sacred. In this song, ivy is likened to a woman and there is no reference whatsoever to Christ. The Latin refrain *Veni Coronaberis,* means, "Thou shalt be crowned." Is this a subtle carol to a pagan goddess, a rebuke against the Christianity of the time?

Canada's Ojibwe people believed in a mythical vine, whose description is very reminiscent of the woodbine. This plant formed a link between the worlds of the living and the dead and could be climbed like a ladder to reach either abode. [7]

Spiritual Traits

Chlorophyll, meaning "green leaf," is the protein molecule that gives plants their green colour. During photosynthesis–the synthesizing of light–chlorophyll absorbs energy from sunlight, which it turns into various sugars for plant nourishment. Because leaves cannot absorb green light, they reflect it, allowing for the dominance of that particular colour in healthy plants. Thus, green represents life, and its energy is conspicuous in Ivy. The Spring Equinox, a time of new beginnings, belongs to Ivy.

In order for the ivy to grow and thrive, it must find a support, often another plant. To do this, it twines in a spiraling pattern, wrapping itself around its host. Likewise, in order to grow and learn, children depend upon adults to help them throughout life's experiences. Thus Ivy, a living green spiral, signifies, in the Talking Forest system, our movement on the new journey of life. Because it gains strength and support from other plants, Ivy is somewhat like the helpless infant who needs adults to nurture and look after it. Like an infant, however, the plant is incredibly resilient and energetic.

The term "ivy league" refers to the tradition of educational institutions such as Yale and Harvard, whose buildings are covered in ivy or creeper. Indeed, European ivy and North American woodbine are fitting embellishments for the institutions that shape young and malleable minds. Buildings festooned in ivy remind us also, that no matter how supposedly "civilized" we become, we can never escape our most ancient home–the forest primeval.

The Rune

The rune is an "S"-shaped double spiral, with a leaf form at each end, illustrating the inward and outward weaving of the vine. The ancient and sacred spiral is a fitting image for the first of the Talking Forest runes. Spirals, in both single and double form, have been found etched on prehistoric standing stones and on cave and temple walls. It is believed to signify the labyrinth–the passage outward from birth through life and eventually inward toward death.

Ivy's spiral reminds us that in order to grow, we must seek knowledge within ourselves, as well as in the world outside. The vine clings to the past, building on older foundations while simultaneously moving to fruition. In order to thrive, ivy must reach ever outward and upward. It is the life force, representing continuum and constant movement.

Kenning: Spiral
Significance: Birth, Inception, Life Force, to Join, to Connect

Ivy is the conception rune, the sigil of creation, moving from the spiral of the former life or prelife into that of the present. In the Celtic Ogham, Ivy or Gort denotes "development." Likewise, the Talking Forest Ivy rune indicates the beginning of the life cycle, the single strands of DNA from the egg and sperm cells that together create the new embryo. Ivy represents the background of what will be, the materials that each of us as individuals have to work with, in order to form our future life and personality. In this way, the Ivy rune is tied somewhat to the idea of destiny. To what structure will this vine attach itself? Who will become our parents? Who will *we* become?

The **upright** Ivy rune in a reading often indicates the beginning of a project or even a new stage in one's life. Always in motion, creative Ivy is tenacious and will not give up until its goal has been reached. Its powerful aura can heal and give vitality to others. In the Talking Forest system, Ivy resonates the vitality of new life and its deity is Pan.*

As earlier mentioned, the Talking Forest S runes are all read negatively or **toppled** when they are upside down.† Ivy in this position, with the dot showing at the top of the rune, indicates a *lack* of Ivy traits—the plant uprooted. Perhaps you are being blocked or are unable to move forward or create.

Ivy lying on its side, however, is read as if it were **inverted.** Here, one can envision the plant as crawling across the ground rather than upward, smothering everything in its path! In this

---

*   Fittingly, the RNA and DNA helixes, the building blocks of life, suggest horns.

†   The other three S runes in the Talking Forest are read in a similar fashion—that is, upside down (with the dot above the rune) indicates a toppled rune and sideways is read as inverted.

instance, Ivy's energies are overpowering the energies of other runes lying nearby.

With unbridled flexibility and tensile strength, Ivy behaves somewhat like an infant, with no experience and hence no understanding of morality. Ivy's primitive energy can run amok, as did the Bacchae of Greek myth. Frequently too, Ivy is parasitical, sometimes overtaking its host and sapping the life from it. People with too much Ivy energy may tend toward "clinginess," becoming co-dependent or, in extreme cases, "users" who sap the energies of others. Therefore, Ivy requires a strong foundation to support and contain its boundless chaotic energy. The attributes of the Talking Forest Beech and Oak, their powers rooted deep in the earth as well as in tradition and restraint, are excellent complements for Ivy.

Reed

Kenning: Cradle, Basket

Significance: Childhood, Innocence, Child

The world's wetlands are a vitally important crucible of life. A multitude of creatures swim, mate and raise their young in relative safety among the reeds. Indeed, the stems of rushes must seem as tree trunks to the tiny insects, fish and frogs who dwell in swamps. And many song and water birds begin their lives in nests enclosed by reeds.

Author Ted Andrews suggests that swamps engender fear in humans.[8] We often feel uneasy whenever passing by a large marshy area. This sense of danger is not all imaginary. Swamps can be dangerous: you can never tell when you will come upon a deep bog or a patch of quicksand. Many swamps also house dangerous reptiles and poisonous plants. But if marshes and wetlands are dank, dirty and treacherous, they have equally proven essential in filtering our water and environment of noxious pollutants. Perhaps the brooding, menacing atmosphere of the swamp is a defense mechanism to keep people away. With humans out of the way, swamplands can continue their essential work as stewards of Earth's fresh waters. Reeds, noble denizens of these environments, make wonderfully competent cleaners, often used to purify grey water from industrial sites. Increasingly, wetlands harbouring reed grasses are employed extensively to help reclaim habitat lost from mining, sewage and other man-made disturbances to the environment.

While in England some years ago, I was amazed by the crystal clarity of many of England's small, crowded, yet celebrated waterways. Rivers like the Avon and Arun all had reeds growing in abundance in their slow-moving depths. And although Southern Ontario is becoming urbanized at an alarming rate, many of its rural rivers still offer good fishing, no doubt due to the extensive swampland scattered throughout the area, replete with reeds and rushes.

Physical Traits and Environment

The Talking Forest Reed represents water reeds, specifically the cattails *(Typha latifolia)* and bulrushes *(Scirpus spp.)*. These plants are very similar, with cattails faster growing and bulrushes more able to withstand drought. Both cattail and bulrush stalks are generally hollow or contain spongey pith; they usually start out as bright green shoots.

Reed in Folklore

Since time immemorial, reeds were used to weave baskets and infants' cradles. Who does not know the biblical story of Moses of the Israelites found by Pharaoh's daughter among the bulrushes? However few people are aware that this story originated from the nativity myth of the Egyptian sun god Horus. When his father Osiris was murdered and dismembered by the evil crocodile god Seti, Horus' mother Isis hid him for safe-keeping among papyrus reeds.

Flutes and pipes made of reeds were held sacred in ancient times and were often played in ritual context. Pan, the Arcadian god of the woodlands, fell in love with the river nymph Syrinx. Sadly, her feelings did not reciprocate his and Syrinx begged the Olympian gods to rescue her from Pan's persistent advances. Much was the shepherd god's disappointment, when Syrinx was transformed into a reed when he caught up with her. Upon observing, however, that the wind made a pleasing sound when it blew over the reed, Pan then set about making this delightful new plant into a seven-reeded pipe or Panpipes, the first musical instrument from reeds. To this day, Panpipes are also called the Syrinx in honour of the shy nymph.

Aesop's fable of the "Oak and the Reed" is a familiar one. A mighty oak, arrogant and rigid in his mien, had mocked a humble reed as being unworthy and insignificant. When a terrible storm later developed, the oak, too proud to bend, was toppled, but the reed, swaying to and fro in the powerful gale, was saved by her suppleness and humility. There is strength in trusting the world and sometimes it is better to bend with the wind instead of wasting useless energy fighting it. Children are very open-minded and resilient and they soon become all too aware of their own smallness and vulnerability. As a result, and because they have not yet been brainwashed into believing instinct is merely childish nonsense, children still trust their "gut feelings." It is this that often keeps them from harm.

Spiritual Traits

Reed has a trusting, gentle energy and is associated with infancy and childhood. Its element is water and its season is spring. Reed is influenced by Luna, our moon, which rules Earth's waters and aquatic plants.

Gods associated with Reed are Horus, Isis, Pan of the reed pipe and of course, the nymph Syrinx. Also noteworthy is Ningikuga, a Sumerian goddess of the reeds. She was fittingly, the wife of Enki, wise god of the waters.[9]

The Rune

The Talking Forest Reed has three branches connected at the base. Each is topped by an oval, representing the fuzzy tip of the bulrush or cattail. The left branch alludes to the time before birth, including past incarnations; the central branch indicates the ever-present moment and the third signifies the future that lies ahead. The triplicate shape of this rune also hearkens to the child flanked by the parents, as well as to the magical power of the number three. Numerous mythologies reference triple goddesses of fate, whose function is to allot newborn children their futures. In Greece they were known as the three Fates or *Parcae*–Clotho spun the thread, Lachesis measured out the length of the individual's life and Atropos inexorably cut short the thread. In Scandinavia, it was the Norns who spun the life of the individual–Urd (Earth) represented the past, Verdandi (Being) the present and Skuld (Necessity or literally, *Should*) the future.

Kenning: Cradle, Basket
Significance: Childhood, Innocence, Child

Where the Talking Forest Ivy rune suggests gestation and birth, Reed stands for the early years of infancy and childhood. Reed speaks to the weaving together of an identity from various strands of experiences. These are learned from a child's surroundings and from life lived with others: parents, siblings, grandparents and playmates. If the Ivy rune illustrates the creation of life itself into a variety of forms, Reed indicates the shaping of each of these into an individual life.

The Reed rune suggests innocence. As water grasses remain clean while cleansing and purifying rivers and lakes, so children begin life "pure"–innocent and trusting. Little children are very honest and candid. We can all attest to truths spoken "from the mouths of babes" that have inadvertently hilarious and/or embarrassing results. However, children grow and become stronger not by being rigid, but by remaining bendable and flexible as Reed, and thus open to new ideas and experiences.

Upright, Reed indicates the beginning of a new project or life situation. The rune suggests one is evolving toward something or developing a new way of looking at the world. In some situations, Reed indicates a child of the querent or alludes to the querent's relationship with their children. It may even suggest the addition or birth of a new family member.

Reed bestows pliancy and creativity; it suggests the ability to "bend" with circumstances. However, too much **inverted** Reed energy–the Reed reflected in the pool–may warn of compliancy or timidity. Here the querent is afraid to leave the pond for further vistas.

Save for the S runes, all Talking Forest runes landing in a sideways position are seen as **toppled.** Here their traits and energies have been attenuated or made null. A toppled Reed rune implies stagnation. There is some blockage or corruption, like a river without reeds to cleanse it. Aggressive runes crossing the toppled Reed may warn of impending danger.

Birch

Kenning: Maiden, Canoe

Significance: Travel, New Experiences

Nothing says "Spring Thaw" quite like Birch. In April, the maple will take its place of honour, with a bounty of sweet, rich syrup. Then, apple and cherry blossoms overwhelm May. Birch however, with her dainty catkins and silvery trunk shining boldly against March's tentative pale browns, announces Persephone's return like no other tree.

Physical Traits and Environment

Birch *(Betula)* is a *pioneer*, sprouting earlier than other trees on open land and she is one of the first to bud in spring. A slender, quick-growing plant, the tree frequently divides into two or more trunks. This is called *copsing*. The graceful branches droop languidly from high above the ground, revealing small, oval leaves that are lightly serrated with pointed tips. The languid leaves and delicate catkins in early spring are like silver raindrops falling daintily from the tree.

The most salient feature of all species of birch however, is their bark. Here is where the tree most expresses her character—whether in the silvery and peeling strips of paper birch, the stark white lenticels of European, or the smooth, uniform taupe of cherry birch. Trunks of white and paper birch are equally lambent by day or moonlit night. The bark's gleam is as bracing as sun on fresh snow, a fitting gown for this proud little denizen of the boreal forest. The inner bark of birch yields an oil much like wintergreen, and with comparable analgesic properties. It is this that gives birch wood its delicate scent, most perceptible in early spring.

Birch in Folklore

Northern peoples such as the Finns, the Russians, and the Saami used the bark of European white birch for writing and for fashioning runes. First Nations people of Canada drew pictographs on birch bark. Thus, people of the Eastern Woodlands held that birch "gave them knowledge through its hidden inner structure and the magical properties of its outer shell."[10] Canoes of the Six Nations and Delaware, made from the bark of paper birch, were deservedly famous for their amazing resilience and buoyancy, in addition to their lightweight, waterproof nature.

Shamans of Eurasia ingested the white spotted red fly agaric mushroom, most frequently found beneath birch trees, as an aid to their spiritual journeys. The Teutons believed these fungi to have sprung from the foam of Odin's eight-legged horse, Sleipnir.[11] Witches were also believed to have used the same mushroom in their flying ointments.

In many parts of northern Europe, brooms or *besoms* were most often made from birch twigs tied round an ash staff with pliant willow branches or *withes*. Since witches' besoms were often made of birch, it is fitting that this tree is linked to goddesses such as the Norse Freya and Greek Artemis–both associated with witchcraft. In Britain, birch was sacred to Rhiannon and Arianrhod–each a Welsh maiden goddess of witchcraft. Many Celtic myths mention the birch tree or thicket as a conduit to the land of Faery. Yet equally, birch could protect one from being abducted by the fairies.

Birch is still held in high regard by northern European peoples. The Norse rune Berkana, meaning birch, is often associated with the Teutonic goddess Berchta, protector of children.[12] One Christian observance that most likely originated from an earlier pagan custom took place in Russia, just before the May holiday of Whitsunday. Here young girls would tie red ribbons to birch branches for good luck and for magical protection.[13] In all Slavic countries, the birch was sacred to yet another witch goddess, Baba Yaga. She is often represented in folk art as a fearsome old hag flying in her giant mortar, steering with a pestle while on the lookout for tasty children. Behind her, she drags a birch broom with her other hand, in order to furtively cover up the tracks of her heinous mission. There is much evidence in the folklore concerning

Baba Yaga regarding her intimacy with herb lore, hence the mortar and pestle. A tree such as birch, with its efficacious magic, would indeed make a suitable besom for this mysterious goddess.

Spiritual Traits

Birch is a feminine tree and air and water are her elements. She has a questing, fearless aura and is particularly associated with the maiden aspect of the Goddess. Birch of the luminous bark resonates solar energy. No tree honours the sun more than her, yet all the same, she defers only to Willow as a lunar tree.

The Rune

In the Talking Forest, Birch is the first of the "T"-shaped runes. These are runes that have branches like horns curving down and slightly inward. This shape evokes the slender, graceful forms and light canopies of the small trees they represent.

The rune specific to Birch sports an additional T shape on the left, or "distaff" side of the main stem, of this feminine tree.* Here is shown a tree that *copses* or develops more than one equal-sized trunk. Hence the rune bespeaks independence and egress. The rune's left-hand trunk, still rooted to the main tree, branches off to form its own shape, to live its own life. Human children can

---

* I have used the classical "Aristotle" system of illustrating "feminine" trees showing their most noteworthy attributes on the left and masculine trees with theirs on the right.

only become truly adult by leaving home; however, they are still connected to the family, keeping in touch with them and indeed, frequently developing closer ties after gaining independence and reaching maturity.

Kenning: Maiden, Canoe
Significance: Travel, Movement, New Experiences

The letter Beth begins the Celtic Ogham array. This rune connotes, among other things, vitality and beginnings.[14] In the Talking Forest system, Birch signifies youth and maidenhood and the launching of a new stage in life—the child's voyage of discovery toward adulthood. **Upright,** this rune addresses learning, the process of initiation, the coming of age and exposure to the lessons of adolescence. It was this tree's bark that was fashioned into canoes to ease the *physical* journey through water. In addition, the bark was used for writing purposes, thus aiding literacy and the *intellectual* journey. In a Talking Forest reading, Birch may indicate someone still living at home with the family, but yearning to strike out for new pastures.

Adolescents, in their eagerness to learn new things and without the sobering lessons of experience, are often heedless of dangers lying in store. Hence, they may take chances they later regret. The **inverted** Birch rune present in a reading may warn of recklessness. However, we all learn from our mistakes, becoming wiser, if frequently sadder, in the process. Alternatively, inverted Birch may indicate someone chafing at the bit or frustrated because they are being held back from exploration.

Toppled or contrary Birch indicates a fear of new undertakings or of leaving the nest. The rune toppled to the left, with the side trunk facing down toward earth, may signal dependency or a lack of the natural curiosity so necessary to learning. Toppled to the right, with the side trunk upward, signifies a new project or journey that has been thwarted–the birch-bark canoe overturned.

Birch is the third rune in the Talking Forest set. Here the child has let go of Mom's apron strings and is now too big to be hefted onto Dad's shoulders. She wants to strike out on her own and is ready to explore the world.

Birch people are often restless and have an eternally youthful outlook on life. However, they must remember to keep commitments. They are eager to try new things, but become easily bored and are often taken by wanderlust. Birches love to travel and, like all travellers, are open to new ideas.

Buckeye

Kenning: Boy, Marble

Significance: Play, Friendship, Loyalty

If Reed corresponds to the infancy and toddler stages of the human lifespan and Birch to its exploratory childhood, Buckeye represents the obnoxious eleven year old, replete with groaner jokes, sneezing powder and fart cushion. Buckeye's aura is imposing, yet somehow absurd. A magnanimous, friendly tree, Buckeye can't make up his mind whether to grow up to be a papaya with five-lobed leaves, a catalpa with showy, deep-throated flowers, or a true chestnut (Castanea) with burnished seed.

Physical Traits and Environment

The buckeye family *(Aesculus)* includes three or four species native to eastern North America, as well as the familiar horse chestnut, introduced from Europe in the eighteenth century. Regardless of place of origin, all buckeyes share the same rounded, handsome crown. Most, but not all, are tall trees. It is unsafe to stand under a horse chestnut during a windstorm, for the branches frequently break off and drop without warning.[15] To add insult to potential injury, this tree has a very rude winter silhouette–each gnarly upturned branch ending in a single huge, knobby bud, gives us the "middle finger" a thousand times over! In late May and June, however, all buckeyes are on good behavior. Like spit-shined boys in their Sunday best, they are densely covered with softly fragrant candelabras of white, yellow or pink flowers.

The large compound leaves of buckeyes are somewhat like a five- or seven-fingered hand. The flowers vary in colour: white with pink centre in horse chestnut, yellow flowers for Ohio and yellow buckeye, and bright pink for red buckeye.

The seeds are enclosed within a green or light brown shell, depending on the species. Only the Ohio and horse chestnut have spiky shells, all other buckeyes have smooth or lumpy casings. The nut, when first separated from its spongey shell, is moist, smooth and silky in a rich, burnished chestnut brown. It begs to be held lovingly in the hand, like a prize marble. The large beige dot on the flattened side of the nut gives the species its name. Unlike the true chestnuts, all buckeye nuts are inedible and somewhat poisonous, at least for humans and livestock. Squirrels however, will eat them.

Buckeye in Folklore

The seeds of all buckeyes have been used as toys throughout history. It was common in Britain for children to take one of the fallen nuts, called "conkers," tie a string to it and recite "Oblionker! My first conker!", while trying to hit another child's conker. Conkers were also used in slingshots or were strung and worn as play jewelry.

In parts of Italy, there is the ritual of burning an effigy of Befana, the kindly witch figure of folklore who brings presents during the festival of Epiphany in January. Horse chestnuts are placed on the pyre to cause an explosion of sparks.[16] A North American belief, carried over from colonial times, is that a conker in the pocket will ward off the evil of rheumatism.

Spiritual Traits

Affable Buckeye conveys an aura of carefree enthusiasm. His energy and habit of mimicking the characteristics of other trees suggests a need to experience everything, much like a curious and eager child. This renders an endearing gawkiness to Buckeye and signals the importance of laughter and cheer, of not taking oneself, or life, too seriously. Buckeye teaches us that we should be able to laugh at ourselves and to see the ridiculous in life. A welcoming tree, Buckeye further denotes friendship and loyalty.

His time of the year is June, when the flowers appear, but also and especially October, when the nuts fall. Squirrels are avid climbers full of comic antics. These aerial nutters are responsible for planting many a forest. They often appear foolish to us. In the process of burying nuts and acorns in the dirt, they blithely forget where their stash is hidden. However, squirrels play a crucial role in creating a healthy woodland environment and deserve our gratitude and respect. Likewise, child's play is no waste of time, but a crucial part of human development.

The Rune

The Buckeye rune is the first of the "F" runes in the Talking Forest. These are asymmetrical, generally indicating trees with a variety of remarkable features. The Buckeye rune has a spiral on its right side, symbolizing a masculine tree with showy flowers. Buckeyes like to make a big production of dropping their nuts, so for this rune, I chose to illustrate the conker as a large dot actually falling from the branch of the rune. A curved line or "shade bracket," capping the upper left-hand branch, indicates a tree with heavy shade.

Kenning: Boy, Marble
Significance: Play, Friendship, Loyalty, Laughter, Cheer

Upright, this rune frequently indicates a sibling or friend of the querent–someone close who will stand by them in a fix. Or it may betoken good times to be had with friends. Buckeye teaches the ability to laugh at life and oneself. The rune may represent a boy or youth who will become salient in the querent's life.

Inverted Buckeye in a reading may indicate the querent is not taking their situation seriously enough. This position further illustrates immaturity and recklessness–a refusal to grow up. It may otherwise warn that the querent is not being taken seriously or is being made the fool!

Toppled Buckeye, lying on its left side, with the flower spiral up, reveals a tendency toward pomposity or taking oneself too seriously. Perhaps the querent should lighten up and lose a few conkers! It can also indicate loneliness, a need for companionship. Toppled to the right, with the flower in the dirt, warns of false friendship. Conversely, it may admonish the querent to be more attentive to good friends. As always, the runic meaning can be more easily discerned from reading surrounding runes.

Buckeye people are youthful and enthusiastic, always wanting to try another adventure. They are genial and loyal to their friends. People with an abundance of Buckeye energy have the enviable capacity of bringing cheer and hope to others. They are often the class clown or the life of the party and may even seek careers as comedians or satirists. Buckeyes are frequently drawn to careers that require creativity, especially of the type that involves game-playing: building or fashioning things, or careers on the stage and in film.

Poplar

Kenning: Oracle

Significance: Speech, Communication

As a child, I was lulled to sleep by the whispering of Carolina poplars swaying outside my bedroom window. When rain was imminent however, this gentle whispering would alter slightly in tone, becoming a compelling, frenetic hiss, evoking monsoons or waves on a wind-tossed seashore.

Poplar leaves speak to us. In some indigenous cultures, the tree is known by a term translated loosely as "woman's tongue."[17] Perhaps originally meant as a put-down of women as loquacious gossips, let us instead take it as a compliment–an acknowledgement of women's role as the primary educators of earlier societies– the mothers and grandmothers who sang lullabies to the tribe's children and related the myths and folktales of their cultures. In any event, it is an honour to have one's voice compared to the gentle calming rustle of poplar leaves!

Physical Traits and Environment

The poplar species *(Populus)* includes all poplars, aspens and cottonwoods. Poplars are members of the willow family, but no two relatives could be less alike. Willow leaves are long, narrow, pointed and tend to droop; but the crisp, yet tender leaves of poplar are either broad- and heart-shaped or round and crenelated. While some willows develop large multiple trunks, all but white poplar grow from a single, usually slender base.

Similarities between the two species are less apparent. The leaves of both poplar and willow are usually a distinctive sage green, often with white or silvery undersides. Both have bark that contains salicin, the magical substance found in aspirin and used as a painkiller since time immemorial. Both species grow quickly and are generally short-lived. Where willow honours water however, poplar evokes air.

The fluttering of each leathery poplar leaf on its long, thick stem is what causes the tree's distinctive rustling. Even the slightest breeze results in movement. All species of poplar bear cottony seeds, each possessing tufts of threadlike tendrils. The wind, ever the tree's loyal friend, carries these seeds far and wide to fertile ground. Cottonwoods earn their name from the white fluffy seed balls that waft on spring breezes, leaving a clean, pleasant scent in their wake.

The shape most often associated with the poplar–an elegant Grecian column–is in fact, limited to the Lombardy and its cultivars, which are planted as ornamental field boundaries and windbreaks. While the outlines of other poplars are not so archetypal, most do tend toward narrow-crowned loftiness.

Poplar in Folklore

It is not earth that has dominion on the prairie, but sky and weather. In some parts of this landscape, cottonwood is the only tree that flourishes.[18] It withstands the drought and sudden floods of the extreme Midwestern climate, can handle harsh winters and is not troubled by strong prairie winds. It is small wonder then, that the first people of the plains held cottonwood in high esteem, using it as a council tree for tribal gatherings. The tree's very shade was credited with great healing powers.

Native people knew well to listen to poplar, acknowledging the tree as a powerful entity, speaking with divine voice. The Oglala leader Black Elk tells us that cottonwood gives prayer to the Great Spirit by rustling its leaves in the wind.[19] The very symbol of the Lakota community, the cottonwood was the only tree worthy enough for the sacred Sun Dance ceremony.[20] During this rite, young warriors would often cut gashes into their chests. Passing leather thongs through the wounds, they would suspend themselves upon a Sun Dance pole, which had been fashioned from a cottonwood trunk. The warriors' suffering was their sacrifice to the Great Spirit.

Unlike the "New World," in Europe, poplar was primarily linked with death and burial rites; its purview however, also implied the overcoming of mortality. The Greeks associated white poplar with the conquering of death, dedicating the tree to Hecate and Persephone, goddesses associated with the Underworld. We remember that Persephone's other purview was Kore–the maiden of spring and rebirth.

Of the Celtic Ogham runes, Edad, often associated with aspen, indicates the overcoming and vanquishing of death.[21] The quaking of aspen leaves was associated with the tremors of fear. In spite of this, its energy was believed to help overcome dread. The holistic Bach Flower system uses essence of quaking aspen to aid in conquering "vague, unknown fears."[22]

The association of poplar with fear and death is pervasive in European lore. Perhaps it was due to the silence of the soft, limp leaves of white poplar, there the most prevalent member of the species. In this way, the tree must have inherited the purview of the silence of the grave. And yet there are some "Old World" associations of poplar with language and communication. Aspen was sacred to Hermes, the clever, loquacious messenger of the Olympian gods, whose duties included guiding the souls of the dead to the Underworld. The Victorian language of flowers signified aspen as representing "scandal, lamentation and fear."[23] Here language and speech are associated with poplar, albeit again in a negative sense.

Spiritual Traits

Regardless of Poplar's gloomy role in European folklore, I sense nothing of fear or apprehension in the aura of any poplars I have met. This is a singularly confident, carefree tree, enjoying nothing better than to stand with its branches swaying in the four winds. Its leaves flutter with an avid curiosity, seeming to speak in many musical tongues, as if picking up tales heard from far-off lands and repeating them in their rustling.

Poplar's element is air. The ability of its leaves to augur rain suggests an affinity with water as well. The tree's ascendancy is in spring, when its resin scents the air and cotton-like seeds waft on the wind—a celebration of the overthrow of winter's deathly silence. Poplar's aura is enhanced during the rainy seasons—in spring, when its voice presages the nourishing April showers, and later in August and September, when it heralds the cleansing rainstorms of late summer. Its traditional association with the overcoming of fear goes hand in hand with the need to talk about what we do not understand. Speaking our fears can help vanquish them. Discourse can be a weapon against both unknown and perceived dangers.

The Rune

The Poplar rune is columnar, illustrating the shape most often associated with this species. The five upswept branches, turning outward at the tips, illustrate the leaves' tendency to rustle in the wind. These branches also represent the five vowels in the English and other languages.

Kenning: Oracle

Significance: Communication, Speech, Language, Eloquence, Counsel

The **upright** rune observed in a reading suggests that adroit communication skills may impress others or be indispensable to an important project. Poplar advises that you should use your gift of speech well. You can be sure that you will be understood and others will seek your wisdom and expertise.

Inverted Poplar advises the wisdom of keeping counsel to yourself, at least for the present. Like a newly planted seedling that needs time to establish itself in its environment, your understanding of the situation has not yet fully developed. Watch and listen carefully. Good observation and listening skills lead to better understanding and more productive dialogue. You may also be in the process of readying yourself to give voice to something that must be addressed—so think before you speak. The inverted rune may also imply indecision.

Contrary or **toppled** Poplar, lying on its side, indicates uncouth or crude speech, arguments and quarrels. People are talking at the top of their voices, but not listening. Contrary Poplar may also warn of gossip, deliberate lies and slander. Ponder what is being proposed and beware of false witness or malicious talk. On occasion, the toppled rune suggests faulty, if well-meaning, counsel.

Poplar trees take their strength from air and water, the elements mediating between the two extremes of earth and fire. Quick-witted and eloquent, Poplar people are capable diplomats and negotiators. Able peacemakers, they have the ability to achieve concord between those who normally cannot see eye to eye. Poplars pick up other languages easily. At times, however, they can be a bit too loquacious.

Poplar is the fifth rune in the Talking Forest system. Our mother tongue is assimilated in early childhood. It is here that we learn to articulate speech, to communicate and develop relationships. How we are schooled to converse with others may mean the difference between invective and diplomacy, war and peace.

Juniper

Kenning: Nest, Nook, Cranny
Significance: Trust, Faith, Humility

Frequently cultivated and just as often overlooked, the juniper bush deserves closer scrutiny. In one of our local parks is a small rock garden that contains something like an avian apartment complex. Here stands a tall redcedar surrounded by other, smaller junipers, like a high-rise building circled by low-rises. In winter especially, these plants accommodate many small birds. Indeed, it is in the midst of winter that homely Juniper becomes less invisible. At this time, nearby or even within her scrubby branches, a bustling community of many small creatures is revealed. Then we frequently hear a cacophony of chirping and the furtive rustling of busy little beings. At this darkest time of year, let us be thankful to this humble plant for providing a haven and food for sparrows, chickadees, mice and other tiny woodland creatures.

Physical Traits and Environment

Juniperus hybrids vary in shades of green from yellowish to grey or almost turquoise. Most are variants of the small, unassuming common juniper. Two however, eastern redcedar and the Rocky Mountain juniper, are small to medium-sized trees. Junipers are tough and able to withstand the extremes of heat, cold and drought found in North America's weather.

Unlike most conifers however, juniper favours strong sunlight and dry soil. Her needles, unlike the flat, gentle, braided scales of her cousins, the cedars, are sharp and prickly to the touch, especially if grabbed tightly. These brusque scales help keep predators away from small animals hiding within juniper's branches. The foliage tends to lie flat across the canopy, thus protecting anything dwelling underneath from extremes of wind, rain and sun. Moisture and light, however, can still permeate the underbrush.

Juniper cones differ from those of other conifers. They look not at all like cones, but resemble berries with a leathery greenish or blue surface. Birds and mammals highly appreciate them, for unlike most berries, juniper cones thrive throughout the winter.

Juniper berries have long been and still are a common ingredient in women's medicine. A bath of these may be taken to induce menstruation, eliminate excess water and alleviate cramps. Tea made from juniper berries and new twigs makes an excellent disinfectant and aid in digestion. Since time immemorial, juniper berries were also used as the salient ingredient in gin, as well as to enhance the flavour of game, especially rabbit, pheasant and venison. Homely little juniper has indeed proven to be eminently serviceable to humans and other creatures. Treat her with respect!

Juniper in Folklore

Juniper's vigilance toward children and small animals is a common theme in folktales relating to this small bush. There is a delightful Danish tale that relates how the evergreens were the only trees who were kind to an injured bird. And of them, juniper also offered her berries as food. As a result of this kindness, the north wind rewarded the evergreens by allowing them to retain their needles in winter.[24]

The grisly Grimm's fairy tale, "The Juniper Tree," tells how a young boy returns from death after being murdered by his wicked stepmother. The spirit of his dead mother, now residing in a juniper, turns him into a bird. The bird sings to his family a song of how he was murdered, thus revealing the guilt of the stepmother, who is put to death. The boy is then returned to his former life by the magic of his mother, the protective juniper.[25]

In parts of Europe, it was believed that a witch could not pass a juniper until "she had correctly counted all the needles on the tree"![26] One wonders if these early "hedge witches" were inspecting the plants for mites or perhaps honouring the little bush for the medicinal and culinary marvel that it is. If the witches were German, perhaps they were using the plant as a sort of wilderness Lost and Found–for in that country, it was believed that Frau Wacholder, the spirit of the juniper, was able to compel thieves to return that which they had stolen![27]

Spiritual Traits

Juniper is a homely, drab little bush, invisible most of the year. She stands out only in winter and even then, you might hear her before you see her. A snow-covered juniper bush suggests comfort and warmth, coupled with a furtive impishness, especially when there are chattering, squabbling birds surrounding her! This scruffy plant's lively, cheering energy charms us in a way the larger, sterner evergreens never could. Feeling cynical? Work with Juniper energy! Juniper helps us rediscover the innocence and wonder of childhood.

Juniper's spirit is ingenuous and trusting, much like that of a young child; thus she is strongly associated with the Maiden aspect of the goddess. Used traditionally in women's magic and as an aid in easing menstrual pain, Juniper is fittingly associated with the rite of passage from girlhood to womanhood. As protector of small birds and animals, appropriate deities for Juniper include Diana and Artemis, traditional guardians of small, wild animals. The Welsh goddess Rhiannon, to whom birds were sacred, is another fitting patron for this small bush, as is Frau Wacholder mentioned above.

The Rune

Juniper's rune is similar to that of Reed, whose purview likewise is centred in childhood. The branches, joined at the bottom, imitate the bush's shape. Three short spiky tines depict the rough scales of Juniper's needles. Each is topped by a cup containing a "berry." The rune's shape reveals that Juniper, although sharp-needled, is trusting, offering her gifts freely to those gentle, considerate souls worthy of her respect.

Kenning: Nest, Nook, Cranny
Significance: Trust, Humility, Faith

This rune **upright** in a reading often suggests that humility is needed. Or you may find unexpected help from one who at first seems insignificant or powerless. On occasion, the rune indicates a girl or young woman in the querent's life.

Inverted Juniper is a warning of vulnerability or naiveté, of being perhaps too trusting. It may also be an indication that others are taking you too much for granted.

Contrary or **toppled** Juniper suggests the querent is unwilling to trust others, or has lost faith. Betrayal from a trusted source may lead to disillusionment or cynicism.

People with Juniper energy are unassuming but dependable. At times shy and retiring, Junipers make good friends and are especially kindly toward the weak and helpless. They enjoy working with children and animals. Many "unsung heroes" do tedious but essential work, which improves the lot of others or the general state of things. These people have an abundance of Juniper energy. Hospital orderlies, office janitors, daycare and homecare workers are Junipers par excellence and are deserving of society's respect.

Juniper's time of greatest strength is January, when we are laid low. Even those of us who like winter sports and love the cold must still, at the end of the day, seek a place to hide from the weather.

Winter has us by the throat and we must submit to it. The best way to do this is to go to ground. Humble sparrows and wrens know that little Juniper can house them. Juniper's resilience, cheer and hopefulness serve us in good stead at this time of year.

Hawthorn

Kenning: Fire, Torch

Significance: Respect, Honour, Anger

I miss the lane that in my youth led to the back woodlot of my parents' farm. Lined on either side with hedgerows of hawthorns, chokecherries and elderberry bushes, it acted as a buffer to the bare, open expanse of field. It was home to chipmunks, voles, field mice, and various species of insects and songbirds. But in later years, most of these hedges were cut down, so that some big-assed, newfangled farm machinery could maneuver its uncouth way into the fields.

Old folktales warn us about the consequences of desecrating trees sacred to the spirits of the land, particularly if they are hawthorns. I must agree that in the case of my family farm, the "little people" showed their displeasure in no uncertain terms. The chipmunks all moved to the back woods; many of the songbirds disappeared–I've not seen an eastern meadowlark since–and on hot, sunny summer days during walks "back the lane," there was less shade to cool one's brow.

Physical Traits and Environment

A small tree, hawthorn likes moist, rich soils in valleys, meadows and upland slopes. Often growing in thickets, hawthorn nevertheless does not fear solitude and is sometimes seen standing alone in a rocky glen or open field.

The demure yet oddly carnal flowers, rosehip-like fruit and sharp thorns establish hawthorn *(Crataegus)* as a cousin of the rose. In most species, the dense thorns appear on the trunk, large branches and joints of twigs. Grown closely together, hawthorns make excellent hedgerows, their spiny branches often intertwining. They don't take kindly to being clipped, which may explain their frequent absence from gardens. Hawthorns were once a common fixture on farmsteads, being used as natural fencing along lanes and between fields. Sadly, the wire fence has in all too many areas replaced this small, sprightly tree, thus reducing the natural habitat for many wild creatures. Prickly as she is, dense little hawthorn provides roost for small birds and animals, while repelling cats, weasels and other marauding predators with her thorns. As such, hawthorn is a superb choice for anyone with some property who wants to restore habitat for small wildlife.

Hawthorn tea from the leaves and fruit is beneficial for heart problems. In particular, it regulates the heartbeat and stabilizes blood pressure, high or low. Hawthorn gives relief from menstrual and menopausal ills, bad nerves, insomnia, varicose veins and hardening of the arteries. The wood burns hotter than that of any other tree. For this reason, in the Talking Forest system, fire is a *kenning,* or profound metaphor for the hawthorn rune. Nevertheless, it is not a good idea to use hawthorn as firewood, as it tends to blow off sparks. Perhaps it was this characteristic that led to all the folktales of fairy reprisal following the injudicious use of hawthorn as tinder!

Hawthorn in Folklore

Hawthorn is a tree of contrasts, with its delicate masses of pale pink or white flowers, its bright red fruit and its vicious thorns. Beloved by the English as a symbol of romance, chastity and young love, hawthorn was feared by the Irish as a bringer of misfortune.

I must say I fear no malevolence from this little bush. Clearly, she does have a mischievous aura. A fellow pagan once told me only half-jokingly, "There are goblins in hawthorns." Indeed, the fairies were said to favour this tree as their abode and many European peoples avoided cutting down or burning hawthorn for this very reason. You incurred very bad luck if you harmed a thorn.

In some parts of the British Isles and Brittany, it was considered unlucky to even take a leaf of any hawthorn that was standing alone on the moor, for fear of angering the fairies. In other parts of Europe as well, solitary thorns were avoided, as they were believed to be witches who had transformed themselves into the little trees.[28] Undoubtedly, actual witches did visit these trees in order to harvest the benefits of the good medicine to be found in the berries and leaves.

Hawthorn was often associated with virginity and female fertility. In ancient Greece and Rome, prospective brides and their retinue carried branches of the tree. Hawthorn was particularly sacred to a number of British maiden goddesses. Blodeuwedd was a flower goddess, created by Gwydion, the Welsh god of magic. She was made from nine different flowers and as she walked, her footsteps left hawthorn blossoms in her wake.

In another Welsh tale, Olwen was the daughter of a hawthorn giant named Yspaddaden. The hero Culhwch slew the giant in order to take his daughter's hand in marriage. This myth may be an allegory for the act of breaking the hymen in order to take a woman's virginity–the hymen being a barrier, much as a hawthorn hedge is. The thorny hedge barring unwelcome suitors from Sleeping Beauty's castle was most likely composed of hawthorn.

Spiritual Traits

On first sight, Hawthorn is not an awe-inspiring tree nor is her great power readily apparent. But her thorns are sharp, her dainty flowers beautiful and her red berries good medicine. Throughout much of history, women have been ignored or scorned yet we, like the hawthorn, frequently prove ourselves tougher and more consequential in the scheme of things than could have been imagined. Without women as the healers, the cooks, the cloth makers, child bearers and rearers, what would have become of the human race? The role of mothers in all societies has traditionally included tasks such as midwife, nurse, farmer, chef, diplomat, undertaker–the list goes on. Although often unsung, women have also been at the centre of great movements throughout history. They struggled alongside their menfolk through many a revolution and social upheaval, and kept home fires and industry going during both world wars. The civil rights, environmental and of course feminist movements could not have succeeded without tough, courageous women.

The tree is at her most beautiful in April and May, when she is in bloom. In Britain and many parts of Europe, hawthorn or "May" blossoms are worn to celebrate Beltane, the pre-Christian spring holiday held on May 1st. Thus, Hawthorn's season is spring, with Beltane in particular, being her time of ascendancy.

The Rune

The Hawthorn, an F-rune, is asymmetrical with a spiral on the left side. This indicates a feminine, flowering tree. A curving branch on the right, similar to those of the Birch rune, terminates in a dot, representing the abundant fruit of hawthorn. The rune's thorn, on the right side, is depicted as a short branch with a slash through it.

Kenning: Fire, Torch
Significance: Respect, Honour, Reputation, Ardour,
Anger, Vehemence

The kenning of fire pays heed to Hawthorn's qualities as a hot-burning wood. Hawthorn illustrates respect, resolve, honour and also, reputation. The rune speaks to standing up for one's principles. Hawthorn, however, is **not** courage, for that trait belongs to Pine, the ethical rune and to Holly, the warrior rune. Courage means facing up to or doing what one fears most. Fearing nothing, ardent Hawthorn needs no courage. Hawthorn does, however, represent anger, in particular a righteous anger–the desire to right a wrong, real or perceived.

The **Upright** Hawthorn rune in the Talking Forest array embodies resolve, determination and passion, as well as respect. Depending on nearby runes, it may suggest righteous anger.

Inverted Hawthorn indicates low self-esteem or embarrassment. It can also suggest resentment and anger held within–never a good thing. Hawthorn energy may be needed to redress these issues.

The contrary or **toppled** rune fallen to the left, with the thorn up, suggests contempt, open resentment, and sometimes, ire. If to the right with the flower upward, bad reputation or dishonour. This may be a warning that the querent has been compromised, either through disreputable behavior on their own behalf or by the deceit of others. The interpretation will of course, depend on nearby runes.

We all have a friend who is a Hawthorn. Frequently, they are a petite, spirited woman who takes no guff from anyone and is afraid of nothing. People with Hawthorn characteristics are stalwart and will take no abuse. They often have no fear, having great faith in themselves and their integrity. However, they can be easily offended and tend to take things to heart, sometimes harbouring resentment. They may be quick to anger, even to the point of aggression. Nevertheless, people with strong Hawthorn energy keep their word and stand by their beliefs and their code of honour.

Cherry

Kenning: Quest, Grail, Odyssey
Significance: Desire, Need, Want

Spring in Vancouver, where the author lived for five years in the mid-90s: picture street after street after street lined with cherry and plum trees heavy laden with blossoms. The ensuing summers were never complete without the agreeably frustrating task of trying to dislodge some of the ripe, luscious fruits. These hung always just out of reach of my makeshift gleaner, a windblown branch. Indeed, it seems the cherry-picker crane was invented because of the maddening elusiveness of this tree's fruit.

Physical Traits and Environment

In eighteenth-century England, the word "cherry" often denoted an attractive young girl.[29] From this, we have the modern-day metaphor for virginity. Cherry deserves her racy reputation. The fruit's disarmingly fleshy texture and colour, coupled with its darkly rich flavour, makes for an unmistakably sensual taste experience. Cherry and all her wanton *Prunus* relatives are inextricably associated with carnality. Neither the wholesomely crisp apple nor pulpy pear manifests the tart sauciness of cherry, the juiciness of nectarine, or the disarming fuzziness of apricot or peach. It is no surprise that these fruit trees are all close relatives of the seductive rose.

Cherry trees are only distinctive and easily recognized when they are in flower or fruit. These are small to medium-sized trees with branches tending to sweep upward from the trunk. The simple oval leaves are like those of many other small trees. To add to the confusion, the smooth bark of cherries resembles that of some birches.

In May, however, the cherries stand out. Like debutantes in flouncy prom dresses, these belles of the orchard flaunt clouds of petals in pink or white. Japanese hybrids are the most spectacular, sporting huge masses of double petals in varying tones of luscious pink. Black and chokecherry, the only shy ones of the bunch, display tiny white flowers held demurely on long spikes.

Like all members of the *Prunus* family, cherries are drupes: each fruit is a fleshy ball containing a single seed in a hard shell. The most familiar to us, sour or "pie" cherries, sport fruit in the suggestive pinkish red called cerise.* Cherry fruits however can range in

---

* Meaning cherry in (appropriately) French, the language most associated with love and romance.

colour from the Rainier's clear yellow overlaid with a scarlet blush, all the way to the purple-black of the ambrosial burgundy cherry.

Cherry in Folklore

More than any other tree, the flowering cherry, with its exquisitely brief blooming season, evokes evanescence and longing. Japan's temperate rainforest is an ideal climate for the Sakura, or flowering cherries, which grow in profusion there. These trees are honoured in spring, during the Shinto rite of the cherry blossom festival. During this time, thousands of Japanese celebrate the ritual of the *Hanami* or "cherry blossom walk." The flowers symbolize womanly beauty and the transience of life. It is in this season that the goddess known as the "Bloom Lady" weaves the tapestry of spring from blossoms of willow, cherry, plum and other trees.[30]

In Britain, cherry had a reputation for wantonness. Here it was believed that to dream of cherries denoted unfaithfulness.[31] Practical New England pioneers associated cherry with a more tangible, if less seductive threat. "Cherry bears" were irate black bears best left alone by any settler hoping to harvest the succulent fruit for pies and preserves. These animals were renowned for becoming indignant when anyone came too close to "their" black cherry tree.[32] And who could blame them!

Black cherry wood is hard and durable. Its intricate burgundy grain vies with that of walnut for beauty and utility, thus it is used in the making of furniture, musical instruments and objets d'art.

Spiritual Traits

Cherry energy is unquestionably feminine and her seasons of power are the blooming time during April and May, and yet again, when the fruits ripen in June and July. She is sacred to love goddesses such as Venus and Aphrodite and to Konohana-sakuya Hime, the Japanese cherry blossom goddess.

The Rune

The Cherry rune is heart shaped, indicating a tree whose manifest energies deal with matters of the heart: passion, need and desire. Each branch depicts a spiral, representing a flowering tree, which terminates in a large dot denoting the fruit. The arms of the rune curve upward and inward, as cherry branches frequently do, making the fruit all the harder to reach. This cautions us that what is greatly desired often hangs tantalizingly out of reach; much effort may be needed to achieve it. Nothing worth having however, comes without struggle. The inward turning of the rune's branches also suggests that frequently, what we seek is already hidden deep within us.

Kenning: Quest, Odyssey, Grail
Significance: Desire, Need, Wish, Objective, Want

The Talking Forest Cherry is not, like Apple, a freely given gift, but rather a challenge or sought-after prize, won only by struggle and perseverance. If this rune manifests **upright** in a reading, you persistently seek or desire something. Cherry positioned next to Tuliptree suggests attraction to another person, but this may be primarily carnal desire. Next to Linden however, the querent seeks a more lasting, loving relationship, although sexual attraction is still at play.

Inverted Cherry implies a desire or wish that may or may not have been thwarted and is not being actively pursued. Fear, laziness or some other factor is keeping you from joining the chase. At the very least, you should meditate on the goal or objective you seek. Is the quest legitimate or worth the effort? If so, do not fear to act on your desires. It is better to seek something and fail in the attempt, than to carry lifelong regret because you did not even try. Climb the tree to pick the cherries!

Toppled Cherry warns of wasted effort, recklessness, questing after chimeras. You've cut down the tree for the cherries but there will be no fruit in later years! It is possible too that what you seek is not needed or even beneficial.

People with Cherry energy are seductive and charming, very extroverted and at ease with others. They may be flirtatious, often employing their considerable appeal to attract others. Frequently, they are dreamers constantly in search of something. However, if they lack the courage of their convictions, they may become frustrated, especially if their plans are derailed.

Cherry begins the second of six sections of the Talking Forest, called *groves*. Each grove comprises seven runes and corresponds to a human life stage. The first grove, beginning with Ivy and ending with Hawthorn, encompasses childhood. This second segment denotes youth–specifically the years following childhood and leading up to adulthood–when the adolescent experiments with lifestyles, beliefs and sexual feelings.

Ironwood

Kenning: Staff, Backbone

Significance: Strength, Endurance, Vigor

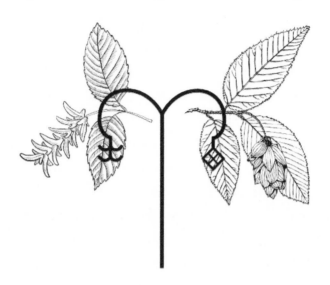

The moniker ironwood usually designates any species of tree whose wood is extremely heavy and hard to cut. In every continent of the world save Antarctica, there is at least one type of tree species dubbed ironwood in the language of the district. In eastern North America, the name refers to one of two species: hornbeam (Carpinus) and hophornbeam (Ostrya). Both are members of the birch family and exhibit that fey charm peculiar to birches, especially during mid to late summer when their whimsical fruits go on display. The word beam, derived from the German baum, simply means wood or tree; thus hornbeam refers to wood that resembles horn—smooth, hard and fine grained.

Physical Traits and Environment

Ironwood at first seems an inappropriate name for either hornbeam or hophornbeam. Both are denizens of the understory–small trees happy to stand in the shade of the giants of the forest.[33] But no other trees in North America have such tough and durable wood. Hard as the wood is, neither species is rigid or brittle and in fact are more resistant to wind and ice storms than many larger trees. Both ironwoods are also disease-resistant.

Hornbeam or blue beech as she is sometimes called, is the arboreal version of the mailed fist in a velvet glove. She has a smooth trunk and low, wide branches that are straight and true like those of beech, whom she resembles on a smaller scale. The sculpted curves of the trunk suggest strong muscle under soft skin, thus giving hornbeam yet another name: musclewood. Hornbeam's strength is much like that of a ballet dancer, lithe and graceful, yet tough and powerful.

Like her close cousin the alder, this tree loves water. She may be found reclining languorously over a stream or pond, thus meriting her other name, water beech. The hornbeam's fruit consists of a string of seeds, each surrounded by three leafy green bracts. These eccentric strings may be anywhere between two and a half to six inches in length and resemble tiny lanterns. The shade of hornbeam is dense and the tree can, on occasion, attain a goodly size of up to thirty feet (9 m). In the fall, the leaves turn a bright red or orange. Such a small tree is not commercially "valuable" but the hard, heavy wood was traditionally used for handles and other tools able to withstand constant striking or pressure.

Hophornbeam is in some ways, the diametric opposite of hornbeam. Small and ramrod straight, his slender trunk stands with the central or *leader* branch erect and reaching almost to the top of the tree. Unlike hornbeam, hophornbeam favours dry slopes. Standing amidst taller trees such as oak and ash, this tree has a "remarkable adaptability in a wide range of climates."[34] Where cousin birch has papery bark, that of hophornbeam is rough and scaly and tends to flake. When burned, the strong wood leaves very little ash. Hophornbeam wood is moreover so dense, it has been known to stop hydraulic log splitters. Little wonder that axe and mallet handles were fashioned from it. The logs were used as levers, giving the tree the name leverwood.[35]

Hophornbeam wears his fruit proudly, like a distinguished little general of the trees displaying his military medals. The "hops," which arrive in late summer, are composite pale green bladders or bracts, each filled with air and containing a single seed. When ripe, these turn a pale parchment brown. Less showy in autumn than hornbeam, the tree's leaves turn either dull gold or the lambent yellow common to many trees, a fitting camouflage for this little soldier of the understory.

Ironwood in Folklore

There appear to be very few myths and folktales surrounding the ironwoods. These humble trees are certainly skilled at not being noticed! Perhaps the difficulty of obtaining the wood and being neither orchard nor fuel trees deemed them less valuable to humans. In addition, both species tend not to form groups but grow singly. Their cousins birch, alder and hazel are capable of forming copses and have been found to be of much use in either their wood, their fruit and/or their medicine. The ironwoods seem only remarkable for the hardness of the wood and uniqueness of the fruit.

Hornbeam was among many trees honoured by the indigenous Ainu of Hokkaido, Japan.[36] Due to her pleasing shape, thick foliage and the ease with which she could be pruned, hornbeam was also one of the most used trees in European topiary of the seventeenth and eighteenth centuries.[37] Many First Nations people apparently used the wood of hophornbeam to frame their dwellings.[38] It would be interesting to know how they managed to obtain the very hard wood for this purpose.

Spiritual Traits

The Djed or ceremonial pillar seen frequently in ancient Egyptian hieroglyphics, was believed to have represented the backbone of the mighty grain and fertility god Osiris.[39] Upon his murder and dismemberment by the evil god Seti, his wife Isis gathered this along with the rest of his body parts for burial. The Irminsul of the Germanic people represented the trunk or backbone of the world tree, Yggdrasil. Many Teutonic tribes possessed a ceremonial Irminsul which represented the tribe centered within their community. Interestingly, the root of the word Irminsul is the same as that of the Greek or Roman *herm,* a word that describes the bust of a deity atop a ritual pillar.[40] Both of these symbols are appropriate for our Ironwood trees.

Hornbeam's aura is feminine, combining the strength of earth with the delicacy of the water she favours. She transmits a still, quiet strength. Hophornbeam, on the other hand, projects maleness and his elements are the strong earth that holds his deep roots in her embrace, together with the air to which his trunk aspires and which fills his hops. He projects a sturdy yet unassuming aura.

The Rune

The Ironwood rune is the first of the four double or *compound* runes in the Talking Forest, formed from a coupling of each of the exclusive runes for Hornbeam and Hophornbeam. The design incorporates the T or "lily" shape common to all Talking Forest runes in the birch family. The feminine Hornbeam is on the left or *distaff* side of the rune. The two smaller inverted "lilies," pendant from this branch, illustrate the distinctive bracts of Hornbeam fruit. The right side of the rune designates the male Hophornbeam. Pendant from its branch is a diamond crisscrossed into four equal sections, representing the hop-like fruit. The runes exclusive to Hornbeam and Hophornbeam (below) are similar to Ironwood, but display their fruit only on the left or right branch respectively.

Kenning: Staff, Backbone
Significance: Strength, Endurance, Vigor, Stamina,
Resilience, Adaptability

The runic meaning of the Talking Forest Ironwood is similar to that of Uruz in the Norse Futhark. It deals primarily with strength, stamina and the endurance to go on. The Ironwoods represent the backbone, the trunk or central locus from which all bodily strength emanates. In other systems Oak usually stands for strength; in the Talking Forest however, Oak's purview is power and sovereignty and its rune implies status. Physical health and hardiness therefore belong to Ironwood.

Upright Ironwood's qualities include adaptability, inner-core strength, the ability to "roll with the punches"; in short, all-round good health.

Inverted, especially if next to Holly, the rune may indicate that the querent will need toughness and resilience in the face of difficulties.

The rune **toppled** to the **left,** with Hornbeam down, implies rigidity or blockage of some sort. To the **right,** with Hophornbeam in the dirt, suggests weakness, inability to withstand pressure.

People with an abundance of Ironwood energy are tough, resilient and stronger than they appear. Hornbeam people are hardy, yet very often graceful. Many dancers would fit a Hornbeam profile. In order to bring their work to fruition, these seemingly fragile artists go through a great deal of effort and pain that would break larger, much "stronger" athletes. Hophornbeam people are frequently smaller than average, but their toughness belies appearances. Marathon runners and decathlon athletes have an abundance of Hophornbeam energy.

The Ironwood rune comes in the early part of the second grove of the Talking Forest. This group of seven runes deals with youth and maturation, the time of life when young people are entering into their physical prime.

Mulberry

Kenning: Spinning Wheel

Significance: Skill, Career, Occupation

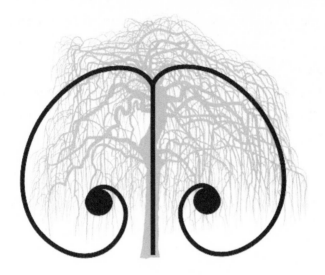

O f all trees not used primarily for its wood, Mulberry was responsible for creating more trade and careers than any other tree. The opulent cultures of China and Japan were built on the silk trade. The Silk Road was a land-based route from Asia to Europe and the Mediterranean. There were many goods carried on that route—spices, precious metals, fruit, rice and incense—but silk was the catalyst for trade between East Asia and the rest of the world.

The voyages of Marco Polo, Christopher Columbus and other Europeans were initiated, in part, to find easier routes to the silk markets of the Far East. Because the silk trade led to the manufacture of garments and a different way for people to attire and thus perceive themselves, in the Talking Forest system, the mulberry tree represents occupation or career: that which you do every day to sustain yourself so that you can live as you choose. Mulberry speaks to how we attire and label ourselves. We are cocooned in workplace uniforms: military, medical or the three-piece suit of the white collar professional. Our occupation becomes the primary catalyst of our self-image.

Physical Traits and Environment

The crown of the mulberry tree *(Morus)* is wide with branches that frequently hang or "weep," somewhat like those of willow. The fruit is an aggregate drupelet resembling an elongated raspberry or blackberry in appearance, but not in flavour.* The fruit of both black and red mulberries are pleasant enough when eaten and the seeds give a satisfying crunch, but the fruit of white mulberry, while edible, is insipid to human taste buds. However, birds and other wildlife enjoy them.

The most salient feature of mulberry is its leaves. They may be notched on only one side, or on both sides of the blade, with two to four lobes, as is usual with red or white mulberry. Black mulberry leaves, however do not always have lobes but display the basic heart-shaped outline and pointed tip common to the species. The asymmetry of the leaves recalls those of sassafras, but where sassafras leaves are thick and succulent, those of mulberry are soft and limp. Since mulberry leaves look as if a worm, finding them tasty, had taken a bite or two, it is fitting that white mulberry leaves make up the total diet of the silkworm caterpillar, *Bombyx*

---

* The brambles, members of the rose family, are not related to the mulberries.

mori. It is this small moth's cocoon that creates the thread that originally led to the Silk Road trade route. For both good and ill, the mulberry tree and its tiny resident would closely bind the histories of Europe and Asia and indeed, the rest of the world.

Mulberry in Folklore

The Chinese first began cultivating the white mulberry over five thousand years ago. They found that the larvae of the silkworm moth created a cocoon made of a very delicate yet strong thread. Women workers removed this thread by drowning the unfortunate creature in hot water. The cocoon would then be unravelled by hand and the thread later spun into cloth. With trade between the two countries robust, silk soon became a major industry in Japan as well.

Not surprisingly, the Chinese held mulberry in high esteem. The art of silk making was said to have begun when a silkworm cocoon fell into the Chinese Empress's tea and she pulled it out by its string. Another Chinese myth relates how the Weaver Goddess wove the Milky Way galaxy. This tale is intriguingly similar to the Navajo and Pueblo myths of Grandmother Spider, who wove the stars from dew.

The Romans deemed the mulberry to be a tree of utmost wisdom, as it did not sprout leaves until after the final spring frost. For this reason and for its use in the art of spinning, the tree was consecrated to Minerva, the goddess of wisdom, who presided over crafts and weaving.[41]

The famous nursery rhyme "Here We Go 'Round the Mulberry Bush" traditionally alluded to the working week and tasks that must be done: Monday we wash our clothes, Tuesday we iron, Wednesday we mend clothes, Thursday sweep and Friday scrub the floor. Saturday is for bread baking and of course, Sunday is set aside for church. It is interesting that of all the trees, it is mulberry that is mentioned in a poem about tasks and toiling, perhaps alluding to the tree's history in trade and commerce.

In a tale by Aesop, a spider quickly made a web and boasted of her craft to a silkworm. The silkworm, giving her the brush-off, said, "I'm too busy to talk. And anyway, you make snares from your thread for your use only. I make thread that is beautiful and from which humans can make other things." Although this is certainly not the message intended in the fable, one could also see it as an analogy of the differences between hunter/gatherer societies and technologically advanced ones. Like the spider, hunters and gatherers and early farming communities took only what they needed for themselves and reused it, as the spider uses her web, wasting nothing and making something as beautiful as it is useful. Like the spider in her web, these societies in essence, "worked from home". Being nomadic, they moved with the herds they hunted, and lived by the waters they fished and the meadows where they gathered fruit and herbs. Conversely, much of the work of "advanced" societies is in the making of articles to be traded to others living far away. Industry develops from this, as silk making evolved from mulberry leaves. Much as the silkworm must be killed to get its silk, societies based on trade and the gathering of wealth are all too often based on exploitation and various forms of bondage.

Spiritual Traits

Mulberry's season is June and July, when the drupes are ripe. The tree has a gentle, yet busy aura. Deities appropriate to her are Minerva, Athena and the Cretan Ariadne, whose thread helped Theseus escape the labyrinth. We may add to this list the Chinese Weaving goddess mentioned above and the Celtic Brigid whose purview was crafts, including weaving.

The Rune

The Mulberry rune, evoking the tendency of the tree to *weep* or droop, is shaped somewhat like an "M" with each branch long and ending in a fruit spiral.

Kenning: Spinning Wheel
Significance: Craft, Skill, Work, Career, Occupation

Mulberry leaves digested by moth caterpillars become silk, which in turn is made into clothing and other necessary items. The Talking Forest Mulberry speaks to that which we *must* do to put food on the table and a roof over our heads. It represents the skills needed for physical survival; the work we must do.

In a reading, the Mulberry rune alludes to career or occupation. **Upright,** it suggests work matters are going well: perhaps learning some new tasks will make your job more interesting or you may be recognized for improving client relations or public service. Perhaps a new career, a raise or a promotion is on the horizon; or a positive change in your present working environment is about to occur.

Inverted Mulberry implies too much time spent at work. The querent is rooted in the job to the detriment of their personal life. Perhaps you need to work longer hours to obtain something desired or needed. The inverted rune may warn of workaholism and frequently counsels that time away from the workplace is necessary to regroup and revisit what is important to you. If you cannot shorten your work hours, you must at least make full use of the limited free time you have.

Toppled Mulberry speaks to an unstable or unsatisfactory workplace or even loss of employment. Or you may need a change of pace, or another position for that desired new career.

Mulberry people are conscientious and creative. They are not happy with "just a job" but often seek out skilled trades or crafts. Mulberries frequently live for their work but must remember to cultivate outside interests: hobbies and relationships that can complement and enhance their skills.

Dogwood

Kenning: Crossroads

Significance: Opportunity, the Moment

Normally unassuming trees, dogwoods grab the eye when least expected, each species with its own unique character. The Talking Forest Dogwood rune signifies opportunity and the need to seize the moment.

Physical Traits and Environment

In British Columbia, a province replete with gorgeous and spectacular flowers, it is the Pacific dogwood that has the honour of being the province's official flower. Few can overlook the elegant charm of the greenish white blossoms, each petal tipped by a pale green or pinkish notch. These "flowers" are in fact specialized leaves or bracts, and they arrive in profusion in the early part of that province's long, glorious spring. The true flowers are the tiny bright green clustered rays within the blossom's central cone. Some hybrids of Pacific dogwood sport pink or red bracts. While this dogwood is the prettiest and most acclaimed of the *Cornus* family, the tree does not bloom for very long and it only shines forth in spring. Later in autumn, the leaves turn a drab brown and simply wither on the branch.*

The eastern flowering dogwood has spring flowers lasting up to a month before they wilt.[42] Our crisp Ontario autumn later bestows the leaves with a splendid carmine that rivals that of sumac. Red osier dogwood lacks the showy flowers of its cousins, but saves its display for winter, when the rich crimson twigs make a startling contrast against the white snow. Dogwood berries are poisonous to humans but enjoyed by a variety of birds and insects. They are bright red in most species. The stark white berries of red osier, however, make an appealing contrast to the tree's red stems and bark. Not to be outdone, the fruit of silky dogwood comes in an intriguing shade of faded denim blue. The smallest of the dogwoods, bunchberry is a tiny ground-cover plant about the size of a trillium. With its large, fleshy leaves and central cluster of red berries, it has the charm of a living floral centrepiece.

Dogwood leaf veins are unique in that they extend vertically to the tip of the leaf rather than horizontally to the sides. This is so the leaf can retain water on its surface. The wood of the tree is very attractive, being fine-grained and white or pinkish. The tree's

---

* The moderate climate of coastal BC does not favour riotous fall colour, lacking the good, hard frosts needed to turn leaves brilliant in fall.

other name, cornel from the Latin *cornus*, alludes to the smooth, horn-like hardness of the wood.

Dogwood in Folklore

This tree's smooth hardness was in ancient times, used in the manufacture of spears. In fact, the wood of the tree was so useful for weaponry that the English name may come from the use of it in making "dags" or daggers, and not, as some believe, from its use in combating dog bites!

During the Trojan War, a grove of dogwood and myrtle sprung up from the spears and arrows that had killed Polydorus, Prince of Troy and son of King Priam.[43] According to myth, many of these same dogwoods were used to fashion the Trojan horse. This hollow wooden contraption was ostensibly made as a peace offering to the Trojans for the desecration of the temple to Athena, which the Greeks had earlier defiled. The Trojans, believing the Greeks had departed, unwittingly towed the Horse into the walls of the city, not knowing it contained an elite force of Greek warriors. The resultant massacre irrevocably changed the course of the Trojan War in favour of the Greeks.[44]

First Nations farmers such as the Iroquois or Haudenosaunee, looked to the May blooming tree as an indicator that it was time to begin planting.[45] The Prussians believed that handkerchiefs soaked in dogwood sap would grant fulfillment of any wish.[46]

Spiritual Traits

Dogwood belongs to spring and fall, the two seasons of greatest change. Opportunity often comes easiest at such times of transformation. Apollo, the Greek sun god and Mars, the Roman god of war and agriculture, are associated with this tree, as is Athena, a goddess often called upon for aid. The Celtic god Lugh is also an appropriate patron for this tree. Known as Lewey Long-hand, Lugh had a sacred fiery spear that never missed its mark.* A thrown spear has momentum; it either reaches its target or doesn't. A good spear thrower must therefore rely on the opportune moment in order for the spear to hit home.

The flower, four petals joined by a circular centre, depicts the crossroad—thus the rune's kenning. The crossroad is the meeting of the four directions and frequently a place between the real and spiritual worlds–the World between the Worlds. Crossroads were the purview of Hermes, Greek god of travel and guide to the souls of the newly dead, as well as Hecate, goddess of witchcraft.

While Dogwood was seen by some Christians as the wood used for the crucifix, the cross is in fact, a very ancient symbol predating Christianity. In pagan iconography it represents the four elements of earth, air, fire and water, converging on the spirit or life force in the centre. It is symbolic also of the union of the Sky Father and Earth Mother–the phallic vertical and the fertile ground of all being. From their union at the centre all is created, all things are made possible.

---

* Although admittedly made of yew, not dogwood.

The Rune

The Dogwood rune's two wavy tines illustrate the broad, gracefully layered branches of this small tree. The branches end in curlicues, each with a small, curved line beneath it, rather than a straightforward flower spiral. This signifies that the bracts are not true flowers.

Kenning: Crossroads, Centre
Significance: Opportunity, Advantage, Action,
the Moment, the Present

Dogwood represents opportunity and the act of seizing the moment. Although the plant usually melts into the woodland background, at some opportune moment, each species displays some advantageous trait capable of grabbing our attention. Some have showy white or pink leaves pretending to be petals. Others display berries in bright or unusual shades. Elsewhere, the osiers choose the drab or monochrome winter in which to shine forth.

The Dogwood rune presented **upright** in a reading indicates opportunity close at hand. Thus it counsels action. You are here at the centre of the crossroads; the time is now for you to make your move. You can go forward or backward, left or right, but you *must* take action. Nearby runes will indicate how the situation can best be handled.

Inverted Dogwood with the canopy downward, suggests you should be on the lookout for an opportunity which is presently hidden but that may soon come to pass. Do as the veins of Dogwood leaf when they seek rainwater at the tip–that is, strive for your goal and do not be sidelined.

Toppled Dogwood warns of opportunity wasted. The moment may be lost or a chance may not come to pass, due to hesitation or faulty judgment.

Dogwood people are industrious and enthusiastic. They are able to see opportunity anywhere and can usually bounce back from failure.

Dogwood is situated in the second, the adolescent or youth grove of the Talking Forest array. Youth is the time when young people set out on the path to their future careers and lifestyles. Here there are many decisions to be made and each will have some lasting effect on you. But here too you have the option of making mistakes and changing your path, as others are more willing to help you when you are young and starting out in life. But while it is true that the journey is the end in itself, yet the wise person does not dally. It is better to seek out what you want while still young with few obligations and with none of the aches, pains and acquired baggage of middle age.

Sassafras

Kenning: Butterfly

Significance: Creativity, Individuality

Sassafras has a habit of sneaking into the oak woods of Ontario's Carolinian forest but it always adds a much-appreciated faery charm. If you step on and snap a freshly fallen twig during your woodland walk, you immediately smell the sap: a clean, spicy root-beery scent redolent of early spring. But the odd-looking leaves, unique to Sassafras, are its most salient feature.

Physical Traits and Environment

Sassafras albidum, a member of the laurel family, is fairly common in the Southern States, growing as much as eighty feet (24 m) in height. In the Northern States and in Canada, it is found only in the Carolinian forest and in somewhat attenuated form. The name is Spanish, or perhaps from a Native word whose meaning is lost. Sassafras was common here during earlier times, but nearly died out in Ontario during the mid-twentieth century. The advent of man-made climate change however, has allowed the small tree to slowly return ever northward back to Canada's Carolinian zone, where it is now thriving. Tolerant of shade, sassafras forms dense, deep-rooted thickets in rich, moist meadowland and by riversides. This somewhat invasive tree is often found in the understory of larger broad-leaved trees such as oak, ash and elm.

Sassafras leaves vary from a plain ovoid "laurel shape," to mitten-like with one or two lobes. All variations usually appear on the same tree and even on the same branch. The single lobe resembles a mitten, hence its nickname, the "mitten tree." A two-lobed leaf always has the second lobe placed symmetrically on the opposite side of the leaf. In spring and summer, the leaves are a rich jade green. In direct autumn sunlight, their colour vies with the sugar maples, varying from yellow, to orange, red and burgundy; but in deep shade they are limited to the clear yellow also found in autumn ginkgos. Numerous bird species eat the navy-black berries that arrive in early fall. Each berry grows separately on a bright red, club-like stalk that looks as if it were made of coral.[47] The sapwood is a pale or golden yellow and the heartwood and twigs are pale brown or orange. Sassafras contains a chemical that hinders the growth of larger species such as elm, thus giving this little tree a slight competitive edge over the forest's giants. The leaves are important sustenance for various moth species as well as for both tiger and black swallowtail butterflies.

First Nations people traditionally used the wood of sassafras for making canoes. An orange dye was obtained from the inner bark as well.[48] The leaves are dried and crushed into a powder called gumbo or filé and used to spice many dishes in Cajun and Creole cuisine.

Sassafras in Folklore

Many First Nations people used sassafras as an aphrodisiac, as did early settlers and African American slaves, who consecrated the tree to Erzulie, the Vodun goddess of love. The Ojibwe also used the root as a narcotic.[49] The wood of sassafras sparks considerably when burned. For this reason, Native people believed that the Great Spirit held the tree in high regard and thus, out of respect, avoided using it as fuel.[50]

At one time, sassafras twigs and roots were made into a tea for a popular spring tonic. They were also used as an ingredient in root beer. On his trip to the "New World," Sir Francis Drake brought back a large amount of this tea to Britain where it was soon touted as a cure-all. As a result, sassafras became the coffee of its day. Because its scent helped keep evils such as bedbugs, lice and disease at bay, the wood was fashioned into cradles, beds, chicken coops and living quarters.[51] Perhaps not the marvelous heal-all the early settlers once believed it to be, sassafras does purify the blood and acts as an antiseptic and stimulant. The tea aids in combating arthritic pain and the oil was in the past, used to relieve toothache.[52]

In the 1960s, the US Food & Drug Administration outlawed the use of sassafras for medicinal purposes because the oil was found to cause liver cancer in rats if administered in "tremendous quantities."[53] Sassafras was once the main ingredient in root beer, but its place is now usurped by so-called "natural flavours," which probably do greater harm.

Spiritual Traits

This solar tree has a youthful boyish aura. His elements are the two most mutable and volatile, air and fire. Spring and early summer are the times of year sacred to him, when the forest's energy is at its peak. There are elements of the Trickster in Sassafras' nature.

The Rune

The Sassafras rune consists of a basic T shape with the down-turned branches shorter than those of Birch or Alder runes. Curving out like horns above these, are two more branches echoing the common upswept silhouette of this small, slender tree. A secondary stem branches out on the right side of the main trunk, illustrating the tendency for Sassafras to copse or develop multiple trunks.

Kenning: Butterfly
Significance: Non-conformity, Creativity, Eccentricity, Individuality

Depending on its placement in a reading, this rune's energy can have either a vitalizing or limiting effect on other runes. For example, the **upright** rune next to inverted Elm may indicate a breaking down of the boundaries of convention created by Elm. This is not necessarily deleterious, especially if the obstructing boundaries are ponderous or too restraining. Next to Birch, Sassafras may illustrate the energy required for a new project or stage in life.

Sassafras in the **inverted** position counsels a need for discipline especially if Pine or Beech–runes of rigor and acumen, are nearby. It may also indicate a creative project in the making that needs thought, discipline and work to come to fruition.

Toppled Sassafras next to another rune speaks to a lack of energy or inspiration. It may indicate stagnation or a creative block, especially if next to Bramble, the rune of entrapment. If toppled to the left with the side branch up, this may indicate that something can be salvaged. Look to your Muse for help.

Like the butterfly or moth that transforms from a simple egg, to an intriguing caterpillar and a refined chrysalis, before its final avatar, great art comes from simple ideas, unusual vision and a desire to create. The sassafras tree of the asymmetrical leaves is unique. Sassafras people–creative and innovative–are likewise one-of-a-kind, often with a non-conformist view of the world. They are quite independent, preferring to march to the tune of their own drum. However, they are also frequently rebellious, stubborn and reckless. Sometimes loud and egotistical, they nevertheless often endow the world with colour, excitement, art and beauty.

It is delightful to have the sassafras copse brightening the forest. The motley leaves counsel us that there is more than one way of looking at the world and more than one way of doing things.

Catalpa

Kenning: Hammock

Significance: Leisure, Holiday, Ease

Standing in the shade of Catalpa is like being stranded in Tolkien's Middle-earth. Beneath her boughs, one feels as overlooked, yet momentous as a hobbit. This large, wide-crowned tree–so comforting, yet exotic as a giant toadstool. Perhaps it is the heart-shaped leaves the size of dinner plates; maybe it is the low-slung, mighty boughs, spreading from the thick trunk; or perhaps the narrow tubular fruit, jarring and equatorial, persistent throughout winter's whiteness.

Physical Traits and Environment

We in the Ontario south, used to our severe, snowy winters, are often surprised to learn that the lush, luxuriant tree growing in our backyard was not an ornamental introduced from the tropics, but a native to the Carolinian forest. While her appearance pays heed to lush, warmer climes, catalpa's other name, Indian bean tree, does *not* refer to India, but instead to Native American "Indians"–most likely the Catawba people. The Catawba, whose name perhaps means "river people," lived in the central-eastern US. The tree requires no river to thrive, however, only an abundance of amiable, sunny weather, frequent rain and relatively mild winters.

Both northern and the somewhat smaller southern catalpa are members of the bignonia family. Both flaunt giant heart-shaped leaves and masses of white blossoms streaked mauve or pink. The flowers bloom from mid-May to June. Although the foot-long pods are called beans, they are not strictly legumes, having tiny seeds embedded throughout a fibrous shell. Forming late in summer, they turn from brown to black and remain on the tree throughout winter. The pods evidently have sedative properties[54] and the Catawbas traditionally smoked them during religious ceremonies in order to induce hallucinatory visions.

As with many fast-growing trees, catalpa is short-lived. Her large trunk often forks low to the ground and the thick, over-arching branches form a graduated, dense canopy. This makes catalpa the perfect hot summer-day tree. However, the weakness of the wood frequently causes the trunk to crack or branches to break off in storms. This same malleability renders catalpa a popular medium for woodworking. Frequently used to make bowls, sculptures and other beautiful objets d'art, the finished product will display a swirled pattern of honey brown throughout a buttery yellow background. Catalpa has also been used in the making of musical instruments.

The female sphinx moth lays her eggs on catalpa leaves. When the black-striped green caterpillars subsequently hatch, they eat the leaves, frequently defoliating the trees. However, these infestations are usually sporadic and infested trees can quickly refoliate. In any event, these "catalpa" caterpillars are highly prized as bait by anglers in areas of the American South where catfish abound.

Catalpa in Folklore

In Japan, women shamans would attract spirits using a bow made of catalpa wood.[55] Along with the acacia, pine and hemlock, catalpa was one of the four major temple trees sacred to the gods of China.[56]

Spiritual Traits

Catalpa's energy is unquestionably feminine and nurturing. Her aura is one of ease and languor. Her element is earth, her season high summer. Deities appropriate to her are the opulent love goddesses Venus and Aphrodite and Oshun, Santería goddess of luxury and pleasure.

The Rune

An "F" rune, Catalpa is the mirror image of the male Buckeye, save that in place of a nut dot, she has a squiggle on the lower left branch, representing the pod-like bean. This asymmetrical rune with large spiral illustrates a shade tree with conspicuous flowers.

Kenning: Hammock
Significance: Leisure, Holiday, Vacation, Ease,
Luxury, Diversion

Upright Catalpa in a reading indicates a need for the querent to experience new and different sensations; you should make an effort to leave the home environment for at least a short time in order to recharge batteries.

An **inverted** Catalpa rune suggests extravagance, indolence, laziness: in general, a refusal to apply oneself, a tendency toward sloth.

Toppled however, the rune warns that sickness, injury or nervous exhaustion may result if the querent does not put aside time to relax and take life slowly. This is especially so if the rune is toppled to the left, with the flower and fruit going to earth.

Catalpa people are affable, magnanimous and happy-go-lucky. However, like the weak-wooded Catalpa, they are frequently lazy or weak willed. Catalpas thus do well with a partner willing to enjoy life with them, who can nevertheless kick-start them into doing the work necessary to achieve this.

Catalpa is near the end of the first third of the Talking Forest set, the triune that deals with youth. People often travel when they are young, while they are still strong and fit, and have not yet taken on debts and obligations. A travel vacation is an excellent form of education; thus Catalpa is a fitting rune for this early part of life.

Locust

Kenning: Sun, Lightning Bolt
Significance: Revelation, Clarity, Scrutiny

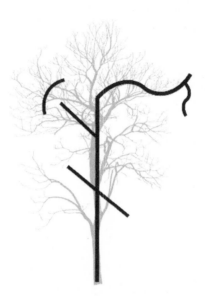

The Locust rune refers mainly to black and honey locust, the only true locusts of Canada. However, other trees in the legume or pea family, grown here only as ornamentals, are also referenced. These include Kentucky coffeetree, the mesquites of the American southwest and the acacias of Eurasia and Africa.

Physical Traits and Environment

The locusts and their relatives have composite leaves similar to those of rowan or mountain ash, but generally smaller, more rounded and lighter in colour. Locust canopy is sparse and erratic, desirable in a yard that seeks dappled sunlight or contrast with darker foliaged plants. Locust's charm is most apparent when standing next to other deciduous trees. Here he can flaunt to advantage his bright, yellow green leaves against the quieter grass green hues of other trees. Locust leaves turn a luminous primrose yellow in autumn and tend to disintegrate when they fall, lessening the need for raking.[57] A characteristic trait of locusts and indeed all members of the legume family is their fruit, which consists of seeds enclosed in pods. These seeds are bean-like and usually black. Depending on the species, they can range from peanut-sized to slightly larger than a fava bean.

Also known as false acacia, black locust *(Robinia)* gets its common name from the colour of the heavily ridged trunk. The sharply angled branches create zigzag patterns like lightning, making the winter silhouette a striking contrast against the sky. The tree, which has wandered from the southern States into the southern edge of the boreal forest, grows quickly and can easily become invasive. Hence, some farmers consider the black locust a weed. Nevertheless, like many members of the pea family, the tree contains nitrogen-building, soil-enriching bacteria in its roots—an asset to any crop field.[58] Whatever rural people may feel about black locust, the tree's resilience and its ability to withstand pollution, even in heavily trafficked or industrial areas, make it a welcome addition to cityscapes.

With their thick, furrowed trunks, black locusts become venerable with age. To see these trees at their spectacular best however, one needs to visit them in their home range–the Appalachian Mountains where they grow well past the eighty-foot (24 m) height limit usually cited in Canada's tree guides.

Prized for its very attractive golden wood, which is mostly sapwood and very strong, the black locust has been used to make many products. The flowers of the tree are pale cream or white and the purplish brown or black pea pods are about three to five inches in length. Both seed and pod are toxic.

Unlike the black, the honey-locust *(Gleditsia)* usually has a smooth trunk, although on occasion, the bark may be plated. Otherwise, he resembles his cousin *Robinia* in shape and size. Where black locust has decorous, rose-like thorns, honey locust brandishes sharp, nasty thorns up to eight inches in length and even wields wicked rosettes of these weapons on his main trunk. Every bit as tough as he looks, the tree easily withstands highway salt and other types of pollution. Appropriately enough, the wood is honey coloured, much like that of black locust. It resists rot and is often used to make artifacts and custom furniture.

Honey locust flowers, similar to those of black locust, are fragrant and creamy white. Blossoms of both species are irresistible to bees and are substantial producers of top-quality nectar. Honey locust pods are about a foot long–much longer than those of black– and depending on the species, they can be wavy or curly, or curved and crooked, like arthritic fingers.

There are many thornless cultivars of locusts grown, I suppose, to avoid injuries caused by people accidentally touching the trunk or branches. But thorns are a salient feature of the locusts, and I find the thornless varieties as much a travesty as roses or hawthorns without them.

If one insists on having a thornless locust, they should try Kentucky coffeetree, which can grow up to 100 feet (30 m) tall. The winter silhouette is similar to that of sassafras, with a profusion of gnarly branches held high overhead. The bark is furrowed and somewhat lighter than that of black locust. A profusion of compound leaves gives Kentucky coffeetree a singularly tropical appearance. Lasting only six months of the year, the leaves turn a clear yellow in fall. The intriguing flower is greenish white, or sometimes mauve. Sadly, Kentucky coffeetree does not live up to his name. The beans must be carefully roasted to destroy any toxicity, and the resultant brew is apparently an acquired taste.

Locust in Folklore

The acacias, which also belong to the legume family and closely resemble locusts, grow on all continents, save Antarctica. Also called wattle, they were sacred to Hebrews, Muslims and Pagans alike. The acacia was highly regarded in ancient Egypt, where it equally honoured the grain god Osiris, his wife Isis and their son Horus. The Egyptian mother goddess Hathor, in her primal form as a cow, gave birth to her children under an acacia tree. The boat of the sun god Ra was comprised partly of acacia wood.[59]

Elsewhere in the ancient world, the Ark of the Covenant was said to have been fashioned from acacia wood.[60] This tree's mighty status in the Abrahamic traditions was partly due to the beauty of its wood and flowers, its abundant honey and especially because it thrived in the arid, semi-desert climate of the Middle East.

Spiritual Traits

Although the pods and trunk are black, this angular, masculine tree has very strong solar energies. More than any other tree save Linden, Locust belongs to the sun. The light green dappled canopy honours the bright solar rays and the white or yellow flowers yield delicious honey.

But while Locust stands for light, he also represents darkness, indicated by the darkness of his trunk and seeds and by his sharp thorns. Shadows can only be seen in sun- or moonlight. Locust therefore relates to contrast and balance. Historically, Locust was equally consecrated to the loving mother goddess Hathor and to the powerful sun god Ra; the dying vegetation god Osiris and the immutable Yahweh of the Hebrews. Other gods appropriate to this tree are Apollo–solar and rational, and his opposite, Dionysus–god of passion and disorder. Locust encompasses both sides of deity–creator and destroyer. In the Talking Forest system, Sunday is the day sacred to this solar tree and his are the masculine elements, air and fire. His season of greatest power is summer, especially the months of June and July.

The Rune

Like the trees it represents, the Talking Forest rune is spare in form. The diagonal line through the trunk indicates the thorns of Locust. The branch on the right ends in a bean pod "squiggle" and the short branch on the left flaunts a small shade bracket, referencing the light canopy of this tree.

Kenning: Sun, Lightning Bolt
Significance: Light, Truth, Clarity, Contrast,
Scrutiny, Revelation

Upright Locust in a reading indicates a disclosure. It may be the "eureka" moment when all is clear or when understanding comes through like the sun through clouds. On occasion, the upright rune will signify some sort of revelation that will fall like a lightning bolt.

Inverted, the rune indicates a desire to seek the truth. It may also suggest something hidden that will soon come to light.

Toppled, the rune implies uncertainty or confusion, especially if to the **left** with bean up and thorn down. If toppled to the **right,** thorn up, it may warn of lies, deceit and falseness. This is especially so if next to the toppled runes Poplar (speech, communication), or Hazel (wisdom, knowledge).

People with Locust energy are very straightforward and actively seek knowledge. Rational, objective and able to see both sides of an issue, they make excellent researchers and detectives. They do not like falsehood or duplicity, but seek the truth and enjoy nothing better than to unravel the mysteries of life.

The Locust rune completes the second set of seven in the Talking Forest, the grove dealing with adolescence and youth, which is the foundation for all that will follow. Locust is the rune that illustrates the beginning of maturity, when we understand that things are not as simple as they used to seem. Truth is often stranger than fiction and there is more to life than meets the eye.

Tuliptree

Kenning: Herm, Icon

Significance: Lover, Beauty

The tuliptree, with his four-point leaves and six-petalled flowers, is symmetrical, asserting the ideals of balance and grace—simple perfection. His beauty and sparseness proclaim a natural icon: branches held high and lofty; a canopy open to the sky; flowers held remote and well out of reach of us lesser mortals; inedible fruit fit only for the gods; a trunk worthy of being shaped into an icon. Tall, stately and beguiling, Tuliptree is a tribute to the gods of grace and beauty... Deity made Manifest.

Leafing somewhat late in spring, tuliptree *(Liriodendron)* towers over the orchard. But he remains aloof from the season's blossoming like an awkward adolescent, embarrassed by all the botanical sex and extravagance. In June, however, the tree matures suddenly into a handsome youth, as lavishly adorned as any lilac, apple or plum. Now, when the orchard trees have lost their blossoms and are busy with the adult responsibilities of fruiting, tuliptree is centre stage.

Physical Traits and Environment

Named for the shape of both leaf and flower, tuliptree's main charm is that his parts suit each other so well, giving the tree a well-formed, spare elegance. Each leaf has four points and looks like the outline of a tulip flower, or as if someone had cut the top point off a maple leaf. These same leaves are a pleasing jade green, summery and soft on the eyes. In fall, they turn lucid buttery yellow or burnished amber. They are a favourite food of many caterpillars, especially those of the tiger swallowtail butterfly.

The large tulip-like flowers are light greenish-yellow with a wide band of peach or apricot orange near the base. On fully grown trees, the blooms sit upright on the upper branches tantalizingly out of reach. They make up for this aesthetic stinginess with nectar that by all accounts, produces a very nice honey. Topping off the Disney cartoon quaintness is the spindle-shaped fruit, reminiscent of a toy top or a thistle flower fashioned out of wood.

Well-proportioned and stately, tuliptree is the tallest plant in the Carolinian forest and in Canada, grows only in the southernmost areas of Ontario. The dove-grey trunk, uniformly latticed, can reach as high as 150 feet (45 m). As befits a relative of the pampered magnolias, tuliptree needs rich, well-drained soil to grow.[61] His roots burrow down deep and the airy branches spread into a high, sparse canopy.

Amiable tuliptree likes to grow with other broadleaved trees and with conifers, enjoying the company of hemlocks especially.

Tuliptree in Folklore

Surprisingly, there is very little First Nations folklore about this magnificent tree. The Delaware made canoes able to accommodate up to twenty people from the trunks of tuliptrees.[62] These boats earned the tree the alternate name of canoe wood.

As noted in the chapter on Ironwood, a herm is a pillar with a likeness of deity adorning it. Originally, herms were standing stones, simple and unadorned. Later, worshippers fashioned pillars made of marble or other stone with the head and usually the torso of a god carved into the top. Food and other offerings were placed at the base of these herms. Although they were named for Hermes, Greek god of travel and communication, these ornate pillars were also erected to other, primarily male gods such as Attis, Dionysus, and Pan.

Author Fred Hageneder adds that the honourary title *Irminsul,* given by Teutonic tribes to their world tree, comes from the same source as the word herm.[63] Deity effigies were originally carved into tree trunks. The earliest herms were frequently endowed with representations of male sex organs, rendering them ithyphallic, thus making them fertility symbols.

Spiritual Traits

With his preference for moist soils and his wide-reaching branches, Tuliptree favours water and especially, air. His season is late spring through summer. Adonis the Greek god of beauty and the beloved of Aphrodite, is a suitable deity for Tuliptree, as is Tammuz or Dumuzi, an earlier Mesopotamian avatar of Adonis. This tree also honours Adekagagwaa, Iroquois god of summer, joy and good health.

The tuliptree symbolizes the beloved, all too frequently placed high out of reach on a pedestal. True love, however, is not blinded by beauty but is able to see through to the person beneath. One who truly loves will respect the object of their affection, flaws and all. They can help them to strive to be the best they can, without fettering them or exalting them too much.

The Rune

The Talking Forest rune is depicted as a tall tree with double branches, the centrepiece at the top being an ample bowl-shaped lidded "flower," held well out of reach.

Kenning: Herm, Icon
Significance: Lover, The Beloved, Charm, Beauty, Grace, Charisma

The **upright** rune represents the beloved, the querent's present lover or spouse, one who is cherished, perhaps even worshipped. Where the Linden rune deals with the *state* of love, Tuliptree represents the *person* who is loved. And while Cherry indicates the *emotional* state of desire, Tuliptree illustrates the *object* of desire.

Either of these runes lying next to Tuliptree in a layout, may be especially revealing of the status of the querent's relationship with the significant other. If the Cherry rune is toppled, the reading may warn of obsession; toppled Linden will conversely show conflict or arguments with the partner.

Inverted Tuliptree often suggests someone worshipped from afar, an unreciprocated love that may not come to fruition. If near an upright Linden, however, it can herald the beginning of a romantic relationship.

Toppled, the rune may warn of a partner who is taking advantage of the querent. Alternatively, it may reveal that the querent is dissatisfied with their partner, perhaps even to the point of "falling out of love."

People with abundant Tuliptree energy are physically attractive, vivacious and often charismatic. Those associated with this rune must beware of vanity or egotism. However, they often have more depth of character than is generally recognized.

At number fifteen, the Tuliptree rune begins the middle third of the Talking Forest. This triune corresponds to the prime of life. At the beginning of this stage, young people's fancy turns to love that is more lasting. As the first rune of the third grove which represents young adulthood, Tuliptree leaves behind the grove of youthful passion begun by Cherry. He begins the search for love in this third grove, which culminates with Linden.

Maple

Kenning: Seasons

Significance: Change, Passages

In the "sugar bush" country of the northeast, maple syruping is still a rite of spring just as it was when I was a child many years ago. While the world turns imperceptibly from stark white and grey to the softer tones of fawn and sepia, the sweet sap courses steadily through the maples' trunks–the magic scent of spring, of life renewing itself–invigorating, euphoric and magical.

The mild days and cold, frosty nights of early spring in Eastern Canada and New England are crucial to the production of maple syrup. These unique conditions allow the sap of maple to run stronger and truer than anywhere else in the world. We can only hope that climate change does not erase the old "maple sugaring" traditions.

Physical Traits and Environment

The maple tree's most salient characteristic is its ability to completely transform itself. No other tree in North America undergoes such profound *elemental* changes. Apple and cherry blossoms hint at the lush fruit they will later become. Tuliptree's unique flower is the logical extension of the leaf's design and foreshadows the eccentric seedcase. But maple *(Acer)* is the tree that best encapsulates *all* the four seasons, transforming itself so that in each quarter, it becomes a different tree entirely. For an all too fleeting moment in spring, the tree billows forth its tiny flowers, gauche and gawky as a six-year-old on the first day of school. These flowers appear in clouds of the most vernal shade of chartreuse and are a perfect complement to the creamy whites, demure yellows and gaudy pinks flaunted by the orchard trees. Shortly after the flowers come the new leaves, unfurling like tiny hands. With these come the strange little seeds, each consisting of conjoined wings. These *keys* vary in colour, depending on the species, from green to beige to red. Hanging in clusters from the branches, they resemble tiny pairs of chaps or harem pants. Many species yield two or three harvests of these amusing ornaments throughout the warm weather. They soon fall to the ground with a spinning, helicopter-like motion, often landing far from the mother tree.

Summer in Canada is unimaginable without maple. We linger gratefully beneath the layered chrome green density of Norway maple, the purple depths of Crimson King, or the sage green glimmer of silver maple. Here we are safe for a while from the hot sun, the leaves of the tree folding over us like hands, caressing us with cool fingers.

Then Autumn...

There are maples that do not display brilliant fall colours. Manitoba maple, whose confounding nondescript leaves have earned it names like "box elder" and "ashleaf maple," has dreary, droopy foliage tinted a halfhearted yellow. Silver maple fares little better, turning a pallid shade easily outdone by the warmer yellows of birch and linden. These maples however, are the exceptions to the rule. Japanese, vine and red maple all paint shocking blood red splashes on autumn's palette. The leaves of Crimson King, a sombre brown in summer, turn any shade in fall from scarlet through to aubergine. But for sheer vividness and beauty, first prize easily goes to the sugar maples. Their technicolour displays are made possible only by the uniqueness of autumn in these parts—dry short days replete with invigorating frosts and chilly nights. Photosynthesis in the leaves shuts down, erasing summer's green. What is left behind is a high concentration of carotenoids, also found in carrots and peppers. The result is the breathtaking yellows, reds, pinks and oranges so familiar to us in Eastern Canada's autumn.[64]

I often consider the splendour of our fall maples as Mother Nature's recompense for our long, cold winters, when once more, maple transforms itself—stark and barren of leaves, yet arresting and regal in its austerity. The winter maple is a gentle grey giant in the white wilderness, elegant in its resolute silence.

Maple in Folklore

Canada's flag, its very identity as a nation, is defined by the maple. This tree is to our country what oak is to Britain or cedar to Lebanon. Yet for such a dramatic tree, maple claims surprisingly little folklore. We know however, that Native people held ceremonies honouring the tree, revering it as the "spring awakener of the forest."[65] An Algonquin tale of Grandmother Nokomis relates how she learned to tap maple trees after tasting the sweet sap oozing from a tree with a fresh gash in its trunk. But her pesky grandson, the trickster Nanabush, poured water over the leaves of all the maple trees, thus diluting the tasty liquid.[66] Thanks to Trickster, it now takes anywhere from thirty to forty gallons of sap to make just one gallon of maple syrup!

A Chippewa story tells of a warrior turning an evil magician into a maple tree. A more primal myth is the Iroquois tale of four brothers who yearly stalk the Great Bear constellation, killing him each autumn. His blood, spilling on the earth, causes the leaves of maple to turn red.[67]

Europe has its own maples. However, they are quite drab in autumn, for the climate there is rainier and lacks the frosty, sunny days needed for showy autumn display. Perhaps for this reason, maple in Europe claims very little folklore.

The dwarves of myth were sometimes identified with the maple.[68] However, I have not been able to discover why. In Teutonic folklore, these beings were reckoned skilled smiths and artisans, using spells and enchantment to craft items of great beauty and renown from gold and other precious metals. Because of this, dwarves have always been associated with the earth element and its mineral riches. Surely any dwarf worthy of his craft would covet such a tree–yielding a sweet, nourishing golden liquid and beautifully patterned wood perfect for furniture and artifacts.

There are many varieties of maples in East Asia, the most famous being the small Japanese maple of scarlet hue. Japanese and Korean people have made a custom of visiting their maple woods in fall much as we do in Canada. This event is a seasonal bookend to their sakura walk celebration of the cherries in spring.

Spiritual Traits

A Scandinavian creation myth mentions four dwarves as guardians of the four elements. Maple likewise belongs to all elements and seasons equally: strong as the earth in winter; offering the liquid food of life in spring; the large, dense foliage bestows the gift of oxygen in summer; and the fiery splendour of the leaves honours the dying sun in autumn.

Always changing, Maple is endowed with some of Trickster's traits. Just when we think things are going our way, the unforeseen happens. Upon later reflection, we come to realize that the unexpected event was bound to happen. We were simply not paying heed to the passage of the seasons.

The Rune

The Talking Forest Maple consists of a vertical stem bisected by two diagonal lines representing the boughs. A bracket on each side and one at the top indicates that this is a large broad-leaved shade tree. The design is elemental, reminiscent of a child's drawing, reflecting Maple's primal, iconic status. The rune also mimics the veining pattern of maple leaves.

Kenning: Seasons, the Year
Significance: Changes, Transformation, Passages

If Maple appears in a Talking Forest spread, changes are about to occur. Perhaps a new stage or passage is imminent in your life. **Upright,** Maple denotes the gaining of wisdom and personal growth by way of life experiences. While the Ironwood rune deals with adaptation to the physical environment, Maple speaks of emotional and spiritual acclimation to changes both within and outside oneself. Many of these changes are unavoidable, brought about by time and nature.

Inverted Maple in a reading suggests the need to look within and accept the inevitable transformation of the self. There is beauty and grace in all of life's stages. Maturity arrives with the wisdom to accept change and the ability to move forward.

A **toppled** Maple rune, lying on its side, indicates fear of change and the inability to deal with upheaval. It may also indicate stubbornness or being "stuck in one's ways." On occasion, the rune in this position may warn of a difficult upheaval in store. Time may be needed to adjust.

Maple urges perseverance through changing times and bestows the ability to face upheaval with grace. These traits are acquired only by living life to its fullest, accepting even the hard times, just as Maple prevails throughout the winter. Indeed, people with strong Maple energy are able to deal gracefully with just about anything life hands them. They accept the inevitability of the seasons and take life's tricks in stride. They are lively, vivacious and open-minded, enjoying life to its maximum. Maple people welcome other viewpoints and cultures and have multiple interests. Warm and generous, they can at times, be moody.

Maple comes near the middle of the Talking Forest set. By the time we reach our mid to late twenties, we find change easier to accept. Indeed, we often seek it out, whether in a new partner, new friends or a new career. At this stage, many of us will now experience one of the greatest changes we will ever see in our lives— the birth of a first child.

Elm

Kenning: Standing Stone, Landmark

Significance: Boundary, Obligation, Duty

A highlight of my 1950s childhood was the occasional family trip to the "big city." For much of the two-hour journey, our ample, dark green Plymouth cruised through woods, farmland and small towns. Along much of the route, stately American elms stood sentry-like along the shoulder of the highway.

Less than a decade later, catastrophe struck. These same placid giants stood leafless, brittle as rotten teeth, victims of the Dutch elm fungus. Fortunately, due to timely and aggressive efforts to eradicate the disease, Ontario's elms may finally be on the road to recovery.

There appears to be fossil evidence that the elms of Europe and Asia suffered a die-back during the rise of Neolithic agriculture and again with the rise of both the Bronze and Iron Ages.[69] Did early humans inadvertently cause an outbreak of Dutch elm disease? In any event, many Old World elms are now resistant to the fungus. Author and botanist Diana Beresford-Kroeger specifies that for elms, the "cycle for resistance emergencies is about fifty to one hundred years,"[70] so perhaps by the 2050s, the American elm will become immune to this disease. Many younger elms so far appear to be resistant. We can only hope that this slow-growing species eventually evolves a means to evade the onslaught of Dutch elm fungus, and that these trees will yet again line our highways in full leaf regalia.

Physical Traits and Environment

Elms *(Ulmus)* are trees of the temperate zone, venturing here and there into the southerly edge of Canada's vast boreal forests. The fruits, small pale green discs, each enclosing a single seed, are called *samaras*. In spring, these are massed on the naked branches in pastel clouds. Shortly after, when the leaves appear, oval, finely toothed and crinkly, they look for all the world as if they had been freshly ironed into tiny pleats. Most species of elm are tall, erect and stately, their trunks ridged and furrowed. A few, like wych elm and slippery elm, are vase shaped, but none have quite the characteristic umbrella shape of the American or white elm. One of the most distinctive arboreal fixtures in Britain's rural landscape is English elm. To this day, it stands as a boundary between fields, as it has for well over a millennium. English elm forms an umbrella-like canopy, but short branches fanning out halfway up the trunk break the columnar simplicity noted in the American species. The English elm's habit of reproducing from a spreading root system endows all members of this subspecies with the same peculiar shape and outline.[71]

As long as elm is given a big enough personal space, she enjoys the company of other trees. Nevertheless, we tend to picture elm as being alone in the landscape, surveying all around her. Throughout human history, in Europe and in North America, on city streets as well as in the countryside, the elm has stood as a landmark tree.

The Iroquois used elms as council trees and believed that a great elm stood at the centre of the Earth. At Shackamaxon, Pennsylvania, Quaker leader William Penn and Chief Tamanend of the Lenape, negotiated what has been described as "probably the only absolutely upright treaty offered the red man."[72]

Later in the eighteenth and nineteenth centuries, American elms would be planted extensively as an edge to farm fields and as an "avenue tree" on city streets and highways. It is now believed that Dutch elm disease spread so quickly because so many elms had been planted too closely together. It is our good fortune that, because of their size and grace, certain individual elms were customarily nurtured as centrepieces on the capacious lawns of institutions and wealthy homes. By their isolation, these trees were provided a safe haven from the fungus. In fact, until recent years, these ornamental elms were virtually the only healthy ones to be found in North America after the onslaught of Dutch elm.

Elm in Folklore

Elm's shade overhangs much of human mythology. The Romans held elm sacred to Saturn, the god of agriculture, and used the wood to build boats and furniture. A Greek myth relates that Orpheus wandered the world grieving and playing his lyre following his failed attempt to rescue his beloved Eurydice from the Underworld. His musicianship was so spellbinding, that elm trees sprang up from the ground where he first played.[73]

Elm is a tree that binds this world with that of Faerie. In European folklore, the tree was believed to be a favourite of the Good People. Smithcraft was deemed a very important science in early societies, due to its purview over horses and metal crafts. Thus in pagan traditions, blacksmiths are often associated with magic and hidden knowledge. As elm wood ably sustains repeated blows, it was used to make blacksmith anvils.[74] Thus the elm's reputation as a magical tree was enhanced.

Elm also binds our world with the Underworld. In Europe, it was planted on burial mounds and the wood was used to make coffins. Perhaps it is due to this association with death that the elm is shadowed by an aura of misfortune lasting to this day. The tree's reputation isn't helped by the tendency of some species to drop large limbs during storms, "on the head of him who leastwise trusts her shade," as Kipling's *Tree Song* ruefully relates.

The Dutch elm disease which destroyed so many trees in Europe and America during the last century, is just another bleak chapter in Elm's often calamitous saga. John F. Kennedy was assassinated in Dallas on Elm Street. Many argue with good cause that this event was a coup carried out by government and secret service forces and that this act precipitated the decline of American democracy. A moving example of elm standing as a landmark to tragedy is the Survivor Tree in Oklahoma City. This elm withstood the terrorist bombing of the Murrah Federal Building in 1995. The blast killed 168 people, nineteen of them children who were attending a daycare in the building. It is believed that because the tree had already toughened out survival in an asphalt parking lot, it was able to withstand being battered by shrapnel that included a car hood. This elm has since become the centrepiece of a poignant memorial to the victims of the Oklahoma City bombing.[75]

But elm is not all sadness and grief! In at least one case, during the medieval period, the elm may have helped to avert disaster. For unknown reasons, the Black Death, which ravaged Europe in the fourteenth century, was stopped just outside of the small town of Senarpont, near Paris. The elms perhaps acted as a boundary, hiding the village from outsiders, thus keeping the dreaded plague at bay. Six centuries later, the citizens commemorate these same elms, placing votive offerings among their branches for healing and beneficence.[76]

Spiritual Traits

Nurturing, feminine Elm evokes "landmark" in a way masculine trees such as stern Oak or craggy Pine cannot. As a tree of the farmstead, she shields the mysteries of the beehive and guards hedgerow and meadow for the smaller trees and their creatures. As a beacon, Elm delineates boundaries. Perhaps more than any other tree, her history shows the outcome of human actions. Air is her element and summer her season, especially hot, sunny July, when her tall shade is most appreciated. A goddess appropriate to Elm is the Norse Skuld, one of the three Norns, goddesses of Fate. Skuld's name means "necessity," or literally, "should" and she was the Norn of the future. Her name also suggests we must fulfill our obligations in order to smooth the path to a well-lived life. Elm is also aligned with deities such as the Greek Hera and Roman Juno. Both are goddesses of family, marriage and propriety–of being socially responsible.

As mentioned, Orpheus, famous for his beautiful music, is associated with Elm. Music often takes us from this plane into another, higher realm. Elm is also complementary with various Celtic deities of otherworld: the goddess Danu, the mother of the Tuatha de Danann, a race of gods who, in Christianized Britain, became the fairy folk. Elm is also appropriate to the Welsh Faery goddess Aine, as ruler of agriculture and fields, and to Gwyn Ap Nudd, a Welsh god of the Underworld, who like Hermes, is a psychopomps of the souls of the dead.

The Rune

The rune has a simple iconic shape. Near the top of the stem two branches curve up and outward from the lofty central trunk. A single large bracket extends over the top of the rune, indicating a parasol-like canopy.

Kenning: Standing Stone, Landmark
Significance: Boundary, Duty, Propriety, Limitation, Obligation

Elm speaks to the boundaries, physical and psychic, between the seen and unseen, but also those boundaries set by society. Elm asks us: what are the limitations of one's abilities? What is possible and not possible? What goals are achievable? What is deemed right and proper? In the Talking Forest system, Elm deals with propriety, civility and obligation: that which helps us to get along with others; while Pine, whom we will shortly meet, deals with morality: that which is ethical, even if socially inconvenient.

We all need boundaries. Children who do not have clearly set limitations often become fearful and insecure, having trouble understanding the "rules of the game." We expect a two-year-old to take a temper tantrum when they don't get their own way. We may not enjoy listening to their screaming, especially if stuck with them in a car or doctor's waiting room! But we tolerate it because, like the little elm sapling who cannot cast a large shade, the toddler does not yet know the boundaries of appropriate behavior. However, an older child doing this is extremely unpleasant and if an adult behaves like this, we call the police!

Elm **upright** in a reading speaks to the establishing of boundaries or limitations, or the fulfilling of obligations and the setting of examples. While this rune often suggests constrictions and duty, it may also imply shade, succor, order, routine—an umbrella or boundary that protects.

Inverted, Elm may indicate an uncertainty as to what one's boundaries are. It suggests a feeling of not belonging or being out of place or out of touch with one's surroundings. The rune may also reveal resentment of doing what is necessary to complete social obligations.

Toppled, Elm may signify degradation, being laid low, uprooted or otherwise having one's boundaries invaded. Perhaps there is a hidden weakness. Otherwise, the rune may imply public reproval due to tactlessness or impropriety. Only occasionally does toppled Elm warn of calamity. In this way, the rune is similar to the Tower card of the Tarot deck.

People who possess Elm energy are calm, stately and graceful. They make others feel safe and at ease. As a result, they are often approached for support and guidance. However, they have a habit of taking on too many problems, which may eventually cause a system overload. Rather than appearing vulnerable, Elms tend to hide their own weaknesses and refuse to seek needed support. It is therefore crucial that Elm people keep their boundaries intact.

Evergreen

Kenning: Sanctuary, Shelter

Significance: Peace, Tranquility, Sleep

The silent evergreens stand guardian in the winter: dark beacons in the white wilderness. When all else is gone, they remain. Overlooked most of the year, Spruce and Fir possess the winter landscape. Hidden within their silence, birds, squirrels and other small animals sleep in safety, perhaps dreaming of the spring to come. Evergreen cones also sleep, closed against the north wind; each scale folded like a blanket over its single treasured seed. There is no artifice about the evergreens: solid, unlovely, unblossomed, unadorned, yet beautiful in their austerity, like the snow-covered world that is their domain.

The silence of winter is a little death, a time when Mother Earth nestles into her white shawl and takes a well-earned rest from the harvest. At this time, we owe it to ourselves to follow her example and not overdo things. We need the Yuletide holiday so that we may draw in, rest and contemplate the passing year and that which is to come. Instead, we run about helter-skelter, shopping and spending, wondering why we become depressed, irritable and run down.

Physical Traits and Environment

Both fir *(Abies)* and spruce *(Picea)* are members of the pine family, growing between twenty-five to sixty feet (7 to 18 m) in height. In both species, the branches tend to slope downward, enabling them to support heavy loads of snow without injury to the tree. The two species are often very difficult to tell apart, the most noticeable difference being expressed through the cones. Those of fir stand upright on the bough. When ripe, they eventually disintegrate, leaving nothing but a pointed central stalk. Spruce cones, on the other hand, hang pendant and do not crumble, remaining intact long after they have fallen from the bough.

Telling the two species apart without the cones is much trickier. The inch-long, dark green waxy needles of both are very similar. They are not bundled together like those of pine or larch. Each needle is instead attached separately to its twig. Fir needles tend to be flatter than those of spruce and are softer and less prickly. When torn from the twig, they leave behind a tiny concave scar. The curmudgeonly spruce's needles, however, leave behind a bristly little peg. There is sap in the needles of both species that safeguards them from extremes of cold. This substance is common to most conifers and it is what gives them their clean, invigorating scent.

The aromatic balsam fir is the most common of its species in Eastern Canada and New England. Its classic steeple shape makes it our most popular Christmas tree. This symmetrical silhouette is common to most fir species. The word "spruce" comes from the Old French word *Pruce* meaning variously, *Prussian* or *dapper, stylish,* and probably alludes to the tree's military bearing.[77] More prevalent in North America than fir, spruce exhibits one of two basic silhouettes. The most familiar shape is the steepled Christmas tree outline common also to firs. Colorado blue spruce and white spruce are two notable examples of this type. So long as these trees grow in the open, their boughs will flare out all the way down the trunk, the bottom ones sweeping the ground. Other spruces, including our native black spruce, prefer to hold their branches in irregular clumps high above a lofty trunk, like dark, clustered storm clouds. Spruce trunks are generally scaled like alligator hide.

Fir and Spruce in Folklore

In spite of the somber mien of these dark-foliaged trees, conifers proclaim a sense of hope, flaunting the green of vitality throughout the Dark Lord's winter. Spruce and fir were frequently planted in cemeteries as symbols of everlasting life.

Native peoples attribute many legends to account for the tenacity of conifer foliage throughout the winter. An amusing Cherokee tale relates how the Great Spirit granted evergreens the right to keep their leaves all year, since they managed to remain awake during winter, standing guardian over Earth. The broad-leaved trees, however, were caught snoozing. As a result, from that time forth, in winter, deciduous trees are now forced to stand naked in disgrace! The Eastern Woodlands peoples considered the spruce to be the tree of peace, for it willingly provided shelter for humans and animals during the cold season.

In autumn, the Votyaks of Finland and Russia honoured their "Spirit of the Forest" by laying offerings to him under a great fir tree.[78] This mighty personage was represented as carrying an uprooted fir tree as a sceptre. Sometimes he used the tree as a club with which to clobber other forest giants![79] A tale from the Harz Mountains in Germany maintains that canaries sing sweetly in gratitude to the fir trees that protect them during stormy winters.[80] In Poland, the fir woods were a favoured haunt of Dziwitza, and her wild retinue of Boruta—female woodland spirits. Their attributes were strikingly similar to those of the Greek Artemis and her nymphs.[81] During classical times, a sacred fir grove flourished in Etruria. This was dedicated to Sylvanus, a Roman god of the woodlands somewhat akin to the Greek Pan.[82]

It is said that the great cathedrals were modeled after the extensive evergreen forests of Europe. Many of the steeples of the old world's mighty churches are certainly reminiscent of the fir's lofty, symmetrically perfect crown.

Our own custom of the Christmas tree originates from pagan practices. At the beginning of winter, the Teutonic peoples of ancient Europe would place dried fruits onto an evergreen tree that they had felled. The tree was a sacrifice to the gods of earth and weather who, it was hoped, would grant an abundant harvest in the coming year. The German hymn, *O Tanenbaum* (O Christmas Tree), bespeaks these pagan origins. No surprise then, that the first North American Christmas trees were brought to New England by German settlers from Hesse and Moravia.[83] From there, the fashion of decorating evergreen trees at Yuletide grew into the lavish spectacle it is today, replete with ornaments, tinsel and electric lights.

In the Celtic Ogham system, Ailm, attributed to silver fir by many modern pagans, indicates birth and beginning.[84] This interpretation echoes the rebirth of the sun at winter solstice, at a time when only conifers seem to thrive.

Spiritual Traits

In the Talking Forest system, Evergreen always refers to the compound rune for Fir and Spruce. The elements for Evergreen are earth and air and its season is mid-winter, especially the month of December. Evergreens radiate a quiet, reposeful aura. Suitable gods for the rune are Hypnos, the Greek god of sleep and his Roman counterpart Somnus. Dziwitza, protector of Poland's forests, and Sylvanus, guardian of Roman woods, are also appropriate, as are

Genetaska, Iroquois goddess of peace and her Huron counterpart Djigonasee. In Scandinavia, where the evergreens thrive, they are sacred to Skadi, the Norse goddess of mountains and to Ullr, a prototype god of winter and the hunt.

The Rune

The Evergreen rune mimics the pyramidal shape of these trees and is the second of the compound runes in the Talking Forest system.* It is comprised of the left half of the rune exclusive to Fir and the right half of the Spruce rune.

Fir, whose softer needles and more graceful form suggest a feminine tree, thus owns the left or distaff side of the compound rune. The upright ovals on the higher branches further denote a tree with upright cones held high out of reach. The masculine Spruce, on the right side, displays downward-turning branches, terminating in hanging ovals, mimicking a tree generous with his pendant cones.

Kenning: Sanctuary, Shelter from the Storm
Significance: Hope, Peace, Refuge, Sleep, Tranquility

Within their dense branches, Spruce and Fir offer safety for creatures needing protection from winter's extreme weather. The Evergreen rune thus deals with peace and repose, as well as

---

* The first compound rune is Ironwood. The others are Hazel and Oak.

sanctuary from the excesses of day-to-day living. This rune also represents sleep, for it too is a type of sanctuary. We need sleep in order for our bodies and minds to remain healthy. The **upright** rune manifest in a reading indicates the attainment of peace and tranquility, even if all around us is in upheaval.

Inverted, the Evergreen rune is an admonition to seek quiet and tranquility. If you are presently experiencing great upheaval, you may need a safe place in which to contemplate the present disruption of your life and how it got to that juncture.

Toppled, the rune suggests ordeal, discord and tribulations. You should at least be prepared to experience some anxiety, worry and inconveniences.

Evergreen people can at times be as brusque as the sharp needles of spruce. In the main, however, they are kindly and well-meaning. They are not particularly glamorous people, tending to fade into the background, like summer conifers. Those around them however, soon come to appreciate Evergreen folk, as they are ever calm and compassionate, and often willing to lend a helping hand. Evergreens frequently prove to be of great service in an emergency. They love a challenge and are tough enough to weather any storms that come their way. They frequently work in occupations offering hospitality, aid and shelter to others.

Ash

Kenning: Well, Aquifer

Significance: Unity, Integration

Venerated in northern Europe since time immemorial, Ash does not boldly announce its nobility. Beech is mightier, Oak more iconic and Cherry more flamboyant. In fact, Ash doesn't even look like a northern tree, its latticed canopy evoking the bamboo stands of Asia rather than the Hyperborean forests of the Dagda or the misty fjords of Odin. But, standing under the sun-dappled shade of a tall straight ash on a warm summer's day in say, Edinburgh or Uppsala, one might easily forget the harsh and bone-chilling winter that was. And the wood of Ash burns long and true—the best fuel around in a cold climate. This alone is reason enough why Ash was so revered in ancient northern Europe.

Physical Traits and Environment

Profoundly symmetrical in silhouette and trunk design, most species of ash *(Fraxinus)* have roots as straight and deep as the branches are high. The bark has a distinctive diamond pattern. Because it favours moist soils, farmers frequently plant ash in order to dry up wet fields, or claim farmland from swamps. This paves the way for trees that prefer dryer conditions. While white ash likes the company of other tree species, the European or common ash generally stands alone and does not often form thickets. In fact, a grove of common ash is a sure sign that a natural aquifer is nearby.

Ash is the exemplar of timber trees, its very name proof of its reputation as fuel. Even when green, ash burns well, due partly to the oiliness of the wood.[85] In fact, the tree is a member of the *Oleaceae* or olive family.

The light-coloured, straight-grained wood is supremely utilitarian, very hard and strong, yet springy. Because of its supple strength, the wood was traditionally made into spears, staffs and other weapons. The spears of Beowulf and King Arthur were both said to have been made of ash and medieval knights jousted with lances fashioned from this mighty wood.[86] Ash apparently draws more lightning than any other tree, save oak–"avoid ash, for it draws the flash," was an old English admonition.

Ash in Folklore

The ash tree looms "out of the murk of legendary time"[87] over the landscape and mythology of Germania and Scandinavia. The mighty Yggdrasil is the world tree from which all life came. An eagle lives in the crown of the tree and a hawk stands lookout on the eagle's brow. Many realms dwell among this tree's branches, the highest being Asgard, the home of the mighty Aesir–heroic, warlike gods of the Norse, whose chief was Odin All-Father. On another branch is Vanaheim, home of the Vanir, elder gods of fertility, land and sea, who were worshipped before the coming of the Aesir. Yet a third branch, Jotunheim, is the home of the giants, enemies of the gods. The Earth, Midgard, is in the centre of the tree and this is the home of men. Deer feed on the branches of Yggdrasil. Ratatosk the squirrel runs up and down the trunk, spreading malicious rumours between the eagle on high and the Nidhogg dragon, who gnaws at one of the tree's roots in Nifelheim, the Norse "hell." Of the other two roots, one is located at the well of the three Norns–Urd, Verdandi and Skuld–who keep record of what was past, what is and what will be. The well of the wise god Mimir, counselor to Odin, is at the third root. While it was believed that the world would end at Ragnarok, the Norse Armageddon, the mighty ash Yggdrasil would continue to thrive into a new and brighter future.

A famous myth from the Norse Hávamál is the strange tale of Odin who, with his own spear, impaled himself on the World Tree for nine days and nights, a sacrifice to himself. He did this in order to gain spiritual inspiration and knowledge of the Norse runes–the Futhark–whose mysteries he in turn, taught mankind.

The Druids honoured ash as the tree representing balance and the "Marriage of Opposites," providing links between the "inner and outer worlds." Author Jane Gifford further notes that due to its erect height and deep roots, the ash denotes a sense of groundedness and belonging to the landscape.[88]

The Askafroa or Eschenfrau was the Ash Wife, who was considered extremely malevolent and destructive. It was necessary to make sacrifices to her on *Ash* Wednesday in order to appease her.[89] Perhaps the Askafroa is a remnant of the belief in the Valkyrie, warrior handmaidens of Odin.

Ash has a strange affinity with the serpent. Native Americans used white ash to cure snakebite as well as other injuries.[90] There was a belief in Europe that snakes would not even go beneath the shade of an ash tree and a popular folk charm against snakebite was to place ash twigs in a circle.[91]

Spiritual Traits

Ash's elements are water–for the tree invariably seeks the pure, clean underground stream; and fire–throughout history, ash wood was preferred as fuel above all other woods. As mentioned, this tree has a strong affinity with the snake. This animal is also associated with water, often living in or close by a water source. In many pagan traditions, the snake was endowed with great wisdom. Indeed we remember that the serpent of the Garden of Eden urged humans to eat of the tree of *knowledge*. Ash is assuredly associated with the god Odin and thus Wednesday or Wotan's Day belongs to Ash.

The Rune

This is a simple, elegant rune for a simple, elegant tree. As with the Talking Forest Maple, the Ash rune has two tiers of branches with brackets at the sides and top, indicating a tree of ample shade. The Ash rune's tines, however, are wavy, differentiating it from the straight diagonals of Maple. In the Talking Forest, wavy lines often indicate a special characteristic about a shade tree's branches or foliage–in the case of Ash, the lattice effect of the leaves. The waviness of the branches also pertains to the clean, running underground streams this tree avidly seeks.

Kenning: Well, Aquifer
Significance: Unity, Integration, Connectivity, Spiritual Awareness, Introspection

Water-loving Ash is the tree of Odin, Norse god of magic and shamanism. As the tree of the Norns from which Odin drew inspiration, Ash's power aids in divination and introspection and it takes its place near the centre of the Talking Forest. The tree also drinks deep from Mimir's well of inspiration and speaks to harmony between the inner and outer worlds.

Upright, Ash represents spirituality, contemplation and meditation. As a tree which often stands alone, its appearance in a reading may indicate that the querent needs to step back and be alone for a while. Perhaps some introspection and reflection is in order. This is even more crucial if the rune is **inverted** and may imply someone experiencing a "dark night of the soul." Nidhogg, the dragon of destruction, lies at the root of Yggdrasil. Looking inside ourselves to our dark half is sometimes frightening, but in order to grow spiritually, we need to understand this side: we must face the dragon within.

Contrary or **toppled** Ash is uprooted. Eagle and hawk, who should be perched on Yggdrasil's highest branch, looking out on the world below them, are busy playing in the dirt! In this position, Ash is telling the querent that they may not be firmly enough rooted in day-to-day reality, nor are they looking within to the spirit. This rune on its side may indicate the querent is living an illusion. Perhaps it is time to seek balance, to follow Ash's example by firmly planting our feet on the earth and lifting our heads into the clouds.

People associated with Ash energy are idealistic, ascetic and spiritual. Those who have experienced difficulties or are seeking higher wisdom frequently need to go within the psyche to find truth within. Ash will help them prevail through this process.

Rose

Kenning: The Goddess

Significance: Secrets, Sanctity, Women's Mysteries

The expansive family Rosaceae which includes cherry, hawthorn, apple, almond, raspberry, strawberries and many other plants, gives the rose proper, the honour of its name. With perhaps more myths surrounding her than any other plant, Rose absolutely stands for the Sacred Feminine.

Physical Traits and Environment

Just as there are many faces of the Goddess, there are many variations of the *Rosa* flower. In addition to our familiar thorny shrubs are wall-climbing creepers, bushes ten feet (3 m) tall, even pygmy roses that fit comfortably into tiny flowerpots. All varieties have small, finely-toothed oval leaves, a few with pink-tinged edges (a feature common to some apple and bramble species as well). The fruit of the rose is a red or orange hip, resembling a small oval crabapple. The large calyx, like that of a pomegranate, is opposite the stem of the fruit and resembles a small crown.

Hybrid rose blossoms come in an astonishing array of colours: sterling silver, apricot, nearly black, white splotched with red and so on. However, the most common colours are still yellow, white and of course, all permutations of red, from the palest pink to the deepest crimson. More than any other flower, the rose owns red. The French word for "pink" is *rose*. Blossoms vary in type from the demure briar, a simple, five-petalled affair, to the tea rose– that well-known voluptuary of the prize-winning garden–with its masses of petals spiraling into the centre of the flower. The damask has the strongest scent of all roses, the petals being a common ingredient in the manufacture of perfumes. Rose water is extracted from the cabbage rose* and used in Middle Eastern and South Asian baking. It is also an incomparable remedy for eradicating wrinkles and softening the skin. Sold in most drugstores, rosewater is very cheap; a simple but effective beauty aid that has been used since time immemorial. No twenty-first century creams or lotions can compare.

---

* So-called for the shape of the large, blowsy flowers.

Rose in Folklore

Roses were first bred for their flowers and scent in Persia, which is now Iran. One caliph, it is said, was so smitten by roses in bloom, that he wore only rose coloured clothing and had his royal carpets sprinkled with rose water.[92] Rose was the sacred flower of Aphrodite, Greek goddess of love and carnality and her Roman counterpart, Venus. One myth tells how Adonis, Aphrodite's beautiful lover, was gored to death while hunting a wild boar. The goddess was inconsolable and red roses grew from her endless tears. Another myth relates how Chloris, the Greek goddess of flowers, was touched by the beauty of a dead nymph she found in the forest. Saddened by her death, she transformed the nymph into the glorious flower we know today.[93] In Scandinavia, rose was sacred to the Norse goddess Freya, whose purview was fertility and whose promiscuity was legendary.

The term *sub rosa,* literally "beneath the rose," means "secret"–that which cannot be divulged. It originated in Imperial Rome, where dining rooms often had plaster roses sculpted into the middle of ceilings. It was established custom that anything said within such a room, where there was much drinking and loosening of tongues, was under no circumstances to be repeated outside.

From the beginning, the voluptuous rose has been associated with women's mysteries, especially those of menstruation and childbirth. In herbal medicine, rosehips were and are often used for women's ailments, specifically to alleviate menstrual cramps or to regulate monthly bleeding. The acidic rosehips, containing prodigious amounts of vitamin C, can be made into a syrupy, carmine red tea. While to some disquietingly suggestive of blood, this refreshing beverage is a taste worth acquiring. Briar rose, also called "witches briar,"[94] is used for kidney problems, digestive complaints and rheumatism, as well as for women's ailments as mentioned above.

Spiritual Traits

Our most celebrated flower, Rose is used to symbolize the Goddess and by extension, womankind. With her voluptuous blossoms and rich, earthy smell, the plant has always been associated with female sexuality and thus belongs to the women's mysteries. Red is the colour we instinctively associate with the rose–the red of menstrual and birth blood, shed by women only: a river of life, allowing the continuation of our species. Rose's element is earth and her time mid to late summer, when this flower is at its height.

The rose's thorns protect the much sought-after flower and remind women that we have a right to protect and defend ourselves. Thorns further counsel men that they must pluck the rose gently and respectfully and only with consent. Roses can grow separately but usually manifest in rows or groups. Likewise, women have traditionally worked together for the good of each other, their children and their communities.

I truly believe that much of our present-day misogyny is because the feminine aspect of the Creator–the Goddess–has been ignored and denied authority for too long. Much of the worst oppression of women in the world appears to be at the hands of extremist cults of the three Abrahamic religions, whose shared deity has been deemed (wrongly in fact), to have male attributes only.

Rose speaks to the natural sanctity of the feminine that is in all humans and teaches women and men to take pride in our sexuality, in all its healthy permutations and to enjoy this important aspect of our lives. Only when the Goddess is relegated to her rightful place alongside the God, will there truly be equality between the sexes and harmony on Earth. Only when Rose comes into her spiritual power and blooms again, will the balance return.

The Rune

This, the second "S"-shaped rune of the Talking Forest, continues Ivy's theme of the life force. The full-flower spirals at top and bottom indicate a rune dealing with fertility. Obviously feminine, Rose faces left, the "distaff" side. The two spirals suggest the fallopian tubes leading from the ovaries to the enclosing womb. Traced from the centre of the top spiral, the rune's path moves through to the centre of the bottom spiral, wherein lies the fruit dot indicating the rosehip, the potential embryo within. The female regenerative organs, unlike the male, are secret, held within the body. Likewise the fertilized egg, created from the shared gametes of male and female, grows in secret in the womb. The female energy builds and nurtures the life created from this shared DNA blueprint. This is part of the magic of the feminine principle.

But all that is born of Woman must die. From birth, we move outward along the road of life and ultimately back inward on ourselves to our eventual death. The thorn bisecting the centre of the rune, guards the mysteries of life and death, pricking all who would profane these mysteries.

Kenning: The Goddess
Significance: The Mysteries, Women's Mysteries,
Secrets, Sanctity

In the present day, secrecy often leads to lies and oppression. It is all too often wielded by those in authority in order to cover up falsehoods and misuse power. In this way, the general public is kept in the dark while corruption and crime continue unabated. Those who try to unveil these acts are frequently harassed and imprisoned. We would be better off with fewer such secrets.

These are not Rose's secrets however. The rune speaks to the profound mysteries of life, something obvious and visible to all but understood only by those who are attuned to the world. In many mystery traditions, acolytes are taught only to the extent that they are able to understand the meanings of that path's symbols and with the provision that they have the maturity to walk the way of enlightenment. Shrouding the teachings in mystery avoids the pitfalls experienced by frivolous and profane people who neither appreciate nor understand the mysteries. The rosebud, protected by its thorns, stays closed until the time is ripe for it to bloom.

In a reading, the **upright** Talking Forest Rose may indicate a momentous life passage, or something precious to the querent that must be taken seriously. Be mindful of your situation before you take action. Rose may also reveal a circumstance where tact or discretion is necessary. Perhaps there are secrets not yet ready to be revealed.

If the querent is female, Rose may imply embarkation upon a woman's mystery: first blood, pregnancy and a new baby or menopause. In order to prepare for this event, in honour and celebration, you would do well to commune with the Goddess or Feminine Principle.

Chosen by a man, the rune may indicate a woman who will presently fulfill an important role in your life. She may be a woman of great spiritual or emotional power or your wife, mother or other significant woman. Or this may simply be the Anima, your female complement coming forth from your subconscious. It is imperative that you heed her. Rose encourages you to nurture or strengthen your feminine side in order to be more fully balanced.

Like all S runes, Rose is read **inverted** when lying on her side. The energies of the rune are similar in meaning, but are weaker or on the subconscious level. Here, Rose is crawling across the lattice, instead of proudly climbing to the top of the fence. For a woman, the rune in this position may imply that you might want to work on developing more self-esteem and contentment with your femininity. A rite of passage may be in order. Alternatively, Rose leaning sideways along the trellis, is simply anyone, male or female, seeking out the Goddess, the feminine within, by moving along Earth, the prime feminine element.

Like Ivy and other S runes, Rose upside down is read as **toppled.** The rune's energies are weakened. The plant has been uprooted, the inverted flower plucked. Indiscretion may be indicated or even disrespect for the feminine principle. Rose in this position sometimes suggests boorishness or profanity. It can stand as a warning of sexual transgression or degradation. Toppled Rose next to Bramble may warn a woman especially, of a manipulative or even abusive relationship. Or it may warn a man against a woman who is not to be trusted in matters of love, or who is needy or will entangle you in her thorns.

People with an abundance of Rose energy are very sensual and enjoy sex. They must, however, remember to use discretion and be sensitive to their partners' needs. What may be a temporary dalliance for Rose could be the love affair of a lifetime for their partner. Rose people must be careful of being too licentious. They likewise need to be wary of being taken advantage of sexually. Roses of either sex generally prefer the company of women to men and enjoy lifelong friendships with women.

Linden

Kenning: Beehive, Chalice
Significance: Love, Bliss, Family

If you are lucky enough to live near lindens, around the summer solstice you will notice a delightful fragrance wafting on the air, arising from the pale creamy yellow flowers. Much like honeysuckle, but deeper, more substantial; cleaner, less cloying… A profoundly yellow scent, linden blossom hearkens back to bliss, the beehive, the mother's touch, the loving caress of a summer's day when the weather is just right.

Physical Traits and Environment

In winter, the elegant chalice-like symmetry of the linden *(Tilia)* is immediately recognizable. The uniformly ridged grey or black trunk frequently divides at mid-height into two symmetrical boles culminating in a harmoniously rounded crown. The gardenia blonde wood–soft, malleable and easy to turn–is a perennial favourite of woodworkers and sculptors. An alternate name for linden, basswood, refers to the fibrous inner bark or bast, which was fashioned by both European and First Nations people into a very tough cord to make rope and basketry.[95]

In Britain, the tree is named *lime* tree, not to be confused with the citric cousin of lemon. Here lime probably comes from the Old English *linde*. This word has connections to the German word *lind* meaning lithe or yielding, and resembles the Spanish word *linda*–beautiful. All these terms are certainly appropriate for this gracious tree. In autumn, linden's soft heart-shaped leaves turn a clear daffodil yellow. But summer is her crowning season, when she regales us with her dense, green shade. It is in this season that the intoxicating scent from the flowers attracts bees of all species. In fact, "bee tree" is yet another name for the linden and with good reason. Industrious little honeybees produce as much as fifteen pounds of honey a day from lindens in bloom. The final product is one of the most ambrosial honeys around.[96]

Linden tea from the flowers is good for digestion, sore throat and kidney infections. Although nothing is to be feared from occasional use, some sources warn that over-consumption of linden tea may cause heart damage.[97] The ecru coloured pods are attached to one or two small round, nut-like seeds. These pods, immersed in boiling water, make an exceptional skin softener. The inner bark was traditionally made into a salve for wounds.

Linden in Folklore

Along with honey production, linden's purview includes healing. The False Face Society of the Iroquois was a secret organization that practiced medicine. Grotesque masks, modeled on the physical attributes of a powerful healing spirit, were frequently sculpted from the bark of a still-living linden. It was of crucial importance that this operation be carried out so that no lasting damage was done to the tree.[98]

The Minoans were known for their beekeeping, and many exquisite items of jewelry featuring bees were found at Knossos and other ancient sites. Although modern-day Crete is too dry and barren for lindens, these trees apparently flourished there during the Minoan era.

A Greek myth concerning linden tells the story of Philemon and his wife Baucis, a generous, kindly and devoted couple who lived during a time of cruelty, selfishness and ignorance. One night, two strangers came to their humble abode. Although they were very poor, the elderly couple gladly fed and sheltered the visitors as best they could with what little they had. But when the meagre food refused to run out and the empty wine pitcher miraculously refilled of its own accord, Philemon and Baucis realized that their guests were no ordinary folk. They became afraid, but the visitors, none other than the gods Zeus and Hermes,* set their minds at ease and rewarded Philemon and Baucis by turning their hovel into a grand temple. Zeus granted the married couple their single, simple request: to dwell as guardians of the grand temple their home had now become, and to die together simultaneously. The devoted pair lived to a very great age, finally dying, as they wished, peacefully and within moments of each other. Upon death, they were transformed into two trees, their boughs eternally intertwined. Philemon became a stately oak tree and Baucis a gracious linden.

As this myth illustrates, in the classical world, the oak represented the sovereign tree, the "master of the house"; the feminine linden was "a symbol of conjugal love and fidelity," as well as of hospitality.[99] It is salutary to remember that this trait of hospitality was far more important to ancient people than to us, in an era where inns and hostels were rare and travel was more inconvenient and perilous than today.

Linden was held in even higher esteem in the dense forests of northern and eastern Europe. The tree was sacred to the Celts and Teutons, as well as to the Scandinavians, Finns, Balts and Slavs. Linden was frequently associated with healing goddesses and high summer. In Germany and many Slavic countries, linden was also deemed the tree of lovers.

---

* In Greek and Roman myth, Zeus or Jupiter, was the god of hospitality, while Hermes or Mercury, of the winged sandals, was the god of travellers.

Lindens were often used as "judicial" trees beneath which laws were enacted and judgments made. Perhaps it was believed the gentle, soft wood and kindly shade of this compassionate tree would temper with mercy the sternness of those passing judgment.

The "rag tree" is a type of sympathetic magic still extant in parts of the world today. Sick people nail items such as clothing and written entreaties to trees deemed to have healing properties. Large powerful trees such as elms, beeches, and oaks are used as such, but lindens are particularly favoured for this purpose.[100]

In Lucheux in the north of France, the "Lover's Tree" was a linden which had a unique double trunk divided at ground level. Newlyweds would walk through it in order to assure a happy marriage.[101]

Spiritual Traits

Save for locust, Linden is the most solar of all the trees. Like the sun who shines on all equally, Linden gives her shade, her beauty and her honey to all who wish it. She prefers full sunlight, as befits a solar tree and her time is summer, specifically the month of June. The summer solstice, around June 21st, when her flowers scent the air, is particularly sacred to her. The mediator elements of air and water are hers. Goddesses suited to Linden are the sun goddesses—Saule of both Lithuania and Latvia and the Norse Sunne. Demeter, Greek goddess of agriculture and, by extension, beekeeping is also appropriate for Linden, as are those two marriage goddesses Hera of Mount Olympus and Frigg of the Norse Asgard. The Minoan mother goddess, generally associated with snakes and bulls, was also a bee goddess. Thus the linden tree honours her as well.

The Rune

Appropriately for such a gentle, loving tree, the upper part of the Linden rune is shaped like a heart. The left branch ends in a spiral, representing Linden's delightful flowers. The right-hand opposite branch is a simple inward curve, paying tribute to the heart-shaped leaves and to the heavy shade of the tree. A squiggly line on the left lower branch of the rune indicates Linden's pod-like fruit. The rune somewhat resembles the ankh, the Egyptian symbol of the feminine life principle. Linden also resembles a Cherry rune with side branches added. Cherry, however, is caught up in herself and in her own desires; generous Linden holds out her arms to embrace others.

Kenning: Beehive, Chalice
Significance: Love, Bliss, Family, Sharing

The Talking Forest Linden appearing **upright** in a reading indicates family and loved ones and a happy home. It may allude to a lover or spouse with whom the querent has strong emotional ties. Representing not only romantic and familial love, however, Linden also hearkens to the altruistic, selfless love that the spiritually evolved hold for other beings and for the world around them.

Linden **inverted** often points to a need to love others more objectively. Juniper near inverted Linden suggests one who is perhaps too forgiving in love. Near Elm, the Linden is not making boundaries clear enough with a child or other loved ones. Perhaps you are too much of a "pushover" and this is a situation where "tough love" is needed.

Linden **toppled** indicates love lost, lovelessness, especially if near toppled Cherry. Near the Hedge rune, it may warn of family problems or a marriage in difficulty.

People blessed with an abundance of Linden energy are affectionate and loving. They tend to strive for utopia and peace in the world. Many great philanthropists and peacemakers are Lindens.

While Cherry is desire that may or may not blossom into love, Linden betokens the lasting love that is strong enough to give support to a partner and children. Cherry begins the second grove, the subset that deals with youth and the learning of new horizons—self-expression and the search for meaning. Linden ends the third grove and is also the last rune in the first half of the Talking Forest set. This part of one's life is primarily spent growing and developing. Now, the second half of life begins, when the individual reaches out to support and mentor others. This is true even if one does not have a partner or children. At this time of life, the mature person becomes less caught up in their own concerns. Rather, the world and others become the centre of their life.

Beech

Kenning Mother, Book
Significance: Teacher, Mentor

When you stand beneath Beech, the immense branches barely clear your head. Beech exudes a comforting, motherly aura and was made for children of all ages to climb. With her smooth, luminous grey bark and profound shade, Beech calls us to our primal, simian home.

Like any decent mother, Beech has made it her duty to educate her human children. In ancient times, messages and poems were etched upon her smooth trunk, much like a chalkboard. Her pale-coloured wood, easy to work with, was most likely the first upon which magical runes were etched and was certainly the first shaped into books. The tree's very name in German, *buche,* is virtually the same as that for "book"–*buch.*

Physical Traits and Environment

The general outline of a mature beech *(Fagus)* is of a large tree with pleasingly rounded crown and perpendicular branches. In an open meadow, the massive branches can easily spread up to thirty feet (9 m). Within heavy thickets however, beech becomes a lithe, dryad-like column. The leaves: oval, lightly toothed and with pointed tips, are attached to very short stems. These leaves angle up and outward upon the branch, as if the tree were offering them to the sky. Leathery in texture, the leaves come in earthy tones of dark green to coppery or purplish red, depending upon the species. In fall, they turn a rich tan colour and stay on the tree well into winter, rustling like pages in the wind. The spring buds on this mighty tree are incongruously dainty, resembling tiny deer hooves. The fruit is a fuzzy, rufous nut. When ripe, this peels back into four sections, much like the paper fortune-telling toy that was called chatterbox. The fruit within, the *mast,* yields two small, hard, buttery sweet seeds that are enjoyed by many woodland birds and mammals.

Most tree species do not thrive in the shade of beech, but she will form copses of her own saplings. These saplings, however, rarely grow very large within the shade of the mother tree.

In the eastern deciduous zone and on the edge of the boreal forest, beech flourishes in the company of sugar maple, birch and hemlock. Beech/maple woods are a common ecosystem in the Carolinian forest. Sugar maple saplings grow up within mature beech forests. When beeches eventually age and die (at around two or three hundred years), the maples, having now reached their prime, take over. The process continues with beech saplings growing between mature maples, thriving and reaching maturity in their turn as the maples die off.

Beeches and oaks are members of the same family. In fact, they are so closely related that on rare occasions, if a beech and oak grow too close together, they join to form a "two-headed hydra of disquietingly hybrid foliage and fruit." Such an oddity is the Bonne Entente ("Harmony") tree in northern France. [102] The beeches in the Faux de Verzy forest near Rheims however, are solely beeches, strangely mutilated as they may be. Their twisted, bent shapes are believed to be caused by the impact from a meteorite that swathed a path through Denmark and northwestern France hundreds of years ago, leaving the trees in its wake uniquely warped.[103]

Beech in Folklore

Throughout its history, beech has had a long-standing connection with pigs. Very old and enormous beeches with hollow trunks were once used as pigsties, and beechnuts are a favourite food of swine.* These animals are sacred to the Celtic crone-mother goddess, Cerridwen and also to that famous mythological mother, Demeter, Greek goddess of agriculture. Beeches formed part of the grove of Dodona and were at times used as oracles, much as the resident oaks were. The sibyls would listen to the rustling of the wind through the leaves and then translate it for those who sought

---

* Let us not forget that most venerable of pigs, A.A. Milne's Piglet, who wisely built his home in a beech tree!

answers to their problems.[104] Although Dodona was assuredly Zeus's grove, it is believed that Demeter too was honoured there. One wonders if there was also a beech grove at Eleusis where the mysteries of Demeter and her daughter Persephone were enacted and where pigs were sacrificed in honour of these two goddesses.

Beech's greatest significance in history and folklore, however, is her contribution to writing. Because of her eminently smooth and *legible* bark, beech has been used as a billboard of sorts throughout history. When the seemingly literacy-challenged Daniel Boone allegedly "cilled a bar on tree in the year 1760,"[105] the unlucky animal was no doubt minding his own business enjoying beech mast. The bear might have taken some comfort in knowing that his obituary would be archived on the trunk of that noble beech. And that this tree outlived the bear's killer.

Some further indications of beech's significance in the history of literacy: Teutonic tribes made runes from the wood of beech. Some centuries later, another Teuton and one of the most influential figures of the German Renaissance, Johannes Gutenberg, is believed to have invented printed type when he whittled a few letters of the alphabet from a beech trunk. He found that when the letters got wet with rain, they left a clear imprint on the paper in which they were wrapped.[106] The rest is written history.

Beech is mentioned in the Celtic Ogham system, not as a rune but as a "kingdom" or aspect that controls how runes are read. These aspects are called *forfedha*. Beech, or *Blath*, is dedicated to the eastern direction and its purview is manifestation, or the final outcome of an Ogham reading.[107] On a further note, regarding the chatterbox toy mentioned above, I believe this item was deliberately fashioned in imitation of the beechnut. As such it was possibly meant as an oracular device, and not just for child's play.

Spiritual Traits

In Europe, Beech is called "Mother of the Forest." Where Oak is king, she is queen. Her month is September, when mast is ripe. Beech radiates a sense of harmony and nurturance. The trunk and branches are smooth and soothing, like a mother's skin. While her main element is earth, the tree encompasses all four—the warming fire from the sun that feeds the leaves; the sky, to which her branches reach; and the water that often pools in the hollows at the bottom of the tree: Beech is mother to all. Her heavy shallow roots often form buttresses on the earth and there are frequently crevasses or hollows in the trunk, where small creatures can live. Goddesses sacred to her are Hera, Hertha, Artemis and of course, Demeter.

Due to her significance in the creation of the written alphabet and books, Beech's purview is learning and education on all levels, including that of the spirit.

The Rune

Beech is a "shade" rune, like Ash and Maple. It sports the characteristic wide, horizontal branches and side brackets representing a shade tree with heavy leaf canopy. The diamond-shaped nut crowning the rune depicts Beech's status as queen of the woodland. The nut is cross-hatched into four sections emulating the pattern of the husk splitting upon fruition. It moreover references the four elements of earth, air, fire and water, all ruled by the Great Mother.

Kenning: Mother, Book
Significance: Teacher, Mentor, Nurturance, Literacy, Education

Where Birch, the Maiden, deals with learning, Mother Beech represents instruction and mentoring. This is the tree of teaching and memory. More than any other winter silhouette, the naked branches of beech in winter recall the grooves of the human brain. The **upright** rune indicates that the querent will act as a guide or mentor to others. This may include teaching others or a situation in which the querent may be able to assist someone, a child or grandchild or other youngster. For women, this rune frequently addresses issues of motherhood.

The **inverted** rune however, warns of a tendency to smother. Just as the tree prevents others, including her own saplings, from growing beneath her heavy shade, the querent may have to learn to allow loved ones and students the freedom to seek their own destiny and to learn from their own mistakes.

Toppled Beech warns the querent that they may be neglecting the next generation if they are stingy in the training and instruction of others. Knowledge gained is useless if not shared. Rarely, the toppled rune may warn of corruption or the teaching of falsehoods.

People with Beech energy make good teachers, educators and caregivers. They typically like children and often settle down, sometimes having large families. It is common for Beeches to adopt or foster children.

Beech and Linden, both of them maternal trees, take pride of place in the centre of the Talking Forest; Linden ends the first half of this system and Beech begins the second.

Apple

Kenning: Gift, Offering

Significance: Choice, Decision

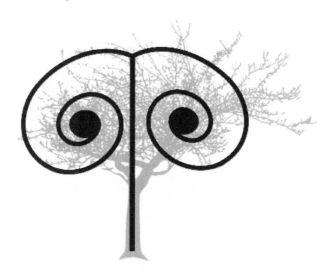

In myth and legend, Apple's purview is choice. And there are certainly a lot of apples to choose from—more than 7,500 cultivars of the fruit![108] Interestingly, domesticated or eating apples do not come by the usual method of simple pollination of female by male flowers. In fact, most of the apples we eat arrive by one of two artificial means. They are either cross-pollinated between two or more different species, or alternatively, produced by grafting—that is, placing a shoot of one species of apple into a slit in the branch of another. These methods of domestication allow for a myriad of apple cultivars. Perhaps Apple's wanton reputation is due in part, to this attribute of tractability. Apple welcomes pruning, thriving best when lovingly cultivated and nurtured.

Physical Traits and Environment

For a plant so steeped in myth and culture, in itself the apple *(Malus)* is a homely little tree. The gnarled, twisted, corkscrew branches and scaly, often scab-covered bark are not exactly captivating. The arrival in spring, however, of masses of large pink or white flowers transforms the apple tree into a ravishing beauty. The five-petalled, seductively scented blossoms, oval, greyish green leaves, frequently edged in pink, and the roseate glow of the grey trunk of many species, attest to apple's membership in the *Rosaceae* or rose family. The tree has an irrevocable association with sex and romance; thus it should come as no surprise that both birds and bees favour apple trees for nesting. This is partly due to the tendency for older specimens to develop cavities in the heartwood or centre of the trunk.

It seems that apple's lot, or perhaps her *choice,* is to channel much of her energy toward yielding flower and fruit for others to enjoy. Most other cultivated fruit trees have comparatively short life spans, due to having expended so much energy in bearing their proportionately large fruit. But apple, generous to the last, can live up to 150 years. In fact, even after losing their heartwood, many apple trees remain surprisingly fruitful for years.

Apples are the most commonly cultivated fruit in the northern hemisphere. They thrive in temperate climates with crisp, frosty autumns and cool to cold winters. Depending upon the variety, apples become fully ripe anywhere from late summer to midwinter. The fruits vary from pale green, to golden brown or deep red in colour, depending on the breed.

All apples originated from the lowly crabapple, a "crab" being any apple with fruit smaller than two inches in diameter.[109] Some varieties, such as the Oregon crabapple, although tart, are quite tasty and refreshing when eaten raw. However, most others are too bitter or sour and are instead made into excellent cider, or cooked into delicious preserves or jellies.

European settlers originally introduced the domestic eating apple to this continent. The most celebrated planter of apples was John Chapman, better known as Johnny Appleseed. A notable eccentric who was said to wear an old tin pan as a hat and a coffee sack for a shirt, he travelled the northeastern United States, planting seeds wherever he went. Upon his death in the mid-1840s, he left behind 1,200 acres of apple trees.[110] Sadly but perhaps fittingly, he died, possibly from pneumonia, after a long walk to fix some of his orchard fences.[111]

The apple is very high in vitamin C.[112] During the height of the British Empire, apple cider was given to English sailors to help stave off scurvy. The fruit is also very high in fibre, thus promoting regularity.

Apple in Folklore

The apple of Celtic and Teutonic folklore is light years away from the forbidden fruit of the Bible.* In many areas of northern

---

* Which in any case, was probably a fig or pomegranate, apples being foreign to the Levant.

Europe, apple is the only large fruit capable of being provisioned as is throughout the long winter. It was therefore, greatly appreciated. It is interesting to note that the farther north an apple myth originates, the more auspicious the fruit is deemed. Its significance as "gift" or "endowment" in the Talking Forest recalls numerous tales surrounding this homespun little tree.

Iduna, the Norse goddess of spring, was the custodian of the golden apples of eternal youth. In order to keep old age and mortality at bay, the gods of Asgard ate one daily. Perhaps this is the origin of the adage, "an apple a day keeps the doctor away!"

In Celtic mythology, the apple is almost always propitious, offering insight and wisdom. Several myths of the Irish and British Celts tell of heroes such as Cormac and Bran Mac Febal being visited in a dream by Manannan Mac Lir, the god of the sea. In most versions, the hero is offered a silver branch with either three or nine golden apples and is transported for a time to the Otherworld, known as the Land of Promise or the Blessed Isles.

The dirne-weibl, a German woodland sprite, was usually seen dressed in white, except in parts of Bavaria, where she favoured red. Anyone lucky enough to be offered one of the apples in her basket would see it turn to money.[113] One wonders if Snow White's wicked queen was a rogue dirne-weibl!

In Medieval Britain, during Twelfth Night, carolers would wassail or sing for food, ale and money. They would subsequently libate apple trees by pouring cakes and cider onto the trunks so that they would yield a good crop in the coming year. In some parts of Western England, a few apples were left on trees that had been harvested, in order to placate the fairies and "ensure their goodwill and friendship."[114] This custom, held over from earlier pagan rituals, actually makes sense. If nothing else, it is a reminder that gifts from the earth should never be taken for granted and we should remember to give back what we take.

Many stories surrounding apple highlight the concept of choice, with frequently a poorly thought-out choice resulting in calamity. Such is the tale from Classical Greece of the Apple of Discord. Indignant at not being invited to an important wedding on Mount Olympus, Eris, the goddess of strife, fashioned an irresistibly beautiful golden apple inscribed with the words "for the fairest," and rolled it toward the three haughtiest Olympian goddesses: Hera, the regal wife of Zeus, wise Athena, who should have known better and Aphrodite, coquettish goddess of love. After much bickering among the three, mighty Zeus, not wishing to be stuck in such an awkward situation, decided that someone else, a mortal, should decide who would get the apple. Paris, a prince of Greece, who just happened to be walking by, was chosen to judge. All three goddesses tried to bribe Paris: Hera offered him power, Athena wisdom, while Aphrodite promised him the most beautiful woman in the world. Paris, being a typical carefree and very attractive young man, chose Aphrodite, eschewing security and wisdom for love. Needless to say, he made an everlasting enemy of the other two goddesses. When Paris was awarded the stunning but married Helen of Troy, he considered himself lucky.

However, his unwise decision led ultimately to the tragic and bloody Trojan War.

A happier Greek myth tells of Atalanta, a princess who did not want to be married. Because she could run faster than any man, she promised her father that she would marry whichever suitor could outrun her. Hippomenes greatly desired Atalanta. Knowing he would never be able to outrun her, and knowing the price of death for any suitor who failed, he prayed to Aphrodite. Always willing to accommodate those in love, the goddess gave him three irresistibly beautiful golden apples.* At intervals during his race against Atalanta, Hippomenes tossed down one of the apples. So alluring were they that each time, the girl was compelled to stop and pick up the golden fruit. Running as fast as he could, the lad won the race and consequently, Atalanta. Some versions of this tale make it clear that the girl chose to pick up the apples rather than ignore them. For she had fallen in love with Hippomenes and did not want him to die.

Whether or not Isaac Newton was bonked on the head by an apple, it is plausible that his theory of gravity came about from watching apples fall from a tree. Newton's formation of the law of gravity and his subsequent study of Earth's place in the solar system were instrumental in the rise of the Age of Reason. It is thus appropriate that this fruit, so maligned by Judeo-Christian mythology, might have played a pivotal role in hastening the Enlightenment, thus precipitating the end of the Church's vast power. From this point on, one could make a choice between

---

*   Not made by Eris, one assumes!

rationality and science on one hand, or superstition and organized religion on the other.

In any event, the Genesis myth of the Fall implies choice. By eating the fruit of the Tree of Knowledge, Eve, and then Adam, gained knowledge, losing the blissful ignorance of the "brute" beasts. They ate the apple and found they were able to use their intellect to reason and theorize about life. They thus *chose* to evolve.

Spiritual Traits

The apple tree has a warm, feminine aura. Her element is water. Friday is sacred to her as it is to Venus, Aphrodite, Freya and other goddesses of love. This tree is at her greatest power twice a year: in spring blossoming time–April and May–and again from late August to October when the fruit of most cultivars ripens. Other deities associated with Apple include Iduna, the Norse goddess of youth, Pomona, Latin goddess of the orchard, and the Celtic sea god Manannan Mac Lir. The tree is also sacred to Hertha, a Teutonic Earth mother goddess. In German fairy tales, she appears under many guises such as Mother Holda and as the dirne-weibl.

Apple's most salient characteristic is that of unselfishness and generosity. Indeed, many Native American people held Apple in high regard. She chose to give her fruits openly to all creatures, and did not keep them out of reach as some other fruit trees do. Apple speaks to choice and decision-making, and to human evolution—our choice to develop the large opposable thumb and adapt ourselves to be tool-makers and users; moreover to develop larger brains, just as we would later cultivate larger apples.

The Rune

The Apple rune implies a simple, unassuming tree with obligingly low, easy-to-reach branches. It is comprised of a simple T shape, both branches curving down and inward into a large flower spiral. Each spiral ends in a prominent dot, indicating the large fruit. Each half of the rune is identical, illustrating that the choices to be made are, in the long run, of equal karmic import.

Kenning: Gift, Offering
Significance: Choice, Decision

While the Talking Forest Cherry rune is a sought-for prize that must be earned, Apple is largesse freely given. The essence of Apple somewhat echoes that of Queirt, Ogham's Apple, whose meaning is more suggestive of beauty or perfection. The Talking Forest Apple also has much in common with the X-shaped Gebo, or Gift, of the Futhark. Coming in the middle of the Talking Forest set, Apple suggests that many of our crucial decisions are made in middle age, when we have growing children, elderly parents, a community—all of whom depend heavily upon the choices we make. Apple speaks to responsibility. One must use the gift as a blessing, not as a curse.

The **upright** rune indicates either that the querent will receive a gift or will make a choice resulting in a positive outcome. Alternatively, the rune may suggest that the querent is making use of their talents, the fruits of which will be shared with others.

Inverted Apple advises the querent that they may have unknown gifts or abilities that should be developed and shared. These should not be kept to oneself but instead brought to fruition. The rune in this position may also signify an inability to make choices or take action: vacillation, uncertainty or indecision.

Contrary or **toppled** Apple warns of a poor or ill-advised choice. Depending on nearby runes, especially the karmic rune Bramble, this may suggest a "left-handed" gift–a crabapple–one the seeker would rather not have received! But gifts may be gleaned even from badly made choices. Experience learned from wrongful decisions can bring wisdom and can help one mature and gain spiritual growth.

Anyone wishing to be more altruistic and less materialistic would do well to meditate on Apple's spiritual energies. Apple people are generous to a fault, giving freely of their gifts and talents. They may at times have trouble reaching decisions and should be careful not to be too accommodating, unless they are sure of the soundness of their goals and of the motives of others. Sometimes Apple people are so eager to please, they allow important decisions to be made for them. They should bear in mind that the best tasting apples always retain a bit of the tartness of the ancestor crabapple. There are times when one must "bite back" in order to retain autonomy and the right to make one's own decisions.

Pine

Kenning: Father, Sentinel, Guardian
Significance: Ethics, Courage, Discipline

The pine is frequently found, in nature and in the human imagination, standing alone on a rocky outcrop or cliff face where few other trees would dare set root. Seeming ill at ease and put off by comfortable and civilized surroundings, pines are at their true glory in rugged wilderness. More than any other tree, it is Pine that evokes the wild boreal forests of Canada's Great Lakes region. Indeed, the Group of Seven's ragged pines are as world-renowned as Van Gogh's sunflowers or Constable's elms.

Physical Traits and Environment

These rugged conifers can and will grow readily on poor soil and in dry, unforgiving environments. The unique shagginess frequently seen in pines is caused by prevailing winds and belongs exclusively to a tree unafraid of the open sky and heavy weather. White, Jack and Scots pines all exhibit this windblown feature. As they grow, the trees tend to lose lower branches, enhancing the spare, windswept silhouette. Not all species of pine display this disheveled profile, however. Some, such as red and Austrian pine are symmetrical and somewhat pyramid shaped. Unlike spruce and fir, however, their branches clear the ground by at least five feet (1.5 m).

Pine is North America's most prevalent conifer, generally growing very tall with a single rugged trunk. For such a dark and dour tree, the bark can be very colourful, frequently displaying shades of teal blue, salmon pink and orange mottled among the grey.

The needles, often a dark bluish green, vary according to the species, from two to eight inches in length. These are held together like tiny brooms in bundles of between two and seven. Pines shed their needles regularly, making a thick carpet of them on the forest floor.

Pine cones, unlike those of other conifers, are rigid and woody. The seeds contained within are dispersed in dry weather. They are usually papery and scale-like but those of edible varieties resemble sunflower seeds. The cones of other species, such as lodgepole pine, are opened by the heat of natural forest fires,[115] thus affirming them as "pioneer" trees that aid in forest regeneration. Pine seeds feed many birds and animals. Seeds of the pinyon pine and others are edible for humans and are delicious. These "pine nuts" are a popular, if expensive, ingredient in Mediterranean, especially

Italian, cuisine. Pine's light coloured, malleable and slightly fragrant wood is highly prized for building and furniture and is essential to the pulp and paper industry.

Pine in Folklore

Pine was sacred to Pan, god of the rugged wilderness. Virgil mentions this in his *Eclogues,* stating that a certain mountain in Arcadia "always has a vocal grove and shaking pines; he ever hears the loves of shepherds, and Pan, the first who suffered not the reeds to be neglected."[116]

The tree was also associated with Dionysus, the god of wine. Frequently allied with Pan, Dionysus carries a sceptre, called a *thyrsus.* This is a rod topped by a large pine cone. Pine was also consecrated to the Earth goddess Cybele, whose lover Attis castrated himself under one such tree. A more refined version of this gruesome myth suggests that Attis was instead transformed into a pine after being gored to death by a wild boar.

Pine was equally revered in northern Europe. Much as Odin sought out the mighty ash Yggdrasil, the wizard Merlin is said to have climbed a pine seeking spiritual knowledge in Brittany's Broceliande forest.

In North America, the Iroquois honoured white pine, deeming it the tree of peace because its branches resembled hands reaching up in prayer.[117] In East Asia, the pine is a symbol of inner peace and tranquility. Pine and cypress have long been popular in Chinese graveyards. The Japanese held pine in especially high regard, as their artwork attests. Many of their myths involve this tree. In one, a young woman falls in love with a handsome young man whose soul is held within a pine tree. Tragically, the young man dies when the pine is felled to make a bridge needed to span a flooded river.[118] Like so many Japanese tales, this one illustrates the necessary suppression of personal happiness for the common good. A somewhat happier tale tells of an elderly couple whose devotion to each other was so great that, like Baucis and Philemon of Greek myth, they wished to die together. Their wish was granted and their spirits melded together into the form of an ancient pine. Sometimes their ghosts could be spied at night raking the pine needles under the tree.[119] The Samurai painted pine trees upon their shields to bestow safety in battle or failing that, immortality and honour upon death.[120]

From time immemorial, amber, the resin of ancient, extinct pines, has been a highly prized gemstone. Pitys, a dryad betrothed to Boreas, the north wind, was beloved by our old friend Pan. When the jealous Boreas changed Pitys into a pine tree, her tears of grief became the amber resin that weeps from the trunk of the tree.[121] This resin is mostly found throughout the Baltic region from Germany to Norway and from Iceland to Russia, either wave-tossed on beaches or dug up from fossilized trees buried within mineral deposits. Amber jewelry has been found in prehistoric gravesites, attesting to the high regard in which primitive peoples held this gem. To this day, witches and other pagans wear the stone as if it were going out of style!

Throughout history, pine was associated with the sea, perhaps partly due to the amber deposits found on beaches. In ancient

Greece, the tree was also sacred to the sea god Poseidon. Its Latin name, *Pinus,* means "raft" and the buoyant wood was used for such throughout the Mediterranean. Native Americans also fashioned pine into rafts.[122] The tall trunks of New England's pines were prized as ship masts for the British Navy. Pitch and tar, obtained from the resin of pitch pine, were used as sealants–hence the common slang "Jack Tar" to denote sailors.[123]

The white pine is the state tree of Massachusetts, commemorating the American War of Independence, fought in part, because the American settlers were tired of handing over their tallest and best white pines to King George's navy.[124] Because this tree is so inextricably wound up in the American struggle for independence from Britain, it has become a common motif on many state flags of New England.

North America's pioneers apparently considered the Jack pine an evil tree, due in part to its habit of growing on soil too poor for crops.[125]. My suspicion is that the curved shape of the cones, which often grow in pairs, reminded the "upright" Christian settlers of the Devil's horns! No doubt, if Jack pine had been native to the Mediterranean, the ancient Greeks at least would have given this tough, useful timber tree the respect he deserves!

Spiritual Traits

Pine's aura is male and his element air. He is sacred to the mother goddess Cybele, as well as to gods such as Poseidon, Dionysus and to Pan and the Roman Sylvanus, both guardians of the wilderness. Pine has a stalwart and protective demeanour–comforting yet stoical. When deciduous trees are bare and tawdry in late autumn,

Pine is still in his glory, bidding us be patient; spring will eventually green anew. In the meantime, like a vigilant father, he stands his lonely watch. While broad-leaved trees sleep their winter slumber, we need not fear so long as Pine guards the land. Author and mystic Ted Andrews warns, however, that we should be careful what we say around pines as they are liable to pass our words on to other trees and to the wind![126] While I have no concerns of any of my deep, dark secrets being bruited about, I do find that a pine forest, its floor heavily carpeted with old needles, emits an alert *listening* quality. Here though, wherever you tread is softly, silently, a temple of peace, guarded by the stern, protective pines.

The Rune

The Talking Forest Pine expresses the unique character and rugged individualism of this masculine tree: three squiggly branches on each side of the stem, those on the right higher and longer than those on the left. The rune mirrors the windblown silhouette of the more iconic members of the species, such as Scots or white pine.

Kenning: Father, Sentinel, Guardian
Significance: Mindfulness, Conduct, Ethics, Courage, Individuality, Discipline

The **upright** Talking Forest Pine denotes moral uprightness, patience, resilience, and courage—all traits necessary for fatherhood.

Pine deals also with independence. Studies show that as children grow, they become less attached to the mother. At this time, the father figure is very helpful in supporting children to develop individuality and autonomy.

To a male querent especially, the Pine rune may indicate issues surrounding children. Perhaps you will become a father, or foster or mentor a child or young person. This rune may alternatively signify one who is watching out for you, either as a guardian or benefactor—a father figure of some sort. On occasion, the rune suggests freedom or liberation from bondage or obligation.

An **inverted** Pine rune suggests the querent is working on the person within. There is a transition toward greater responsibility and a strengthening of character, especially if runes such as Elm (Duty) or Ash (Introspection) are nearby. However, inverted Pine may also warn of loneliness, or an inability or unwillingness to connect with others.

Pine lying sideways or **toppled** suggests apathy or even moral laxity, especially if toppled to the right. It may warn that you are not doing the right thing, either from fear of standing out from the crowd or perhaps you worry that taking a stand may lead to unpleasant repercussions.

People with strong Pine energy are tough, stalwart and dependable. They are observant, with good instincts. It is hard to "pull a fast one" on Pines. They are generally not afraid of doing the right thing and standing up for what they believe in. However, too much Pine energy may lead one to become too independent or reclusive or too self-righteous. Pine is useful spiritual medicine for those who need to strengthen their moral fibre or who must steel their courage to do the right thing.

Walnut

Kenning: Treasure, Harvest
Significance: Wealth, Plenty, Generosity

No tree affirms man-made wealth and luxury like the walnuts, especially the Circassian, or English walnut. Much of our historical use of the species speaks to the gaining of wealth: ships for empire building, fine furniture for the upper classes, gunstocks to protect valuables and privilege.

But the working classes were also sustained by walnut, especially the white walnut, commonly known as butternut. Those living close to the soil used butternut to fashion the items they needed: the nuts for food and cooking oil, the wood for hives for honeybees and dyes from the husks for quilting, cloth-making and decorating buckskin leather. In the Talking Forest system, the Walnut rune references the dark wood walnuts of both old and new worlds, as well as the white walnut, or butternut of North America.

Physical Traits and Environment

Walnut *(Juglans)* is a large handsome tree with a thick trunk and broad, symmetrical crown. With spreading branches, walnuts display open, spacious canopies. This characteristic bespeaks a tree of generous spirit. The composite leaves of the walnuts resemble those of ash. But while ash's canopy is latticed like bamboo, the leaves of walnut whorl dizzyingly around their twigs. This is especially apparent looking up into the branches of the tree.

While generous with its shade, walnut often stands alone. It is greedy of the soil it grows in, which of course, must be only the deepest and most fertile. The tree exudes a toxin, *juglans,* from its roots, which gives walnut its Latin name. It also makes it difficult for other plants to grow in walnut's shade.[127]

The durable, beautifully textured wood of the walnuts, black or English, is justly famous and highly prized for making furniture, decorative objects and gunstocks. Due to the oily wood's resistance to decay, it was used in shipbuilding and fashioned into wheels for water mills.[128] When mature, the trunk of walnut is grey with intersecting ridges. As befitting such a high-status tree, the rich green leaves of black walnut turn gold in autumn; those of English walnut are a paler yellow. Black walnut is considered by many to be the most valuable timber tree in North America. In fact, it is so prized for its wood, that in some areas, larger specimens have been stolen by helicopter![129]

The walnuts are considered nut trees par excellence. The round fleshy casing of English walnut is smooth and bright green; that of black walnut similar, but olive green with frequent dark spots. In both species, the husks leave a brown stain on the hands. The hard inner shell is tan and slightly bumpy in the English walnut, and black and heavily ridged in our native species. In both cases, the shell is difficult to break open to get to the actual nut within. The nutmeat is composed of two halves, each resembling a tiny human brain, especially in the English walnut. The nuts are very rich and oily and somewhat bitter tasting.

The white walnut or butternut is limited to the Carolinian forest. While the leaves are similar to black walnut, the wood is light. The ridged bark, light brown when young, turns nearly black when mature. The soft husk of the fruit is green and oblong and, like other walnuts, stains the hands. Its hard inner shell resembles that of black walnut but is a rich golden brown and has deeper ridges. The nuts, smaller and more oblong than those of black walnut, are oily and rich in flavour. A yellow dye was obtained from the husks and used in the making of "butternut jeans," which were common among working class people in the early 1900s. Thus, butternut can be seen as the "working class" walnut. Unlike the "upper crust" walnuts, this tree is happy to share its space with many others such as maple, beech, oak, cherry and pine.

Walnut in Folklore

The word Juglans means "Jove's nut" and the walnut was in fact, consecrated to Jupiter, supreme god of Rome. The walnut was also sacred to Carmenta, the Roman goddess of childbirth, motherhood and fertility. Later, in Medieval Italy, witches of the town of Benevento would hold their celebrations under a huge walnut tree. Perhaps they were honouring Carmenta! The tale has it that even though St. Barbatus had the tree cut down, a large walnut would obligingly and immediately spring up anywhere the witches decided to hold their "unholy revels."[130] These witches must have had amazingly potent magic, for in nature, walnuts take at least ten years to mature!

The walnut was also sacred to the pre-Hellenic goddess Carya. In later myth, she was a princess of Laconia in Greece, who was transformed into a walnut by Dionysus.[131] The caryatids, companion nymphs of the goddess Artemis, resided in walnut trees. Statues of these nymphs were a common fixture in classical and neoclassical architecture, where they served as supportive columns and were usually fashioned from walnut wood.

In many parts of the Mediterranean, a walnut tree was planted on the birth of a daughter. The tree would later be cut down and made into the girl's marriage bed.[132] In Britain, to dream of a walnut tree was said to denote unfaithfulness,[133] however dreaming of gathering nuts prophesied "unexpected wealth."[134]

Spiritual Traits

Earth is Walnut's element. As the tree fruits around Harvestide, she belongs to September, the month of the Harvest Moon. With her tasty, nutritious fruit and attractive wood, Walnut is a feminine tree. She is sacred to Carya, Artemis and to Carmenta. And of course, the walnut is also Jupiter's tree.

The Rune

The Walnut rune is similar in shape to that of Ash, with the addition of a dot at the end of each branch, indicating the nuts of a heavily fruiting tree. Another nut crowns the Walnut rune. A bracket on each side, but not on top, suggests it is a large shade tree with spare, open foliage.

Kenning: Treasure, Harvest
Significance: Wealth, Success, Plenty, Largesse, Generosity, Magnanimity, Resources

The **upright** rune indicates wealth and riches, and the attainment of security. Throughout history, elegant, beautiful items proclaiming status were created from both black and English walnuts, while indigenous and working-class peoples used butternut to create more practical items. The Walnut rune therefore indicates not only treasure, but also thrift and the wise use of resources. In addition, the walnut tree's tendency to destroy other plants growing too close to its shade warns of the dangers of having too much wealth. Conversely, butternut's habit of growing in cooperation with many other trees instructs us to be generous with our riches.

The **inverted** rune suggests greed, miserliness, or keeping one's wealth to oneself. More often however, Walnut in this position recommends being frugal for the time being. Perhaps now is not a good time to paint the town red.

A **toppled** Walnut rune may indicate poverty, want or a loss of income. It can, however, simply indicate money spent on an item that is needed or very much desired—perhaps a new house or a child going to college. A walnut tree is being cut down to create necessities! As always, nearby runes will help with interpretation.

People possessing Walnut energy are magnanimous and generous. They enjoy luxurious items and things of value, frequently sharing them with others. However, too much wealth unearned or gained dishonourably, all too often makes one greedy and avaricious.

Walnut lies near the end of the second triune of the Talking Forest set. The fourteen runes contained within these two middle groves represent the prime of human life. Here many of us are comfortably settled into a career or are steadily and gainfully employed. We are now able to put aside assets toward our estate and posterity.

Hedge

Kenning: Cottage

Significance: Homestead, Pride of Place

The Talking Forest Hedge rune refers specifically to the following plants: privet, boxwood and forsythia as well as spirea and barberry. These bushes can and do grow wild. For centuries, however, humans have primarily grown them to provide a living, green fence. Privet, boxwood, forsythia, spirea and barberry are all plants that are easily shaped and can take pruning well. The latter two have species native to North America. The others were all introduced from Europe and Asia.

Physical Traits and Environment

All five of our Talking Forest Hedges are short, bushy plants.* Boxwood *(Buxus)* and privet *(Ligustrum)*, the two traditional hedges, are the "plain Janes" of the lot. Both have glossy, dark green leaves, those of boxwood being more leathery and privet

---

* Note that while juniper, hawthorn, cedar, holly and yew are all frequently planted as hedges, the unique character of each of these plants necessitates its own special Talking Forest rune.

leaves longer. Privet's very name indicates its long use as a fence and enclosure. Its quick growth makes the plant perfect for topiary. Boxwood, the most common hedge plant, is the smallest at rarely more than four feet or one metre in height.

The oval, jade green leaves of forsythia *(Forsythia spp.)*, slightly pointed at the tips, appear soon after the masses of canary yellow flowers. In Southern Ontario, these bright blooms are among the earliest harbingers of spring, arriving as early as mid-March, depending on the mildness of the weather. The blooming season lasts about three weeks to a month.

Spirea *(Spiraea spp.)* blooms in the summer, with mostly white blossoms, but there are pink varieties as well. Depending on the type, the leaves are small and lobed, somewhat similar to those of hawthorn, or long and oval with a pointed tip. These plants usually grow to about five feet (1.5 m) in height.

Barberry *(Berberis)* is a joy in winter, with oval scarlet berries shining forth like Christmas lights on the leafless but thorny bushes. In warmer weather, barberry leaves resemble those of box.

Hedge in Folklore

Hedge is all about the art of shaping the home environment. You grow a hedge primarily to mark off where your property ends and someone else's, or the commons, begins. It is this trait which makes hedge plants the most domesticated of all of those featured in the Talking Forest, save for apple, vine and rose. Incidentally, the latter two are also represented as S runes in this array.

In the Victorian language of flowers, privet indicates defense.[135] It is perhaps salient that most of the hedge plants grown for ornamental purposes today are native to Europe or Asia, but few to North America. Most were brought over by white settlers, who also brought with them the idea of land as *property*. The First Nations people generally did not believe in owning the land. Mother Earth was no one's possession. Beyond the planting of certain nut trees and food crops such as corn, beans and squash, Native peoples did not force plants to grow to their bidding. With the European settlers, however, this all changed, with sadly many wars fought, and blights such as genocide and slavery the result. Forest and grassland were razed for tillable fields. Workers, willing or otherwise, were essential for harvesting crops. Fencing was needed to show boundaries.

No study of hedge would be complete without a quick overview of the history of *topiary*: the reshaping of botanical nature to suit our own desires. Historically in Europe, boxwood and yew were most often planted as topiary, although hornbeam and holly were frequently employed as well. This art form may have originated in the first century CE with the Romans.[136] It appears to have lost favour during the bellicose chaos and the porous boundaries of the Dark Ages.

Topiary didn't become popular again until the relatively peaceful times of Renaissance Italy.* From there it moved on to France and the Netherlands where the Dutch, "constrained by space and wind

---

* It is noteworthy that during the medieval and early Renaissance eras, the commons–land open to all people–came under attack from the upper classes. At this point, much of the public lands, especially woodlands, were taken over by feudal lords and gentry. The warfare of the commons continues today with condo developers, large corporations and other private interests threatening public land and parks.

would create tiny, complicated topiaries of painterly perfection."[137] William of Orange and his consort Mary brought the fashion to England in the 1600s. In the next century, horticulturists such as the eminent Capability Brown, were the first to introduce wealthy landowners to the fashion of vast naturalized estates, replete with open spaces and large trees. Interestingly, these gardeners were influenced by the horticultural practices of some of North America's First Nations people, who had developed the custom of planting oak, hickory and walnut savannahs as food sources and to attract game animals.[138]

Spiritual Traits

Hedge is primarily a fence, meant to keep out those not welcome in the household, as well as providing protection from the elements. It is difficult to break through a hedge without discomfort. The branches are thick enough to block entry to larger life forms, yet are supple and soft enough to provide shelter to small creatures. Hedge provides beauty to the beholder and safety for tiny indwellers. This plant belongs to all seasons but specifically to late winter, when it protects the home from the cold winds and storms of February and March. Each of the species represented by the Hedge rune casts the cheerful, busy aura of one who takes pride in their house and home.

Hedge has three major purviews, corresponding to the triple aspects of the goddess of hearth and home. Firstly, it acts as a form of protection against wind, nosy neighbours, etc. This aspect is the Crone's purview. Secondly, Hedge may act as a doorpost. Frequently, you will see a bush planted on either side of the front door of a house. Plants most often used for this purpose include forsythia, cedar and lilac. While still acting as a guardian, Hedge as doorpost confers a welcoming aura and this is the Mother's purview. Finally, Hedge is frequently artistic and expressive. We note this especially in some topiary design. This creativity and playfulness belongs to the Maiden.

Hedge is sacred to hearth and home goddesses such as Teutonic fertility goddess Hertha; Frigg, who was the Norse matriarch of the Aesir; Hestia, Greek goddess of the hearth flame, called Vesta in Rome; and Juno, Roman goddess of marriage and family.

The Rune

Hedge is the third "S" rune. These runes epitomize plants that in some way, express *procession*. Hedges are generally planted in rows; their implicit movement is primarily left to right; therefore, the upright rune is horizontal. The three diagonal lines through the Hedge rune indicate the fence that becomes the plant's main function. Upright, with the dot below it, shows the flower swirl on the left, indicating a feminine rune.

Like Elm, Hedge deals with boundaries. But whereas Elm is a landmark, a geographical boundary, indicating where you stand in the world, Hedge deals with possessive, chosen boundaries that enclose and keep things in or out. Elm compels us to look into the middle distance to the tall signpost and whatever lies beyond. With Hedge, however, we are simply content to deal with our own backyard.

Kenning: Cottage
Significance: House and Home, Possessions,
Pride of Place

Upright, Hedge speaks to the home, pride of ownership and aesthetic appreciation. It also implies the responsibility of looking after one's own affairs.

Inverted Hedge, standing on end, with the flower swirl on top, evinces a very tall, narrow growth. It is much higher than it needs to be and looks rather ridiculous. Hedge in this position implies snobbishness, materialism, a need to "keep up with the Joneses." The rune inverted the other way with the flower spiral at the bottom suggests one who values their privacy, perhaps to the point of reclusiveness.

As with all other S runes, the **toppled** Hedge rune is upside down with the dot on top. Here, the hedgerow has been dug up. This indicates a house in disorder, a home in disarray and possibly, unprotected. Perhaps you are not looking after your home or following up on important tasks. Things like the leaky roof or faulty electrical wiring, if not fixed, will cause larger problems. The rune in this position may additionally warn of security issues. Perhaps you need to get new locks on your doors and windows. Alternatively, Hedge toppled may indicate trouble with noisy or disrespectful neighbours.

People with Hedge energy are often highly creative and generally thoughtful of their surroundings. They will frequently create useful and beautiful things simply for the sake of adorning the world around them, leaving their mark on it in a benevolent way. Hedge people are often designers or engineers.

Hedges however should beware of snobbishness, or worrying about appearances and what others may think. They may try to regulate their environment to the point of becoming "control freaks." We all know of people who take great pains with their hedges–pruning them into silly shapes, imposing a "crew-cut" on the poor plants at every opportunity.

The Hedge rune appears halfway through the fourth grove, representing middle age. At this time in our lives, we frequently hope to settle down in our final abode before the nursing home or cemetery. Here we express the desire to stay put. As we age, however, we can become so attached to our home that, before we realize it, we are housebound. We get into the habit of not socializing enough for our physical, mental and spiritual wellbeing. This often leads to premature old age and senility. While Hedge does protect the home and helps keep it private from prying eyes, it is *not* a houseplant. Hedge is a *border* between our domicile and the outside world. It reminds us that while we should look after our home and personal life, it is crucial to get outdoors and remain in touch with the rest of the world. All our hedge species originally were and still grow wild, a reminder that Mother Earth is our real home.

Cedar

Kenning: Besom, Sweat Lodge
Significance: Cleansing, Purification

The arborvitae or cedar has a cool, clean scent that frees and opens the lungs. Profoundly uplifting and healing, nothing can beat a cedar forest for the purity of its air. With their acid green boughs spreading out like lace fans, a forest of cedars in spring is as much a celebration of Earth's awakening, as are the orchard trees.

Physical Traits and Environment

The Cedar rune of the Talking Forest references the arborvitae *(Thuja)* and their close relatives the cypresses *(Cupressaceae).*

The true cedars or *Cedrus* are not native to Canada and are rare ornamentals here. There are two species of *Thuja* native to North America—white cedar in the east and Pacific or redcedar in the west. There are no native cypresses in Eastern Canada and the yellow cypress, also called Nootka or Alaska cedar, is the only one native to Western Canada.

Unlike the clumpish junipers, the stately cedars are generally larger, with a conical silhouette. Their trunks resemble those of juniper however, being reddish in colour, ridged and fibrous. The bark has a tendency to shred from the tree in long vertical strips. The wood is soft, pinkish, light enough to float and easy to split.

The flat, scaly needles of cedar are softer than those of prickly juniper. Cypress boughs, like those of most conifers, are dark and sombre in colour, but those of the *Thuja* cedars display a brighter shade in the winter landscape. The density of the layered branches makes the cedar windbreak every bit as effective, but without the dark, brooding aspect of the sterner evergreens. As with all conifers, cedar needles are jam-packed with vitamin C.

The cones of *Thuja* cedars look like small green flower buds before they turn beige and open up, woody and scaly. The somewhat larger cones of cypress resemble tiny green or purple soccer balls. They ripen to beige or brown, with the woody scales splitting open from the central core.

Cedar in Folklore

Because of its high vitamin C content, the northern white cedar *(Thuja occidentalis)* was an excellent cure for scurvy among First Nations and early settlers. Thus the tree was named arborvitae or "tree of life."[139] Some believe that the tea that saved Jacques Cartier and his explorers from death by scurvy may have been brewed from the needles of this tree.[140] In any event, the oil is still made into salves and ointment for sore muscles and colds.* Northern white cedar was traditionally used as a purgative and an abortifacient. By acting as a "sudorific, diuretic and expectorant," it was moreover effective in reducing fevers.[141]

Native American peoples have traditionally used cedar sprigs to line the floors of their sweat lodges. Both First Nations and white settlers also made use of *besoms* or brooms of fresh cedar boughs to sweep their dwellings.[142] As the smoke from burning cedar bark made an excellent vermifuge, beekeepers often fumigated their hives with it.[143]

Tall and aromatic, western redcedar is revered by the First Nations of the West Coast. People such as the Haida, Tlingit, Nuxalk and Kwakiutl employed the soft, easily worked and waterproof wood to make ample canoes holding up to twenty people. The giant tree trunks, which can reach a height of 230 feet (70 m), also formed elegant lodges and totem poles, a few of which still grace the lush forests of British Columbia, Oregon and Washington State.[144] The totem pole was a type of family crest, a history of the tribal lineage, as well as a spiritual guardian for

---

* Oil of cedar or thuja is poisonous and should never be taken internally!

the people. Their totem animals were proudly depicted upon the trunk, one above another. In addition, redcedar's sacred wood was used to create the highly ornate masks and costume appendages used in the complex mystery plays that recounted the myths and legends of the West Coast peoples.

The ancient Greeks had a cypress grove sacred to Hebe, handmaiden of the gods. Here liberated prisoners offered up their chains to her. Aesculapius, the Greek god of healing, also had a cypress grove consecrated to him.[145] These trees, often used for healing purposes, were eminently appropriate to such a god.

Spiritual Traits

Our *Thuja* cedars do vital work in cleansing the environment. Many inhabit swamplands that, while not fit for human habitation, are crucial to the health of the environment. As mentioned earlier, swamps are amazingly effective at alleviating pollution caused by nearby industry. Thus, Cedar is an essential tree in the process of purification. Cedar wood was historically deemed appropriate to house sanctified objects and the oil from its needles has been used as a disinfectant and healing agent throughout human history.

All the species named cedar are noteworthy for their ability to cleanse physically, mentally and spiritually. Our own arborvitae has elements of both fire and water. The wood floats readily and burns easily. Cedar's aura burns away impurities, while simultaneously allowing the subject to relax and dismiss the pain or problem at hand.

The Rune

Like Poplar, this is a "candelabra" rune. It has six branches, three on each side. These begin lower down on the left, indicating a feminine rune. Each branch turns slightly out and then upward, simulating the upswept outline of the tree. This narrow rune resembles a torch bearing flames of purity burning away negativity and bringing cleansing energy where needed.

Kenning: Besom, Sweat lodge
Significance: Healing, Cleansing,
Purification, Preparation

The appearance of this rune **upright** in a reading indicates that a healing process is underway. It may not always be pleasant, but it is necessary and for the best. The healing may be physical, or it may involve mental, emotional or even spiritual purification. Cedar's energies can be used in healing magic, for example, to clean out impurities in the aura. Both kennings of the rune indicate the spiritual purview of Cedar. The witch's besom, used in circle, sweeps away negativity and unnecessary dross before the rite can begin. The sweat lodge, with its carpet of cedar boughs, cleanses the body and prepares it for the spiritual journey of enlightenment.

Inverted Cedar suggests an internal healing, usually spiritual or emotional. This position frequently advocates that now is a good time to heal and rest up. "Going to ground" is an effective process used by wild animals to heal themselves and to keep illness from spreading. Here the rune suggests you follow their lead.

Toppled Cedar indicates sickness, malaise or impurity. Depending on other runes nearby, Cedar counsels the querent to look after their health.

People associated with Cedar often make good doctors or nurses. They can be somewhat brisk in dealing with others, but generally are of kindly disposition. Cedar is not as gentle a healer as Willow, the next rune in the Talking Forest. However, the two complement each other. They can be used together for healing work, as well as with Elder, the great unifier and harmonizer. Cedar comes near the end of the fourth grove of the set, when the aches and pains of our middle years remind us to look after ourselves. Now is an optimum time to purify and purge bad habits and negative energy we have accumulated throughout our lives. At this juncture, we may need to effect a change in lifestyle in order to maintain our health and remain productive in the world.

Willow

Kenning: Moon, Water
Significance: Intuition, Grieving

Willow evokes most continents and graces many of the great rivers of the world. In the mind's eye this languid tree leans beside the Zambezi and Amazon Rivers alike, draped in humidity and summer heat. Half a planet away in the white depths of January, golden stems of osier blazon along Russia's Volga in the east and Canada's Red River in the west. There are willows by the reed beds of England's Avon and gracing the shores of China's Yangtze,–all worthy models of willow ware pottery.[146]

Physical Traits and Environment

The tree is in fact, native to all continents save for Australia and, of course, Antarctica.[147] Thus it comes as no surprise that this genus is very large. There are more types of willow in North America than any other tree species.[148] Willows vary in size from the tiny groundcover Arctic willow to the mighty black willow that can reach a height of 120 feet (36 m) and a diameter of eight feet (2.5 m). Osier's twigs in shades of gold or emerald green add colour and cheer to winter's stark landscape. Most emblematic of all the willows, however, is the weeping or Babylon willow, originally from China. To this day, the weeping willow has remained a popular ornamental tree in Europe and North America.

Lithe and supple, gracing stream bank and lakeside, willow *(Salix)* is married to water. Throughout history, the tree has been renowned as a harbinger of this element. The journals and diaries of early pioneers "are full of happy exclamations of sighting willow trees."[149] Many species have shallow, broadly spreading roots that tend to mat, thus preventing erosion. Like the ash, willow dries up soggy fields. She holds the watershed and cleans the riverbank.

Like most fast-growing trees, willows are short-lived. However all, particularly the osiers, grow with such ease that a twig, stuck in moist ground, can soon become a sapling. Many willows have heavily fissured grey bark. The leaves are long, very narrow, elliptical and pointed at the tips. They terminate in a short stalk that is attached to a very pliant twig. It is this feature that causes willow's languid or "weeping" quality. These supple whip-like twigs are called withes or withies, and were traditionally employed to make rope and baskets.

The most renowned of anodynes, the bitter tasting bark of willow is famous for its salicylic acid. Used since time immemorial as a painkiller and to combat fever,[150] this medicinal ingredient is found today in Aspirin and other painkillers.

Willow in Folklore

Due to her inescapable association with rivers and water, willow was afforded great honour by many North American peoples. The Plains nations used the malleable wood for lodge poles, sacred pipes, water jugs and snowshoes.[151] The Aztecs of Mexico also held willow in high regard. There, the trees were invoked during severe storms to protect the community.[152]

The Ainu of Japan believed the human backbone was made of willow. They reasoned that people were supple as a willow sapling in youth but as they grew older, they became rigid and bent like the tree in old age! Accentuating this bond between humans and willows, the Ainu made fetishes from willow wood to protect newborn children on their journey through life.[153]

In Ireland, travellers carried the "Sally rod" as a good luck charm.[154] The word "sally" comes from the Celtic Sail or Saille, which is also the name of the fourth Ogham rune–Willow– representing intuition and clairvoyance.[155] In many parts of Europe, forked willow rods were used to dowse for water, a further indication of the tree's tie to this element.

Willow was associated with witches and in ancient Greece, was sacred to Hecate, the triple goddess of witchcraft, the moon and the Underworld. It is not surprising that witches or anyone skilled in the herbal arts would honour a tree of such noteworthy healing and dowsing properties.

The watery element is associated with the emotions, especially that of sadness. Water forms the tears we weep and is also a large component of "sad" places such as swamps and marshes. For these reasons, willow is frequently deemed unfortunate: a tree of grief and sadness. In the Victorian language of flowers, willow indicates "forsaken love."[156]

Spiritual Traits

Because of her association with water, Willow is irrevocably tied to the moon. She likes full sunlight, but I personally believe that this most lunar of trees in fact craves above all, the naked light of the moon in all her glory and mystery.

Willow leaves are the first to arrive in spring and the last to fall in autumn. In late fall and in winter, the bare pale yellow branches lend a cheery lambent gold to the stark landscape. Truly, Willow is a tree of compassion!

Willow's sweeping branches purify the waters, washing away psychic dross. Monday, through long tradition both washday and the day of the moon, is thus sacred to Willow. The menstrual cycle is also within the moon's purview. Many scientists hold that the function of the menses is to cleanse the womb of excess blood and material and any bacteria that accumulate during ovulation. Thus, Willow is strongly tied to women's mysteries. She is sacred to lunar deities, such as Artemis, Hecate, cat-headed Bast, and cow-headed Hathor, both of Egypt, and also to Myesyats, the Slavic moon god.

The Rune

This is the second of the two "M" runes in the Talking Forest, Mulberry being the other. The branches of the Willow rune simply curve down and slightly inward, like willow withes reaching for water.

Kenning: Moon, Water
Significance: Healing, Grief, Intuition, Compassion,
Compliancy, Fluidity

Upright Willow in a reading suggests a healing is taking place. Pain and suffering are being washed away. This is sometimes a grieving process, but one that is good and necessary. Willow looks at her reflection in the water and sees her inner self. She is the tree of introspection and intuition, a frame of mind that accords with the healing process as well as with grief. Willow's purview also lies with the moon and magic associated with it.

Inverted Willow suggests intuition and perhaps lunar magic. It occasionally warns of grieving that has gone on for too long or that is being held within. Here the querent must learn to let go. The moon cannot stay forever in waning phase and the river must flow if it is not to become stagnant or dry up.

Toppled Willow often implies sickness, especially if next to inverted Cedar or toppled Sassafras. Here the rune urges the querent to look to their health. Alternatively, the toppled rune may indicate a lack of sympathy, especially if next to toppled Linden. The waters of compassion have dried up and the tree has therefore fallen. Working with Willow energy will help replenish the well of empathy.

People associated with Willow are graceful and gentle. Many Willow people turn to social work, medicine—especially the alternative paths, and psychotherapy. Being influenced by the moon, Willow people are frequently psychic and many are empaths.

Willow closes the fourth grove of the Talking Forest which deals with the prime of life, that chapter of life that for most middle-aged people, centers on family, security and stability.

Vine

Kenning: Festival, Celebration

Significance: Hospitality, Social Life

Of all foods created by human agency, none other except perhaps cheese, comes in such an astounding array as wine. It is fitting then, that wine and cheese go so well together and that wine growing districts are frequently home to dairy animals that are raised explicitly for cheese making. Even those other symbols of civilization—coffee and tea—do not come in so many varieties as wine. No one ever talks about such-and-such being a good year for Earl Grey tea, nor do they discuss the "nose" of a specific brand of espresso.

Wine from grapes is world famous as an aperitif and as a digestif. In recent years, it has been discovered that the French, whose rich cream- and sauce-filled diet should give them all heart attacks and strokes by age forty, are among the healthiest people in the world. This is in part due to their *moderate* consumption of wine. It appears that drinking one or two glasses of the beverage daily during a meal prevents blood clots and arteriosclerosis.

Beer cannot match wine for the distinction of its varieties of lagers and ales. Nor can that other great civilization-bringer, apple, and its cider. Perhaps this is due to snobbery, for there *is* a class distinction between the beverages. Wine has always been considered the drink of the aristocracy, while beer and cider belong to commoners such as myself. The logic in this is that grain can be stored for winter and is the staple ingredient of the bread we live by; likewise apples, which are good keepers and can be eaten virtually all year long. Grapes, however, must be eaten upon ripening in late summer and early fall. The only way to keep them from going bad is to dry them for raisins—or make wine. Winemaking is a lengthy, time-consuming process. One needs wealth to afford the vineyards and servants to tend to them.

Ritual and recreational drugs were substances commonly used by indigenous peoples. No matter how "primitive" they were, hunter-gatherers made good use of nature's extensive pharmacopeia. Tobacco, peyote and other naturally growing mind-altering or stimulating plants do not need extensive and exacting preparation, as do grain, hops and especially grapes for wine. To make bread, beer or wine takes land, and an *agrarian* society that brings with it a sense of rootedness. The result is a momentous transformation of human cultures from nomadic hunter-gatherers to more sedentary agricultural societies.

Physical Traits and Environment

Native to both Europe and North America, the grape *(Vitis)* is a climbing vine with lobed leaves resembling those of maple or sycamore. Some grape hybrids have beautiful leaves sporting pinkish veins and undersides; others have leaves large as dinner plates. In autumn, many species display gorgeous shades of orange, pink or red. Common to all grapevines are tendrils; similar to those of ivy, these spiraling branches twine themselves tightly around the host tree or trellis.

Grape species come in a dizzying variety, almost all of which are grown for eating or winemaking. The fruit may vary in colour from tender yellowy green Rieslings, to blush pink Muscats, nearly black Cabernets or the misty blue of Concord grapes. In most species, the grapes hang on the surface of the vine canopy, the better to ripen in the sunlight they crave.

Vine in Folklore

In the classical world, the vine was held sacred to the god of ecstasy, called Dionysus in Greece and Bacchus in Rome. The purview of Dionysus included divine inspiration and the art of the theatre. He was the son of Zeus, king of the Olympian gods. According to the Eleusinian mysteries, his mother was Persephone, who was corn maiden during the warmer seasons and queen of the Underworld in winter.

Other myths held that Dionysus was son of the mortal woman Semele. Goaded by the jealous Hera, Semele insisted upon seeing her lover Zeus as he really was. As a result, the unfortunate woman was scorched to death by the sky god's divine majesty. Zeus rescued his unborn son Dionysus from the ashes and sewed him into his thigh until it was time for him to be born.

This latter tale elucidates the life cycle of grapes. The vine appears to ripen best in the scorched earth of the Mediterranean climate, also known for its violent thunderstorms. The grape needs heat and dryness in order to ripen. Zeus, god of air, thunder and lighting, is thus a fitting father for the grape. His action of sewing the vine god into his thigh can be seen as an analogy of the custom of using the oak, Zeus's tree, as a trellis for the vine. The trunk of the tree is therefore its "thigh." The earth, Semele, goes fallow and may appear to die when the vine ripens in autumn, but, like Persephone, is resurrected in spring. Indeed, some versions of the Semele myth mention that the adult Dionysus rescued his mother from the Underworld.

To the Greeks, wine was the very blood of Dionysus. As the grape is crushed to make wine, so the god was torn apart by the Titans, pre-Olympian gods who were sent by the resentful Hera. They lured the infant Dionysus with a thyrsus or sceptre, then tore him to pieces and ate all but his heart. The angry Zeus slew the Titans with his thunderbolt and retrieved the heart, in this version feeding it to Semele, who subsequently became pregnant. Thus, Dionysus was twice born; no doubt a mythic reference to the practice of gleaning two grape harvests within the same year.

Most people familiar with Greek myth know that the Sibyl at Delphi was the priestess of both Apollo the sun god and the earth goddess Gaia. What is less well known is that she was also a priestess of Dionysus, who many classicists deem as Apollo's darker aspect.

The cult of Dionysus became very popular in Greece. Depictions often show him with satyrs and maenads. The latter were women said to partake in ecstatic orgies of wine drinking, dancing and singing. These maenads or *bacchae,* after chewing ivy leaves, would frequently tear men and wild animals to pieces.* Not surprisingly, the cult was denounced in both Greece and Rome. As is often the case with nonconformist groups, however, the truth about the rituals may have been distorted.

Wine was offered at the alters of other Greek gods, especially Aphrodite, the goddess of love. In Rome, narcotics such as belladonna, henbane and opium poppy were added to wine as stimulants along with water, surprisingly, to avoid "becoming drunk too quickly"! [157]

Spiritual Traits

Late summer and early fall—the time of the wine harvest, and most particularly Harvestide, or autumn equinox—belong to Vine. All elements, and especially fire and water, have an affinity with the vine. Gods associated with the plant are of course Dionysus or Bacchus, Aphrodite and Venus, as well as Silenus, the jolly satyr who was the elderly companion of Bacchus.

The Rune

Vine is the final "S" rune in the Talking Forest. The shape recalls the grape tendril—like Ivy, growing and moving constantly. The

---

*   As previously noted in the section on Ivy, this plant is very poisonous if ingested.

rune horizontal, as shown above, is in the upright position. This alludes to the manner in which grapevines are arranged for ease of harvesting–along trellised fences or on low-growing, pollarded trees. At the end of each spiral are three dots representing a cluster of grapes. The double spiral of this rune reminds us that there are two sides to the vine god and the gift of wine is double-edged. It may be benevolent, a bringer of cheer and social pleasure–the solar aspect; or it can become destructive as a maenad, especially in the hands of an alcoholic or someone drunk behind the wheel of a car.

A final note on the four S runes in the Talking Forest: two, Ivy and Vine are masculine, while Rose and Hedge are feminine. When upright, Ivy and Rose are vertical while Vine and Hedge are horizontal.

Another S rune sacred to Dionysus, Ivy began the first grove in the Talking Forest. Vine now begins the fifth and second-last grove of later middle age. It is at this time of our life we are expected to be fully responsible and able to "hold our liquor." Youth is spent in a frenzy of learning and sensation. Our prime involves the hard work of planting our life harvest. Now we settle down into the subtler mysteries, where hopefully, we appreciate the gifts of the ecstatic god without losing control. Many of us are also now at a stage where we can afford to entertain our friends and neighbours more lavishly than before. Hence the final third of the Talking Forest. These fourteen runes, heralded by Vine, represent the later years.

Kenning: Festival, Celebration
Significance: Social Life, The Arts, Inspiration, Creativity,
Civilization, Hospitality

Where Buckeye indicates an *individual* friend or associate who may have a strong influence on the querent, Vine represents social skills: our relationships within *groups* and how we mingle with others. Mulberry's purview is the *skill* needed for physical survival, whereas Vine speaks to the *arts,* an emotional and spiritual necessity that completes us as humans. As viticulture was the prelude to highly structured civilization, Vine indicates pleasures that are only fulfilled by interaction with others. Thus, **upright** Vine next to other runes suggests social skills and artistic abilities adroitly brought to bear on a situation.

The upright rune next to a toppled rune, however, may indicate that grape, twining along the fence, has run wild and taken over the orchard. Perhaps the querent is involved too much in socializing and not enough in setting their own house in order. It can also warn of addiction or drunkenness, especially if next to toppled Pine.

Inverted Vine, looking like an upright "S," is climbing from the sky and tunneling into the earth. Dionysus seeks his mother Semele in the Underworld. Likewise, we take nourishment from the conscious upperworld as well as from the earth of the subconscious in order to make good harvest. The rune in this position suggests the querent should turn to the arts and to the Muse to create something. By making beauty tangible, we touch the divine spirit.

The **toppled** Vine, with the dot above the rune, indicates one who is introverted and not socializing enough. Vine in this position advocates getting out in the world to meet others. Only then can you refresh your view on life: invigorating mind, body and soul and giving pleasure and celebration to your existence.

People associated with Vine are sociable and enjoy being with others. They are great entertainers and coordinators, often capable of inspiring others and acting as their Muse. However, if they do not discipline themselves, they may get carried away, behaving outrageously or recklessly.

Sycamore

Kenning: Commons, Village Square
Significance: Community, Civic Matters

Author Marie-France Boyer mentions the public or "palaver trees" in Africa.[158] These are large shady trees beneath which people gather to socialize, tell stories or perform plays and discuss issues important to the community. In many areas of France, the sycamore, in French, platane, is the "palaver tree" nonpareil. Indeed one could say that "le platane" is to France what the maple is to Canada. In this most gracious of countries, the tree can be found everywhere: lining city streets and country roads, and shading busy afternoon cafes. Virtually every town I visited during my trip to the south of France had one or more of these elegant giants holding place of honour in its town square.

While walking in a public park or woods in the Carolinian region, you may come upon a large tree with familiar looking five-pointed leaves, but whose bark appears to be peeling. It is not a diseased maple, but a sycamore *(Platanus),* also called plane tree. The species bears no relation to either maple or to the sycamore fig of similar bark, whose name it shares.

Physical Traits and Environment

The largest tree in the Carolinian forest, the American sycamore, our only native species, is fast growing, reaching a height of 180 feet (55 m), and having a large open crown. A pioneer tree, it is one of the first species to grow in places such as barren fields and strip mines.[159] In fact, all members of the sycamore family are highly resilient, being able to withstand pollution and amenable to pollarding or pruning back to the trunk. Small wonder then that plane trees were planted along the busy streets of many European cities. One such species became such a fixture of Britain's capital, that it is called the London plane.

Like catalpa, the American sycamore has few branches, but each is very large, making for an open crown with sparse canopy. The leaves, the size of a man's hand or larger, resemble those of maple.* The name *plane* from Latin *platanus,* or "broad" *(platy),* most likely refers to these sizable leaves. Older members of this

---

* So much so that there is a maple called sycamore maple!

species sometimes manifest burls–protuberances growing out of the trunk–giving the tree the impression of venerable old age. By contrast, the smooth patchy bark, light grey in parts and peeling to a celadon green elsewhere, presents a vital, youthful mien. The lively chartreuse colour we know as French green must have been named for the vibrant colour sunlight makes as it shines through France's sycamore leaves.

Although sycamore trees are long-lived–to more than 500 years–trunks will frequently hollow out. Some of the more prodigious specimens in Europe were used as houses, pigsties and stables.[160] Because the wood is tough-grained, it was traditionally used for kitchen implements and especially for butcher blocks.[161]

In Western Europe, the sycamore was honoured for its massive size,* unique beauty and speedy growth. Plane trees flourish in arid places in the Mediterranean where other broad-leaved trees cannot thrive. Unlike other fast-growing trees, they also can reach a venerable age and, as the London plane attests, they are able to withstand industrial toxins and city grime.

The sycamore's fruit is made of thousands of tiny seeds, all contained in a tightly packed golden ball. These eventually blow apart causing much sneezing among those susceptible to allergies. Most plane species yield two or three balls on a stem; however, the North American sycamore has only one per stem.

---

*   French sycamores are generally larger than those found in Southern Ontario, being up to fifteen feet (4.5 m) in diameter and with much denser canopies.

Sycamore in Folklore

The sycamore tree was highly regarded by the ancients in Europe and the Middle East. However, mention of sycamore in Biblical, Egyptian and Classical myth usually refers to the sycamore fig of the *Ficus* family, so no relation to plane trees.

It is believed that an ancient sycamore had survived in Chios from Classical Greek times. Under this tree's shade, Hippocrates, the renowned physician taught his students. There is also a famous tale that when Alexander the Great was in Persia, now Iran, he sought his future of a large double-trunked plane tree famed as an oracle. This tree "of the sun and the moon," accurately foretold his early death far from Greece.[162]

The French writer, Jacques Brosse, mentions that icons of Dionysus, the Greek god of wine, were carved into the trunks of plane trees that had blown down in storms.[163] Brosse adds that the sycamore was sacred to both Dionysus and the Great Mother, as were other plants with five-lobed leaves, such as the fig, the vine and the ivy.[164] Plane trees were common to Greece and the *platanus* is an appropriate tree to honour the god of wine, because it makes such a good trellis for the vineyard. During my sojourn in southern France, I saw numerous instances of pollarded *platanes* supporting grapevines.

Spiritual Traits

Sycamore's elements are earth and air and its high season is summer. As noted earlier, the trunks of large specimens were historically used for butcher's blocks. Sycamore of the pale luminous trunk therefore also belongs to the Blood Moon of November, when animals were traditionally slaughtered to avoid having to feed them over winter, when food was scarce. The leaves, like those of maple, are five-pointed and somewhat resemble hands. Human hands create the human community and the plane tree has witnessed much of our history.

The Rune

The Sycamore rune has four wide branches, similar to the other shade tree runes. The waviness of the lines here alludes to the tendency of the branches to zigzag. A dot representing the button-like fruit hangs from each of the two lower tines. A solitary shade bracket at the top of the rune signifies a tree of sparse canopy with a large open crown.

Kenning: Commons, Village Square
Significance: Public Duty, Civic Matters, Community

Because Sycamore has been used so much as a shade tree of the commons, it takes its place as the Talking Forest rune representing community. Whereas the Hedge rune deals with one's private space, Sycamore presides over the public sector. Hedge represents the boundary outside the house but is still part of the home. Sycamore is the boundary of the city street and the commons. The use of plane tree wood for butcher's blocks brings to mind the former pagan practice of public sacrifice, with the whole community witness to the slaughter of animals that were sacred to the gods. This was a communal event. While we do not sacrifice animals publicly today, one's involvement in the community is a type of sacrifice. Thus, in the Talking Forest, Sycamore stands as the tree of public duty.

Upright, the rune indicates the querent's involvement in their neighbourhood. Here we see an activist or volunteer who believes strongly in helping the community grow and thrive. However, an upright Sycamore rune next to inverted Hedge may indicate someone who is too involved in other people's business. It might be time to back off and give the Hedge some sunlight!

An **inverted** Sycamore shows someone overly taken with their own ideas and not willing to listen to the opinions of others nor to cooperate with them. Unfortunately, in the activist community, we often see this type of individual. These are people who tend to be overly forceful in having their ideas put across, often to the detriment of others.

A **toppled** Sycamore rune manifests as apathy, unawareness or lack of involvement in one's neighbourhood. It may also suggest burnout for those too heavily involved in their community, especially if next to toppled Ironwood.

People associated with good Sycamore energy make good neighbours and are often involved in public affairs. Good city councillors and volunteer firefighters are examples of people who are moved by the power of Sycamore.

Sumac

Kenning: Horned God

Significance: Wilderness, Men's Mysteries

Antler-like branches that shade, fruit that sustains wildlife, and thickets that provide ready shelter: all contribute to making Sumac an appropriate symbol of wilderness. If Apple speaks to our taming of nature, and Sycamore our interaction with others, Sumac reminds us of the wild that was our first home.

Within the last two centuries, we have lost our very sense of place in the real world. We are fascinated and saddened by stories of people such as Christopher McCandless and Timothy Treadwell, who died in part, because they did not pay heed to

Mother Nature's harsh and unforgiving laws.* We see ourselves mirrored therein and stories such as theirs make us all too aware that the wilderness, once our beloved home, has become alien to us. Sociologists note too how our children and grandchildren are the first generations that have been increasingly cut off from nature. Regrettably, instead of daily walks in the woods or city parks, they spend all their time at the mall, in front of a computer screen or fiddling with a mobile device. I believe that this self-imposed exile from the natural world is a huge factor in our present angst.†

Physical Traits and Environment

With slender, curving branches and reddish or dark brown bark, sumac *(Rhus)* rarely grows more than twenty feet (6 m) in height. It is easy to see where staghorn sumac got its name: its winter silhouette against the sky immediately evokes an adult buck deer replete with a full rack of antlers. These "antlers" are created in part by the fruit pods, which stand upright on short stems. Each pod is composed of many furry, one-seeded fruits, called drupes. In summer, before the pods become too noticeable, staghorn's

---

* Both died in Alaska–McCandless from possible starvation, when he was stranded in an abandoned bus thirty miles from help; Treadwell was mauled to death along with his partner Amie Huguenard, by brown bears in the Katmai National Park. Both men were known for taking chances in the wilderness.

† One good thing that may have grown out of the Covid-19 pandemic is the public's renewed craving for outdoor activities and time taken to experience local parks and other semi-wild areas.

dense green, palm-like leaves give it a tropical mien. This effect is enhanced when a group of these trees grow together; for they then form a low arching canopy, much like rhododendron bushes. Each compound leaf is composed of anywhere from nine to twenty-one leaflets. Fittingly, the fawn coloured branches of the tree have a fuzzy surface, much like the "velvet" of a deer's antlers.

Sumacs flourish across North America. Because they favour moist soil, they are liminal trees, frequently found by riverbank and stream, on the forest edge and in meadows. All sumac species tend to thicket, staghorn being particularly invasive, frequently taking over an area via new shoots or "suckers" growing out of the roots.

Smooth sumac, so called because its twigs are not hairy, closely resembles staghorn in all other aspects, with hybrids frequently occurring between the two species. Shining or winged sumac lacks the deer-like tines of its relatives. However it makes up for this shortcoming with unique leafy "wings" lining the stems between the leaflets, giving the twigs the appearance of fat, green paper twist ties. All red-fruited sumacs provide essential winter food for many birds and animals. All have rich green leaves that turn a brilliant, bloody crimson in autumn.

The swamp-dwelling poison sumac has oval, white fruit and its compound leaves are more rounded and leathery than those of other sumacs. Young stems stand out bright red against the brilliant green of the foliage—a strident warning that this, our most toxic native tree species, must be avoided at all costs. The painful itching and skin rash caused upon contact with the plant reminds us that all sumacs are members of the *Rhus* genus, including poison ivy and poison oak, two very unwelcome guests at the campsite. This toxicity is a recurrent feature of the cashew family, to which *Rhus* belongs.[165]

While poison ivy is a member of the sumac family, it behaves like ivy–creeping about, putting down roots and generally taking over. Understandably, we loathe this very inconvenient plant, all too often a literal pain in the butt! However, poison ivy serves an important role in nature. It and other native plants poisonous to humans allow for safe, pristine and human-free habitats for plants and animals that are generally immune to the toxin.

Sumac in Folklore

First Nations people chewed the fruits of both staghorn and smooth sumac to quench thirst. From these, they also made refreshing "lemonade" for a hot summer's day.[166] Indeed, much of the plant is high in vitamin C and the roots and bark were used in medicine as a purgative and disinfectant. Indigenous peoples used all parts of sumac to make red, yellow or black dyes. The leaves were often dried and added to ceremonial pipe tobacco.

Spiritual Traits

Sumac's phallic pods proclaim this a masculine tree. October and November, when the fruit is fully ripened and the leaves have turned, is Sumac's time of greatest power. These are the months of the Hunter's Moon, when men traditionally took the first of their winter treks to hunt large game as food to sustain the tribe. Sumac's elements are fire and water, both strongly associated with blood. Water is the blood of Mother Earth, and Sumac grows along the rivers and streams that are her arteries. Gods appropriate to this tree are Pan, the protector of wild creatures, Herne the Hunter and Cernunnos, a Celtic horned god worshipped both as god of fertility and of the Underworld–life and death held in balance.

Sumacs tend to grow in thickets and we recall that men from the earliest times have found it advantageous to hunt in groups. The red of sumac's fruit and autumn leaves represents also the blood that is shed each time we slaughter animals for food. With present-day monocultural farm practices, we have lost touch with the process of obtaining our food. We are not familiar with how animals are slaughtered and how the meat is processed. In ancient times, animals raised expressly for food were publicly slaughtered with great honour in outdoor temples. Modern "civilized" people look with horror upon these sacrifices, and upon present-day halal and kosher practices. In fact, they are probably more humane than those found in many of our modern abattoirs.

People of ancient times paid tribute to the animals they ate and used as livestock by attributing to their gods the physical and emotional qualities of domestic and game animals. Hence cow-headed Hathor, goat-footed Pan and the antlered Cernunnos, among many others. The respect First Nations people had for the animals they hunted is well known. Food animals such as bison, deer, turkey and salmon were regarded as mighty totems. As much as was possible, all parts of killed animals were used, with hardly any waste. Even parts unusable were treated with honour. For example, West Coast people customarily threw salmon bones into the sea, believing that by doing so, they were ensuring these fish would be reborn and populate the ocean again. Porcupine quills, grouse feathers and bison horns became part of ritual headdresses and regalia.

Sumac reminds us that all are interrelated: tree, stag and human. As technological creatures, modern people forget that we are ultimately prey as well, even if only for the maggots that will devour our flesh or the fire that will reduce our bodies to ashes.

The Rune

With its four tined branches, the Talking Forest Sumac is an imitative, *iconic* rune, like Pine or Elm. It mimics the tree's silhouette, with an oval at the end of each branch representing the flowering spikes.

Kenning: The Horned God
Significance: Men's Mysteries, the Natural World, Wilderness

In most early cultures, men were the hunters. Furthermore, while women were busy with the care and welfare of the children and elders, and looking after hearth and home, the men took it upon themselves to protect the tribe and to keep them safe. Talking Forest Sumac therefore signifies men's mysteries. While the red of

Rose in the women's mysteries represents the blood of birth and life, Sumac's red hearkens to the blood of death and the sacrifice of the hunted animal. It references as well the personal blood that may have to be shed to protect the tribe against outside dangers. While the men's mysteries did eventually encompass battle and defense of the people against other tribes, Sumac's scope does not include the battlefield–his most salient energies are from the Horned God archetype of ancient hunter/gatherer societies. It is now commonly believed that these societies were not particularly warlike. It is our next rune Holly who speaks to defense of the self and others.

As Sumac often dwells by streams and rivers, he provides the emotional support that the water element gives, especially for anyone trying to find harmony with other species. Although interactions between the sexes have changed immensely in the last few decades, men in our culture are still under pressure to be unwaveringly stoical and invincible–an impossible expectation for anyone. Men too need nurturing and support and Sumac's wild energy will keep a man in touch with his instincts and feelings. Women who have had negative experiences with men would also do well to meditate on Sumac's wholesome male energy: protective yet liberating.

In a reading, **upright** Sumac indicates the hunt–both hunter and prey. In modern parlance, it generally denotes our kinship with the wilderness and how we interact with nature. This rune may also indicate a career working in the wild or with animals or plants, such as veterinary medicine or field biology. Sometimes the upright rune signifies fatherhood or another imminent male passage: the youthful "rut" of the teenager or the male "menopause" of middle years. For a woman, the rune may signal a man who will become important in her life.

The **inverted** Sumac rune may counsel a man to make communion with the Horned God within–that is, to seek out his inner male self. This is especially crucial if the man has issues of low self-esteem or of being disconnected from the natural world around him. Likewise, the inverted rune may suggest to a woman that she make contact with her *animus*–the god within; for all humans are male and female in part, within the psyche. We all partake of the god and the goddess.

Toppled Sumac often warns of an artificial lifestyle, of being out of touch with the natural world. It may be necessary for the querent to seek the wild for a time, to get away from the bustle of the city and the man-made world. The rune on its side sometimes warns of insensitivity or lack of empathy for other beings. It can on occasion, even clarion danger within the natural environment. Let instinct be your guide. The animal mind knows the lay of the land and whether or not something is amiss.

People associated with Sumac energy are nature lovers, such as hunters, anglers or environmentalists. Regardless of their sex, they generally prefer men's company, just as Rose people favour being among women.

A compelling "hunter's triad" can be made from Juniper, protector of humble creatures, Sumac, the hunter and Yew, the rune of death. Anyone who hunts would do well to meditate on these runes.

Holly

Kenning: Warrior, Battle

Significance: Conflict, Struggle

War as an "art form" that went beyond the intermittent tribal skirmishing of early peoples did not fully develop until the advent of agriculture. Holly is the tree of warrior energy, although it must be stressed that the Talking Forest Holly does not glorify militarism or conflict for the sake of war. The holly's leaves are only spiky lower down on the tree to prevent foraging by animals. So too the rune speaks to self-defense and protective energy rather than unbridled aggression.

Physical Traits and Environment

Evergreen holly *(Ilex)* is not a gentle plant. Many species of this tree have prickly leaves whose spines come to a point, making them sharp as thorns. Leaves of the European or English holly become gradually less spiky as they move higher up the tree, suggesting that these points may be a protection against foraging animals. The yellow or white flowers are quite fragrant and appear in the spring. The berries, a bright clear red and a favourite of birds and wild animals, are inedible to humans. English holly and his American cousin both thrive in southern and central US and on North America's west coast. They are not common in the rest of the States or in Canada, but can grow in the Carolinian zone. Both English and American hollies are of middle height and columnar in shape, with the characteristic leathery, glossy, spiked leaves familiar to all. They have the mien of hussars from the Napoleonic War standing in full, arrogant regalia. The wood of holly is amazingly white, and so richly uniform in texture that it resembles ivory more than any wood. It is easy to work and often used to make decorative boxes or sculpture.

Holly in Folklore

The tree, being evergreen, retains both its leaves and bright red berries throughout the cold months. In Europe since time immemorial, holly has been used to proclaim the winter solstice and the vanquishing of the dark time of the year. Revelers wore holly boughs during the Roman Saturnalia feast in December. Many of our modern Christmas customs originate from this festival, including that of placing holly wreaths on doors and as centrepieces.

Although holly is usually regarded as a masculine tree, he shares his name with Mother Holly or Moder Holle as she was known in Dutch and German legend. In early English folklore, she was an aspect of the earth, specifically the protective goddess of winter. She shelters the earth and its creatures during the cold months, offering the red berries of holly to birds and other animals who are in need of sustenance at this time of year.

The myth of the battle between the Holly and Oak Kings illustrates the eternal struggle between winter and summer. In the common version, they struggle eternally for ascendancy and for the favour of the Goddess. The Oak King holds sovereignty throughout spring and into autumn, but at Harvestide he is vanquished by the Holly King who represents the colder time of year. At Yule, during the Holly King's ascendancy, the Oak King is reborn and the cycle starts over.

With the coming of Christianity, the holly tree became a symbol of Christ. It was believed that the leaves were used to make the crown of thorns Jesus wore at the crucifixion. The red berries symbolize the blood he shed and the evergreen qualities of the tree are a reminder of his promise of resurrection after death. Regardless of the carol's popularity among Christians, "The Holly and the Ivy" may actually reference an older pagan tradition alluding to the *dyad,* or sacred marriage between god and goddess. Here, ivy represents the feminine principle and the promise of summer, while the masculine holly is ascendant in winter, when the Lord of the Hunt holds sway.

The wood of holly was used to make spears and arrows. The Roman writer Pliny believed that if a holly staff was thrown at a wild animal, the creature would return and lie down by the staff.[167] In the Victorian language of flowers, holly means foresight,[168] a fitting trait for a warrior.

Spiritual Traits

Holly is a solar, masculine tree and his time is the Yule festival at winter solstice. In early winter, courageous Holly is the defender of the sun's fire and stands guardian of all he surveys. You cannot penetrate his defenses; thornless as he may be, his very leaves are weapons. He is sacred to Mother Holly who guards all creatures during the winter. Warrior gods such as the Roman Mars and the Norse Tiu are appropriate to Holly, as is the Celtic goddess Morrigan. Note however, that Holly's energies are more suited to Athena, Greek goddess of strategic and defensive battle than to Ares, a god of violent, chaotic war. Holly speaks to physical courage, whereas Pine deals more specifically with moral courage.

The Rune

The Talking Forest Holly is another candelabra rune, but it has a unique feature. Each berry dot is placed just below the tip of its branch's spike, illustrating Holly as our only non-needled tree with sharp and prickly leaves. The branches of this masculine rune start on the right. The six branches recall the five fingers of the human hand, capable of making weapons, controlled at the top, by the mind.

Kenning: Warrior, Battle

Significance: Test, Struggle, Strife, Conflict, Ordeal

Upright in a reading, Holly represents conflict, as well as the strength and courage to face it. Here, struggle or sacrifice may be needed in order to achieve a desired goal. The upright rune also implies the querent will be successful in their endeavour. Holly is actively struggling and doing battle, whether with others or with the querent's own inner fears or personal issues. While Hawthorn is also an aggressive rune, she deals more specifically with issues of anger and self-respect. And where the Evergreen rune, as shelter from the storm, bestows *placid* security, Holly provides protection by active means.

Next to prudent runes such as Pine or Beech, the Holly rune may indicate that vigilance is needed. Sometimes Holly illustrates someone who is daring to the point of recklessness. This is especially so if the rune is next to the inverted Buckeye.

Inverted Holly indicates one preparing for defense. The rune in this position often warns of conflict with others. Here the warrior is shielding himself and sharpening his weapons in readiness for a struggle.

Toppled Holly warns of quarrels and disputes with others. It may also indicate timidity, an unwillingness to engage or a weakening of morale, especially with toppled Hawthorn. On occasion, it may signal danger, especially if next to Bramble, the rune of entrapment.

People associated with Holly are often in the military, are peace officers or emergency personnel such as firefighters. They are generally courageous, frequently idealistic, sometimes rushing into a situation in order to set things right. If they are not careful, they can be brusque or blunt to the point of being insulting or disdainful of those who appear weak or timorous. Holly people must be careful not to take offence when it is not meant. It is helpful for them to remember that holly leaves are prickly only on the *lower* parts of the tree. In other words, aggression is only necessary when one is actually under attack.

Bramble

Kenning: Trap Snare

Significance: Consequence, Obstacle

The hedges that sprang up suddenly to surround Sleeping Beauty's castle were probably hawthorns, but brambles would have been just as effective. These matted, clingy bushes grow best in meadows and make themselves at home here in the maple/beech forest system of eastern North America. They include many varieties, of which raspberry and blackberry are the most renowned.

One of the most notable characteristics of the brambles is their tendency to cling to and scratch anyone who tries to traverse them. They form virtually impenetrable thickets, the branches often overarching smaller plants. However, as they rarely grow over five feet (1.5 m) in height, one can usually see beyond them.

Physical Traits and Environment

Typical of most members of the rose family, the leaves of bramble *(Rubus)* are small and oval, sometimes pink-tinged, resembling rose or apple leaves. In most of the numerous varieties of bramble, there are three leaves to each stalk. Loganberry, a cross between the blackberry and raspberry, has oblong red fruit. Dark purple boysenberry was developed by hybridizing blackberry, raspberry and dewberry, the latter a groundcover North American bramble. Other species native here include the thimbleberry with shallow, pink, fuzzy berries, and salmonberry, native to the West Coast. The latter resembles a bright pink cross between thimbleberry and raspberry. No matter their shape or colour, bramble fruits are always aggregates composed of tiny drupelets. They closely resemble mulberries, however the two species are not related.

Brambles are often a haven for nettles, wasps and in some areas, poisonous snakes. As a child, I was once stung on the neck by a wasp while picking raspberries on my parents' farm, and had a good cry about it.

Bramble in Folklore

Befana was a benevolent witch in Italy, who brought gifts to children (including coal for those who were naughty), much like that other venerable pagan figure, Santa Claus. On the night of Epiphany in January, an effigy of Befana was burned to herald the end of the old year and the beginning of the new.[169] Befana's pyre consisted of many things including brambles, which would certainly have made good tinder. The prickles represent the harshness of winter, just as the fruit promises the eventual sweet harvest.

Blackberries have long had a close historical association with the Devil. In Scotland, when the berries went sour on the vine, it was because the Devil had thrown his cloak over them. Old Nick was more rambunctious in Ireland where he would stomp on the plants in order to sour the berries![170] Robert Graves states that blackberries were not eaten in Wales after September 30, because the Devil was believed to have entered into them at that time. He adds that in Brittany however, they were taboo at all times, "because of the fairies."[171] Due to its tendency to cling tenaciously to passersby, the bramble became a symbol of remorse.[172] Not surprisingly with all of the above, it was believed that to dream of brambles foreshadowed bad luck. Dreaming that one passed through them unharmed, however, presaged triumph over an adversary.[173]

Spiritual Traits

Bramble belongs to August and especially Lammastide–August 1st, when the berries begin to ripen. At this, summer's first harvest, we begin to reap what we sowed earlier in the year. Bramble is the Talking Forest rune of karma and consequence and is every bit as much a gift as Apple, the rune of choice. Bramble's gift of payoff however, is often one we would prefer not to accept. Brambles are not tall plants however, and no matter how thorny the problem or how much we may be trapped within Bramble's spines, there is generally a way out or around the issue. But it is not always the way we would have chosen.

There is an element of obligation with Bramble. In the past, hunter-gatherers learned to invent traps to catch food, particularly when more straightforward hunting was difficult or inadequate. This extra food and clothing source was shared among the tribe, thus aiding in the development of more complex cultures. Whether we live in a close-knit, "primitive" society or the current digital world, we are forced to be helpful or at least considerate in some way, sacrificing our time and expertise. We are snared by obligation into helping the family and community flourish. But it is also true that if we cooperate with others, we harvest the fruits of friendship and love. It is often when we resist natural law, are selfish or untrustworthy, that we eventually get caught in karma's thorns.

Growing among North America's beech/maple forest, Bramble reveals to us the growth that comes from life's lessons, as well as the changes this learning brings. Treated with respect, the bush gives us lovely delicate flowers and delicious fruit. The stinging insects usually leave us be and continue to do their necessary work as pollinators and predators. The hidden nettles are good medicine. Likewise, we gain both the sweetness and the barbs of experience from the mistakes we make in life. Ripening around Lammastide, Bramble reminds us that we are harvesting the result of actions taken earlier in the year.

Deities appropriate to Bramble are Trickster Coyote, the Haida/Tlingit Mouse Woman who helps people get out of a variety of sticky situations, Befana who brings gifts for all, good and bad, and of course, the Greek goddess Nemesis.

The Rune

The left-hand spiral of Bramble is smaller than the one on the right, showing that these bushes vary in size. It also helps distinguish the rune from Hawthorn and Rowan, both of which are similar. Each of Bramble's flower spirals ends in a dot, befitting such an abundantly fruitful species. Like Hawthorn, Bramble has a thorn on the right side.

Kenning: Trap, Snare

Significance: Consequence, Karma, Obstacle, Barrier

Bramble's purview is much like that of Straif, the Ogham Blackthorn, or Isa in the Futhark system. **Upright,** it represents circumstances that cannot be avoided: either outside forces acting on a situation, or actions resulting from past karma. It may warn, if next to Holly, that the querent is open to attack or at least, is vulnerable with weakened defenses. If close to Elm, the rune signifies *geas,* a magical prohibition or obligation. As such, Bramble suggests karmic outcome, good or bad, from action taken in the past.

Inverted Bramble carries the same intent in milder form. The effect will be less incisive than that of the upright rune and the problem easier to solve, albeit mitigation may be necessary. Inverted Bramble next to toppled Reed however suggests inertia, an inability to take action. Here, the querent is thwarted and can do little but wait out the issue.

Toppled to the left, Bramble may presage removal of a problem, escape from a sticky situation or freedom to move after a time of inertia. However, there will likely be consequences: here the thorn is sticking up ready to poke the querent. Bramble **toppled to the right,** with the thorn downward, indicates a difficulty easily avoided. Here the trap is already sprung, the snare with open egress, which the intended victim need not fear. With either toppled position however, the querent would do well to learn from the experience, assessing how it happened in the first place.

Bramble energy is not to be feared and can be helpful in enabling spiritual growth. Like Elm, it is a boundary rune, but where Elm indicates *social* boundaries, Bramble is a *spiritual* and sometimes even a *magical* boundary, as were the thorns surrounding Sleeping Beauty's castle. In protective magic, one might meditate on Bramble as protection against physical or psychic attack. Bramble is a guardian like Pine, but where Pine is a shield, Bramble, the snare, is somewhat more combative, if not as evidently so as Holly's club.

The Bramble rune closely resembles the Talking Forest Hawthorn and occasionally can be as aggressive as its cousin. Hawthorn deals with standing by one's principles. Bramble is about the *consequences* of doing just that. The outcome is not always fortunate or "just." Indeed, many good people have died for their principles. But the law of karma works in the long run for the common good. The world is better for the work of upstanding and honourable people, even if they die in the doing. Like Hawthorn, Bramble evinces respect. Hidden among bramble bushes are intrinsically beneficial, but potentially afflictive creatures, such as wasps and stinging nettles. When we disrespect karma, eventually we are stung by its laws.

Bramble likewise resembles the Talking Forest Rowan–the "lucky" rune. What often appears to be simple good luck however, is actually the result of "what goes round comes round." The good luck brought by Rowan is often karmic payback for previous good deeds. Bramble is, in effect, Rowan with a thorn! The briars of Bramble compel us to walk in balance with the universe. Rowan's energy happens when we learn to stay in step with it.

Bramble directly follows the Sumac and Holly runes in the Talking Forest. These three I refer to as the *struggle* runes. Sumac represents the natural struggle between predator and prey, Holly the human conflict of war and Bramble the battle between the individual and their soul. Centred in the fifth grove of the Talking Forest, these are runes of late middle age/early elder years. At this stage, time is catching up with us and the natural process of aging shows up in aches and pains and sometimes, more serious illnesses. Finally, this time of our lives is a struggle with how we have snared ourselves into our present condition by decisions made earlier. Many people have regrets in middle age because they did not previously take an alternate path. Others are now thriving and enjoying the harvest of their middle years because they followed their hearts.

People associated with Bramble are often aggressive and cantankerous. They are usually scrupulously honest and willing to help those whom they perceive as being worthy of aid. Reticent and less edgy than Hawthorn people, Brambles can tend to be judgmental and will hold others to their promises.

Hazel

Kenning: Wand, Divining Rod
Significance: Wisdom, Intellect

In Europe since time immemorial, "water witches" have used forked branches of hazelnut trees to find natural reserves of underground water. When the first white settlers came to North America, they mistook the native witch hazel for the small tree they remembered from Europe. They made similar use of this new tree, with apparently similar results.

The mix-up is understandable as the species, though unrelated, share a very close resemblance. For the sake of clarity, this book adopts the word "Hazel" to indicate the compound rune representing both trees. "Hazelnut" refers to *Corylus* or "true" hazel, as well as its exclusive rune, while "Witch Hazel" pertains to the *Hamamelis* genus or its particular rune. "Cobnut" and "filbert" are terms that refer to the fruit of the hazelnut tree, as well as to specific *hybrids* of this plant.

Physical Traits and Environment

Both hazelnut *(Corylus)* and witch hazel *(Hamamelis)* exhibit a fey, magical aura. Both are small trees that tend to form thickets in maple/beech forests, preferring stream banks and woodland clearings. On occasion they will even share the same meadow. Both plants possess toothed oval leaves that are pointed at the tips and turn burnished gold in autumn. The true hazel or hazelnut, a member of the birch family, grows here and in Europe, with the native species being hardier here. They thrive in Lower Mainland BC, Eastern Canada and much of the US, but are not as common in the northeast as the witch hazels. The catkin flowers somewhat resemble those of cousin birch. Witch hazels are native to North America and Asia, but not to Europe. Our native species ranges naturally over east and central North America. The stringy bright yellow flowers bloom from late fall even into January, when most other plants are dormant.

By far, the easiest way to tell the two trees apart is in the fruit. Hazelnut sports frilled or beaked papery pods that grow singly or in groups of two or three. Each one of these oddities contains a savory, reddish brown nut, called a filbert or cobnut. Not to be outdone in peculiarity, witch hazel sports a chambered beige seedpod shaped somewhat like a miniature turban squash. Each of the two black seeds bursts out of its chamber with such ferocity they have been known to fly a distance of thirty feet or nine metres! Perhaps it was for this reason the tree was called *witch* hazel. These seeds, however, don't need brooms to fly!

Hazelnut and Witch Hazel in Folklore

According to the Irish Celts, the Boyne River was overlooked by seven, some say nine, sacred hazelnut trees. Here lived the Salmon of Knowledge, who had obtained his wisdom from eating the hazelnuts that frequently fell from these trees. After seven years, the Druid who presided in that area finally caught the salmon and had it roasted. His acolyte, Finn McCool, while testing the fish to see if it was cooked, burned his finger. Putting the sore digit to his mouth to cool it off, he gained knowledge of all things.

Hazel's significance as the Coll rune in the Ogham system is similar to that in the Talking Forest–wisdom and knowledge.[174] Like its close relative alder, hazelnut has a strong affinity with water. Forked branches of hazelnut were used as divining rods to find hidden underground streams. It was believed the bite of an adder could be assuaged by use of a cross that was fashioned from two hazelnut twigs.[175] Interestingly, the snake represents the bringer of knowledge in many myths, including the Old Testament Book of Genesis. As hazelnut was deemed a tree of wisdom throughout Western Europe, this is no doubt an example of sympathetic magic.

In the New World, both First Nations people and European settlers used the hazelnut primarily for food and the witch hazel specifically for medicinal purposes.[176] The Iroquois in particular, used witch hazel as a panacea. The Menominee of Wisconsin used the seeds "as sacred beads in their medicine ceremony,"[177] no doubt due to their amazing ability to fly from the pod. To this day, the juice from the bark and leaves of witch hazel are sold by drug stores to act as a vulnerary for bruises, injuries, stiff muscles and insect bites.

Spiritual Traits

Air and water are elements associated with both Hazels. Late summer is their time of greatest strength, particularly August through late September, when the filberts are harvested and the witch hazel seeds begin to disperse. This time of year corresponds to middle age: that chapter of our lives when we achieve wisdom garnered from our years of experience. Gods associated with the Hazel rune are Hermes, Athena and her Roman counterpart Minerva; Nechtan, Irish god who guarded the waters wherein dwelt the Salmon of Knowledge; and Cerridwen, Welsh goddess and keeper of the cauldron of knowledge and inspiration.

The Rune

Because witch hazel so closely resembles hazelnut and the aura of each is so similar, I felt justified in uniting them into the Talking Forest Hazel, even though the trees are unrelated. The resulting compound sigil is formed from each of the runes unique to Hazelnut and Witch Hazel.

The filbert is shown falling from the branch into the stream of consciousness, for Hazelnut gives knowledge to those who seek it.* The three dots on the right-hand branch of the rune are the seeds of Witch Hazel, springing from the pod in a burst of inspiration. This is the third of four compound runes in the Talking Forest set. The runes exclusive to Hazelnut and Witch Hazel are shown below.

Kenning: Wand, Divining Rod
Significance: Wit, Wisdom, Knowledge, Intellect,
Focus, Cunning

This is the rune of intelligence, with Hazelnut denoting "book-learning," whereas Witch Hazel suggests native intelligence. If Hazelnut refers to academia, Witch Hazel's alma mater is the university of hard knocks. The **upright** rune's appearance in a reading suggests knowledge that will come to the seeker. Perhaps the querent will return to school or otherwise broaden their education—by travel, a new interest or hobby, or even self-guided research in the local library. All are worthy ways of learning.

Inverted Hazel directs the querent to use the intelligence they were given. Dive deep into the pool of knowledge within. Let the seeds of inspiration burst forth and disperse where they may. When one looks into the subconscious, ideas are often dredged up which

---

* Save for Buckeye, this is the only rune with the fruit detached from the rest of the rune.

compel the seeker to explore formerly hidden knowledge. This in turn leads to more understanding along with an even greater thirst for learning.

If the rune is **toppled to the right,** with the Hazelnut side on top, the tree has been cut down and the filbert is lying on the dead branch. This indicates the querent is not thinking clearly. Stupidity is not a lack of intelligence, but what happens when smart people do not use the wits that were given them. We all know well-educated people who still do stupid things and don't seem to learn from their mistakes. In order to avoid repeating errors, you must eat of the hazelnut of knowledge.

The rune **toppled to the left,** with the Witch Hazel side up suggests cunning, subterfuge, or untrustworthiness–intelligence used to negative results. Here yes, the seeds of Witch Hazel are dispersing far and wide, but the source of learning–the tree–has been cut down. Knowledge without understanding is cunning. One may discover nuclear fission, but if it is used to start a world war, where is the wisdom in that?

People associated with Hazel are quick studies, very intelligent, with boundless curiosity. They are frequently, but not always, members of academia. Able to see the larger pattern behind things, they can however become overly intellectual. People with too much Hazelnut energy are in danger of being locked in the "ivory tower," becoming too arrogant and disconnected from the everyday world to be of much use to it. Those with a surfeit of Witch Hazel energy are perhaps too clever for their own good. Many con artists and swindlers have this proclivity.

Oak

Kenning: Door, Scales

Significance: Power, Judgment, Law

Save for the redwoods and sequoias of North America's West Coast, no tree in the forest can compare with the might and majesty of the great Oaks. Massive in trunk, out-flung of branch, monarchs of endless sky and roiling weather, they defer only to the kingly sun and the lightning bolt. And yet, well rooted in the bountiful earth, the Oaks magnanimously toss the largesse of their acorns on all subjects alike.

Physical Traits and Environment

There are two mighty branches in the *Quercus* family: the white oaks and red oaks. Although each is named for the colour of its wood, this is not very accurate. Wood from some species of white oak is brown, while some red oaks have white wood! There are more definitive ways of telling the two apart. White oak leaves generally have rounded lobes and the edible acorns are an annual crop. Red oak leaves are pointed at the tips and the bitter tasting acorns appear only in alternate years. Most oak leaves, a sedate olive green in summer, turn gold to brown in fall, but some red oaks are showier in autumn, with the well-named scarlet oak especially resplendent.

Like all members of the beech family, oak casts a mighty shadow. Red or white, most oaks have large, heavy branches perpendicular to the single, main trunk. In white oaks especially, these branches become gnarled and twisted with age. Of all trees, the oaks have the deepest and most massive of root systems* and, fittingly for such majestic trees, they prefer rich, heavy clay soils.

We are all familiar with the roundish or oblong acorns. These are attached to the twig by a cross-hatched lid or "cap" that looks amusingly like a tiny beret. A popular food source, acorns have been eaten by cows, pigs, moose, deer, bears, mice, as well as turkey and other game birds. Like many trees whose fruit is a large nut, oaks are extensively planted by squirrels. Without these wee beasties forgetting where they hid their stashes, we would not have the glorious oak/hickory forests that cover the eastern US and the southern tip of Ontario's Niagara Escarpment.

---

* The Greeks honoured oak as an oracular tree in part, because its roots were set so deep in the ground. It thus had direct contact with the Underworld. Nathaniel Altman, *Sacred Trees*, p. 167.

Oak–hard, heavy and refined–is among the world's most highly prized woods. It has been used for furniture making, in architecture and in shipbuilding. England's great navy was originally built from the wood of the mighty English oak. When that timber tree became scarce, Britain looked to the white oak of the colonies for their shipbuilding program. So long-lived is oaken wood, that Winston Churchill's Second World War bunker was shored up by the ribs of one of Lord Nelson's flagships built more than 100 years earlier.[178]

Oak in Folklore

Save perhaps for the apple, the mighty oak is the most storied and revered tree in European mythology. Invariably sacred to the male patriarch god of each pantheon, oak thus came to symbolize the king or chieftain—the "father of the country." The oak is a natural lightning rod; thus, it was an appropriate tree for the Greeks and Romans to dedicate to their respective weather gods, Zeus and Jupiter. To the Celts, oak was sacred to Dagda, the great Earth/Solar father of the Tuatha de Danann. The Norse and Teutonic cultures named the oak as Thor's tree, while the Slavic peoples dedicated it to their god of thunder, called Perun or Perkunas.

Oak as an attractor of lightning is a common motif in both European and North American legend and it is based on fact. The oak is struck more than any other tree save perhaps, ash. "Avoid the oak for it draws the stroke!" as the saying goes. Apparently, the oak's thick, rough and ridged bark traps water inside, thus attracting electricity from the air.[179] The large heavy branches of this mighty tree tend to fall during gales and heavy rainstorms, making it even more dangerous for one to stand beneath during heavy weather.

Seemingly, thunderstorms in Greece occur with the most violence and frequency at Dordona. Perhaps this is why the famous grove to Zeus was built there. Gongs fashioned of bronze were placed in oak trees throughout the grove to imitate the sound of thunder.[180]

In ancient Italy, the nymph Egeria, possibly an aspect of the goddess Diana, was the wife to King Numa, who was the ancient lawgiver of nascent Rome. In Nemi, a sacred grove was dedicated to her.[181] Here, it is said, the title of Rex Nemorensis or King of the Sylvan Glade was held by a runaway slave. It was essential that he carry his sword at all times in order to defend himself from would-be usurpers.[182] For if another such slave could break a bough from a certain sacred oak of this grove, he could challenge the reigning priest to a duel to the death, only ruling in the latter's stead if he succeeded in slaying him.

In Britain, there is a persistent belief that King Arthur was buried in an oak tree, although no one seems to know the exact locale: some say Glastonbury, others cite various places in Wales or in England's West Country. But if no one in Britain knows where Arthur lies, the French at least are certain that Merlin's tomb is located in Broceliande, in the west of Brittany, near a great oak tree, le Chêne des Hindrés. It was here the Lady of the Lake was said to have enchanted the famous wizard.

With the advent of Christianity, many pagan oak groves were usurped for Christian worship. It has been suggested that the Scottish word for church–*kirk,* may originate from the Latin *quercus* meaning oak. This name suggests a throwback to pre-Christian times in Britain, when the Celts and their Druid priests worshipped in oak groves.[183] In any event, we know that the Celtic word for oak, *duir,* has the same etymology as the English *door* and the German *tür.* Moreover, it is said that Durrow and Derry monasteries, established in Ireland by St. Columba, were named for sacred oaken groves that had originally stood there.[184]

Oak is irrevocably tied with England's sovereignty and its monarchs. It is said that Elizabeth I received news of her imminent enthronement beneath an English oak. During the Civil War, Charles II reputedly hid from the Roundheads in another tree of this species. For this reason, English oak is often referred to as Royal Oak. During the seventeenth century, it was also believed that oak leaves changing to an unusual colour, or fading too soon in the fall, was a sure sign of impending civil disaster.[185]

In both Europe and North America, of all trees, the oak holds the purview of justice. Legal cases were tried and people either freed or condemned most frequently under oaks, although elms, lindens, sycamores and chestnuts also served as "justice trees."*

---

* It would be interesting to do a study of "justice trees" to see if the type of tree used had any effect on judgment. Were, for example, oak judges more likely to be "hanging judges" and linden judges more merciful?

In pagan Lithuania, priests carried out their official duties, often presiding as judges, at the foot of large oak trees.[186] In Germany, Switzerland and other places, local magistrates would sit under the town's oak when giving judgment.[187]

However, this judicial aspect of oak has a darker side. The tree's high, perpendicular branches, capable of supporting heavy weights, makes it peculiarly suitable as a gallows. I posit that in Europe at any rate, this tree was more often used as a "hanging tree" than any other. Marie-France Boyer concurs that the oak often was a gallows tree. In one town in Belgium, an oak was named "Triche-en-Gibet"–"Cheating the Gallows,"[188] something one suspects many hapless people in this locale didn't do! The Wolves' Oak at Condé-sur-Risle in France, took its name from the quaint custom of hanging not only reprobate humans from its boughs, but also wolves unlucky enough to have been captured![189] In spite of all this, however, the oak has mostly positive associations. The "umbrella oaks" of France served as symbols of sanctuary during the oppression of the Protestant Huguenots during the seventeenth century.[190]

In North America, the famous Charter Oak of Hartford, Connecticut was a council tree for the local Iroquois.[191] For hundreds of years, this venerable landmark acted as a sort of seasonal clock. The people knew "to plant corn when the acorns were the size of a mouse's ear."[192] Later, the white settlers used it for their town's landmark, as well as a symbol of their sovereignty, free of the English yoke. When the tree finally blew down during a storm in 1856, the settlers used pieces of it to make gavels and office furniture for the State Capital building nearby.[193] It is not

**Sell your books at
sellbackyourBook.com!**
Go to sellbackyourBook.com
and get an instant price
quote. We even pay the
shipping - see what your old
books are worth today!

Inspected By: Viviana_Gutierrez

00048978957

to be wondered that the colonists would wish to preserve this particular tree's *mana* in their symbols of office. For at one time during the War of Independence, the trunk of this same tree was used to hide the town's new charter, when the British were threatening Hartford.

Spiritual Traits

This most masculine of trees has a powerful aura: aloof and majestic. Oak's season is September when the acorns appear. Thursday, named after Thor and traditionally assigned to many thunder gods, belongs to Oak. The tree's deep roots and heavy branches reach out and shelter many living things. This illustrates that true power never fears to give of itself and never forgets what gave it life–the sheltering earth and the broad-horizoned sky. The tree is sacred to the many weather and sky gods mentioned above.

The Rune

Oak is one of the unique "iconic" runes of the Talking Forest. This is the final compound rune of the set. It is composed of the specific rune for White Oak (below left) and the rune for Red Oak (below right). Two branches reach out and upward from the main trunk; the left branch with two curved or rounded horns emanating from the tip, represents the rounded lobes of white oak leaves. The right-hand branch terminates in an arrow tip, symbolizing the sharp, pointed lobes of Red Oak. The grey shaded* acorn crowning the tree signifies Oak's status as king of the woodland.

White Oak   Red Oak

There is an intriguing dichotomy between the White and Red Oaks. The White suggests the solar and sky gods, with gently lobed leaves and edible acorns, while the Red Oak denotes the harsher aspect of the god: the dark lord, with horned lobes and bitter acorns. The White Oak is perhaps mercy while the Red suggests rough justice. The Oak rune illustrates that justice can prevail only when both sides of an issue are pondered. In this way laws can be instigated for the good of the people. Edicts that are carelessly lenient, cruelly draconian or cynically corrupt ultimately serve no one. The scales must be level and balanced.

Kenning: Door, Scales
Significance: Power, Justice, Sovereignty, Judgment, Law, Majesty

The Celtic word for oak is duir, meaning door. When a decision is taken or judgment made, it is as if a door has opened and a threshold has been crossed. Even if eventually reversed, the judgment made will have a lasting effect, for good or ill. Oak thus carries with it a strong element of karma. Often growing on hilltops, the tree

---

*   The acorn for the specific White Oak rune is not shaded and for the Red is shaded black.

is periodically struck with lightning. Nevertheless, it frequently survives the lightning bolt. Likewise, those who carry power well can take the slings and arrows of fate and opinion equally. But they must remember that being a large target renders them easier to strike.

In a reading, the **upright** rune suggests success in public life; perhaps a career or situation in which the querent has public authority and often has to make decisions crucial to the lives of other people. This may also indicate a powerful and just person who will have a positive influence on the querent's life.

The **inverted** rune illustrates a situation in which good judgment is needed. The querent must ponder carefully, going to the deep root of the issue, before deciding on the proper recourse. Depending on nearby runes, Oak in the inverted position may indicate the overcoming of a seemingly insurmountable situation— the uprooting of an unjust or arbitrary barrier, especially in legal or civil matters. A new seed of justice is being planted.

The contrary rune **toppled to the left,** with the Red branch up, suggests harshness, inflexibility, judicial rigidity. If **toppled to the right,** with the White branch up, there may be injustice or a weakening of the querent's autonomy, due to legal laxity or corruption. Toppled on either side next to Reed or Juniper, Oak may express power laid low; if next to toppled Hawthorn, it will have been brought down by ill repute.

People associated with Oak believe in propriety and following the rules. Often working within the legal system, they are lawyers, police officers or judicial reformers, strong and stalwart in their beliefs. Being generally traditionalists, Oaks don't like to buck the status quo, but prefer to change society from within.

Oak people are sometimes inflexible to the point of intolerance, forgetting the spirit of the law by following the letter too closely. These people would do well to remember Aesop's fable the "Oak and the Reed"–Oak will do well to learn flexibility from Reed. Linden trees often grow together with Oak in the wild, and their energies are highly complementary. The gentleness and mercy of Linden will mitigate Oak's rigidity.

Oak is man's law while Bramble is karma, the law of the universe. Likewise, Oak deals with social mores among humans, while Sumac suggests the laws of nature and man's attitude toward the wilderness. Where Elm illustrates the mores of the smaller community, Oak represents the laws of society as a whole.

The Oak rune ends the fifth and second-last grove of the Talking Forest–the final years of middle age and entry into the elder years. Indeed, older people with their greater experience, are often slower to pass judgment but also more difficult to hoodwink.

Larch

Kenning: Ladder, Shaman
Significance: Spirituality, Mysticism

One small yet profound element separates Larch from all other conifers. Around mid to late November, this tree chooses to cross autumn's veil to experience the "little death" reserved for deciduous trees only. The green of summer fades from the needles and they eventually fall to the ground like so many golden pins. It is thus that Larch joins the broad-leaved trees in their long death-like sleep of winter.

Physical Traits and Environment

At first glance, larch *(Larix)* is simply a pine with added grace. The tree, like many other conifers, is pyramidal in shape. But the branches are frequently longer, more perpendicular and higher from the ground, lending an air of indolence that most conifers lack.

Depending on the species, larch needles form in bundles of ten to forty. They are attached to a tiny peg projecting from the twig. In contrast, the needles of its closest relative, pine, cluster in groups of two to seven directly on the twig. Larch needles are usually no more than two inches in length, brush-like and an attractive misty green—a contrast to the darker needles of pine, which are longer and coarser. Larch needles perch upright on the branch, blanketing the upper section of the bough. Most larches also possess smaller solitary needles along the end of each branch, giving the tree a feathery appearance.

Throughout winter, however, the grey branches of larch are left forlorn, naked and twiggy. The renowned naturalist, Donald Culross Peattie, describes in detail this dreadful transformation, noting that these trees change to "corpselike forms... rooted in the muck."[194] In contrast, the "tenderly beautiful" larches of spring reveal new, succulent jade green needles resembling tiny silicon bottle brushes. As if this isn't enough, the cones, appearing in March or April, are soft to the touch and come in a delightful shade of rose pink. The smaller male cones are smothered in bright yellow pollen. This vernal paraphernalia gives the larch as much right to join in spring's Easter parade as any of the flowering trees!

Although larch prefers the company of other conifers, particularly hemlock, it also grows in aspen and birch groves. A denizen of the boreal forest, larch thrives from North America's tundra to the southern Great Lakes and all along the Cascadian West Coast. The tree prefers damp, boggy areas and muskeg, but is adaptable to other soil conditions, so long as it grows in direct sunlight.

The cones of eastern larch, also called tamarack, are about an inch in diameter and, when mature, look much like tiny, gilded rosebuds. Cones of western and subalpine larches are bigger and more spruce-like in appearance, with a long, slender, hair-like bract protruding from each scale. In all species, the cones sit upright on the branch.

Larch in Folklore

Larch is held in great esteem in the taigas of northern Eurasia, Alaska and Canada. It is world tree to the Saami of northern Europe, as well as to numerous Siberian peoples. This is most likely due to its being one of the very few trees that can survive on the tundra. The Tungus believed their medicine people were formed from a larch and that when they died, their souls would return to this mighty tree before reincarnation. Shamans cut ceremonial drums from living larches, making sure the tree was left whole and unharmed after the operation.[195]

The Turanians, people of central Asia related to the Turks and Iranians of present day, placed offerings of reindeer hides, pelts, cloth and household implements beneath or in the boughs of sanctified larch trees.[196] The larch groves of the Siberian Ostyaks were so sacrosanct that hunting, fishing and even drinking from a stream that adjoined any of them were prohibited. It was furthermore imperative that those who merely entered the groves left offerings behind.[197]

Larch does not impress one as an easy tree to climb, nor is it the only one that grows in the taiga. Spruce, aspen and birch also dwell there. The birch, also sacred to Northern peoples, may even be easier to climb. Yet during their vision quests, shamans ascended the larch. There are a few reasons for this. First, larch's needles and cones arrange themselves on the branch in a spiral fashion, a trait birch does not possess. As we know, the spiral is an ancient and sacred symbol of life revered by many hunter-gatherer peoples. Second, most shamanic peoples have rites of passage in which the neophyte endures a symbolic death. By shedding its needles each autumn, larch experiences the winter dormancy, the "little death" usually reserved for broad-leaved trees. This leads into the third reason for larch's high status. During their trances, shamans frequently visited the heavenly spheres of the gods. However, they also habitually travelled in the opposite direction, to the Underworld. Here they would visit their esteemed ancestors. How like a shaman larch is! Spanning two worlds, it crosses the boundary that divides the unchanging, seemingly immortal conifer from the broad-leafed tree that experiences winter's deathly sleep.

Spiritual Traits

Larch honours all four elements. It stretches to the sky, to which one climbs to gain insight, and is rooted in the water that is hidden in the boggy, muskeg underworld. A solar tree that seeks out the sun's fiery gaze, Larch makes its abode in the forests of the North– the direction traditionally assigned to the element of earth.

This tree is most noticeable in early spring and in late fall: times when the veil is most tenuous between the physical and spiritual worlds. All visible parts of the larch–needles, cones, branches–seem to turn spiraling up to the heavens. Yet the roots auger deep into the muskeg. Larch's energy is cosmic and connected to the astral world. On pondering the otherworldly qualities of this tree, one might almost wonder if the seeds of the original arrived on Earth as an extraterrestrial thirty-five million years ago, embedded in the soil of the great meteor that caused Siberia's massive Popigai crater.

The Rune

This Talking Forest rune is more symmetrical than that of windswept Pine. The rune resembles a ladder, with the three rungs slanting upward diagonally from left to right. Conjoined to both earth goddess and sun god, this tree knows the muskeg and sky equally and is at home in both the underworld and in the upperworld of the stars.

Kenning: Ladder, Shaman
Significance: Spirituality, Spirit World, Mysticism, World between the Worlds

When early peoples in the northern hemisphere looked up to the cold, crystalline night sky, they saw Ursa Major, the great bear goddess and her cub. Here was the Great Mother watching over her children both in the sky and on Earth. Well-rooted in the underworld, Larch looks up to the reeling stars and sees the hidden code that relays the mysteries of the cosmos to us. **Upright,** this rune represents philosophical or metaphysical matters, that which is separate from day-to-day existence. It also suggests a spiritual awakening or vision quest.

Inverted Larch indicates the querent is embarking on a spiritual journey; but for now, the tree is entering the underworld of the subconscious. Pay attention to the inner voice, but do not cut yourself off from the everyday world. The inverted rune may also imply an initiation process or entry into the clergy or priesthood.

Toppled Larch indicates one who is out of touch with reality, spiritual or otherwise, and may need to seek enlightenment. Perhaps they are so involved in the mundane world that they cannot see beyond it. Alternatively, the rune in this position may warn the querent to watch out for those who would cynically misuse their trust in order to gain spiritual control over them.

People associated with Larch are spiritually inclined, frequently entering religious orders. At times unrealistic, with heads in the clouds, Larch people must learn to keep their feet on the ground. They also should be on guard against intolerance toward others whose beliefs do not correspond with theirs or whom they deem less enlightened.

Larch begins the sixth and final grove of the Talking Forest. This represents the elder years. At this time of life many people, feeling the encroachment of death, the final great mystery, turn to the spirit world.

Alder

Kenning: Bridge, Crannog

Significance: Instinct, Dreams

Wherever Alder thrives, there too dwell the salmon. There is a powerful symbiosis between the two. Salmon swim from the ocean into rivers guarded by alders. There they lay their eggs and die on the riverbed, its soil rich and replete with nitrogen from the tree roots. The alders in turn gain nourishment from the corpses of the salmon. The young fry dwell among the protective roots of these riverine trees before swimming down river and out to sea to continue their life cycle. It is only fitting then that salmon meat is often smoked over flames of alder wood.

Alder reminds us to never forget the ancestors and what they taught us. The knowledge of past and present is retained in our instincts, our intuition. To this day, the salmon return from the sea to the rivers that spawned them. Likewise, we return to the river of the subconscious, where our animal instinct always leads us true.

Physical Traits and Environment

Alder *(Alnus)* is a small, unassuming tree whose silhouette, leaves and male catkins readily mark him as a member of the birch family. Like birch, alder tends to form thickets, but shuns the higher ground of birch for the riverside and stream bank. In this moist environment, the short roots of the tree are often visible above ground. These roots contain micro-organisms that can convert nitrogen gathered from air and soil into vital nutrients.

Wise foresters understand that planting alders by the water will combat erosion and help to control stream flow.[198] Indeed, alder shares such an affinity with water that the wood will not rot when submerged in the element, but will harden "to the toughness of stone."[199] For such a water-loving tree, however, most alder species prefer to grow in full sunlight and can survive drought-like conditions.[200]

Red alder has smooth pale bark similar to that of white birch, while the smooth, light brown bark of speckled or river alder resembles that of cherry. The plant's most striking feature is its fruit: a tiny, hard, bright green oval appearing in spring, eventually turning dark brown and then black. This hard little catkin, called a *strobile,* resembles a miniature pine cone, even down to the scales, which open up in fall to disperse the seeds. Many birds eat these seeds throughout the winter, the strobiles remaining on the tree until spring. Fittingly for a tree whose fruit resembles that of the evergreens, alder likes the company of conifers.

Alder in Folklore

The Karok people of Oregon believed that the salmon were born of speckled alder, partly due to the symbiotic relationship between the two species and also because the inner bark of the tree is salmon red and speckled.

In Celtic mythology, alder was a symbol of spiritual generosity. Like his cousin hazelnut, alder could provide egress into the land of Faery. However, it was unlucky to fell a sacred alder and doing so might cause one's house to burn down.[201] The Ogham's alder rune, Fearn, deals with aspects of foundation and steadfastness.[202]

Alder wood bleeds bright red or orange sap when cut; thus it has often been associated in myth with sacrifice and life after death. Alder was sacred to the Welsh oracular god Bran. Mortally wounded in battle against the Irish, Bran ordered that his head be cut off and returned to Wales where it continued to advise the Welsh tribes via oracles. It is a common belief that Bran's head was buried where the Tower of London presently stands. To this very day ravens, birds sacred to Bran* are kept at the Tower as mascots.

---

*   In fact, the name is Welsh, meaning raven.

It is held that if the ravens leave, Britain will fall into ruin; for this reason, the birds' wings are clipped to keep them from flying away. Alder was also associated with the Norse god Odin,[203] who coincidentally, owned two ravens—Hugin (Thought) and Munin (Memory). These creatures informed him daily of all goings on in the world.

Alder leaves refresh feet tired from walking, and its water-resistant properties made it a worthy wood for clogs that carried people through mud and marsh. Hence the line in Kipling's famous song: "Alder for shoes do wise men choose." The wood was formed into shields, presumably after being hardened in water. Alder wood was also fashioned into dairy vessels and other articles whose function necessitated contact with liquid. However, its most famous historical use was in the building of bridges, docks and jetties over water bodies. Marsh-dwelling Celts used the wood to build walkways and pilings for their *crannogs* or lake dwellings. The old city of Venice was built on alder piles.[204] The Dutch later used abundant supplies of alder from their bogs and swamps when building the original canals and bridges of Amsterdam, Den Bosch and other cities.

In the past, alder woods were often associated with ghosts and malevolent witchcraft, perhaps in part due to the wood's ability to bleed. Alders also thrive in swamps that may hold various dangers such as quicksand and bogs. Goethe tells of the Erlking or Alder King, who carried off hapless children to their deaths. This elven lord was leader of an ancient race believed to live in burial mounds and sacred woods, much like the fairies and the Tuatha de Danann of Celtic mythology. Although also associated with elm and elder–both sacred to the fairies–the Erlking was specifically connected to alder because of the tree's association with swamps and bogs. These places are home to diseases, including many varieties of fever that affect humans, children especially.

Spiritual Traits

Alder's aura is masculine and his season is late winter to early spring, when the new cones first appear. After all, it is in the drab mud of March that the vitality and beauty of spring arises.

This is a lunar tree whose element is water. Gods sacred to Alder are oracular ones such as Bran, Odin of the wise ravens, Morpheus, Greek god of dreams and Faunus, Roman woodland god of prophetic dreams.

Providing the best wood for bridge making, Alder represents the link between the conscious mind and the subconscious. Dreams are a sort of bridge between the otherworld and the so-called "real" world. They are the mechanism whereby the subconscious speaks to us. It is essential to pay heed to dreams, especially if they are vivid, for they are the gods' way of communicating with us.

The Rune

The Alder rune is shaped much like Birch save that the side shoot is on the right, indicating a masculine tree. In addition, this side branch bends downward toward the water's edge, seeking what is hidden beneath the surface of things. Almost a mirror image, the Talking Forest Alder is Birch revisited: the wisdom of old age returning to instruct youth. Alder's spirit, like that of Locust, is very perceptive and able to see both sides. But where the Locust rune is solar and intellectual by nature, Alder, being lunar, is intuitive. As a *liminal* tree, Alder lives between worlds, knowing both land and water, being deciduous but bearing cones like the conifers.

Kenning: Bridge, Crannog
Significance: Support, Foundation, Instinct,
Dreams, Intuition

Alder speaks to the need for a strong internal foundation. In a Talking Forest reading, **upright** Alder indicates a need to pay close attention to one's intuition. This rune may also suggest hidden influences or unforeseen benefits to come.

Inverted Alder instructs the querent to pay special attention to dreams that are recalled upon waking, as well as to images that recur in daydreams. The subconscious is speaking clearly and must be heard.

The **toppled** rune implies decaying foundations or an inability to see what is really happening. It may caution the querent against willful blindness or denial, especially if toppled to the right. On occasion, the rune may suggest hidden influence or unforeseen circumstances working against the querent. The rune toppled to the left, with the side branch up, is telling the querent to look stalwartly into the pool of the subconscious to overcome obstacles. In particular, recurring nightmares, a result of hidden fears or anxieties, should be examined. By confronting the Erlking within—by facing our inner fears—we come to grips with and conquer them.

People associated with Alder are unassuming, but no less important to their community. They often work tirelessly for the good of all, simply out of a desire to help and an understanding that strong, well-supported people are a community's best resource. A career spent helping others—providing a bridge for growth and nurturance—is never wasted. Many Alder people are engineers and municipal planners.

All the conifers have an affinity with Alder, especially Larch, who helps Alder bridge the gap between the mundane and the spirit world. Larch is a conifer that upon shedding its needles in fall, shares the winter dormancy of the broad-leaved trees. Deciduous Alder relates to the conifers by yielding "cones." Larch seeks the universal mind for answers: the gods out there in the heavens as well as those in the underworld. Alder seeks answers from within: in the muck and mould of the human mind; and in dreams, where the gods speak to us through our subconscious.

Hemlock

Kenning: Sage, Elder
Significance: Age, Grace, Gratitude

The immediate impression of this graceful tree is of acquiescence. Rooted gently in the earth, Hemlock takes the rain into himself, letting the drops fall delicately from his soft needles. The whole plant, from drooping crown, to cones hanging at end of bough, to gently sloping trunk, suggests compliance, a downward flow to earth.

Physical Traits and Environment

Contrary to some misinformed people, the hemlock tree *(Tsuga)* is not poisonous. This is not the hemlock that killed Socrates!

The Greek philosopher drank the deadly brew from the *Conium maculatum*, the water parsnip, also called hemlock. This herb looks nothing like a tree and closely resembles parsley or Queen Anne's lace. The hemlock tree may originally have been named as such simply because the needles smell somewhat like *C. maculatum*. But there is no harm to fear from this gentle conifer.*

Like fir, hemlock is steeple-shaped, with branches growing low to the ground. If removed from their pegs, the needles, also like fir, leave indented scars; however, they are flatter than fir needles and the branches tend to droop. These traits, in addition to the delicate taper at the top of the central or *leader* branch, give the mature hemlock the semblance of a venerable wizard wearing a long robe and conical hat.

Although it prefers a cool moist environment with well-drained soil in shaded woods, hemlock grows under a variety of conditions and enjoys the company of other trees, both conifer and broad-leaved. The eastern hemlocks have been called the "redwoods of the east," due to their height at maturity: up to seventy-five feet (23.5 m).[205] These trees, however, are dwarfed by their western cousins, which can reach dizzying heights of 200 feet (60 m).[206] As is seemly for a tree of such venerable mien, eastern hemlock can live to 600 years of age, taking as long as half of those to mature.[207] Western hemlock has been known to reach a lifespan of over 1,000 years.

Hemlock can be distinguished from other conifers by his cones. These grow on the tips and not along the branches as with other evergreens. The bark, often purplish, contains a high level of tannin.

---

* So long as one is absolutely certain they are dealing with *Tsuga* hemlock and not the poisonous yew!

We are often told that predation–to eat or be eaten–is Mother Nature's ultimate driving force; that the wilderness consists only of the constant struggle "red in tooth and claw." But while predation is certain, life on this planet would not survive without cooperation– the ability for species to interact with each other to the advantage of each. We are reminded of the relationships between flowering plants and the insects that fertilize these plants, while harvesting pollen and nectar. All plants give off oxygen for animals to breath. Animals in turn exhale carbon dioxide needed for plant respiration and photosynthesis. Higher life forms, including humans, could not survive without the myriad bacteria in our bodies that help us digest food and complete other biological processes.

It has been recently discovered that young hemlocks deep in old-growth forests were thriving without sun. Fungi, using *mycelia* or threadlike appendages, growing into and on top of the soil, had been transferring excess nutrients and photosynthesis to the hemlocks from birches and alders that were growing far off along sunny stream banks. Mycelia can grow for miles and they connect fungi to trees and other plants. Paul Stamets, the mycologist who made this discovery, holds that "the entire earth is wired with such intelligence promoting sustainability."[208]

Other fungi, in the form of mushrooms, grow on dead hemlocks. One in particular, the reishi, although not edible, is extensively used in naturopathic medicine.

According to botanist Diana Beresford-Kroeger, the hemlock's mandate is "to have regenerative synchronicity with maturing trees."[209] She describes another symbiotic relationship involving hemlock–this time with the trees of the maple/beech forest in

Eastern Canada. The young eastern hemlock, protected by the shade of old maples and beeches, thrives when they die off. In turn, the hemlock provides shade for beech and maple saplings.[210]

Hemlock in Folklore

First Nations people used hemlock in their sweat lodge ceremonies, as well as for medicine to alleviate coughs and colds. A tea was made from the bark and applied externally as a hemostatic.[211] Hemlock was deemed one of the four main trees in Chinese mythology,[212] perhaps due to the tree's aura of deference and wise old age—traits generally more valued by Asian cultures than our own.

Spiritual Traits

Hemlock's aura is male and water and earth are his elements. Winter, especially the quiet, snowy depths of January, suits this tree. Deities associated with Hemlock are Cronos and Saturn, gods dealing with time and its passage. This conifer has a serene and peaceful spirit. He bestows calming energy to those suffering from nervous illness or who are under a great deal of stress.

The Rune

The rune illustrates the "stocking cap" taper that adorns the tip of the hemlock tree. The branches are on the right side only, befitting a male rune. The overall design, while mirroring the shape of elegant Hemlock, also indicates the wisdom and grace of acquiescence when it is necessary.

Kenning: Sage, Elder
Significance: Age, Grace, Tolerance, Benevolence,
Gratitude, Experience, Empathy

The **upright** appearance of this rune in a reading indicates gentleness, tolerance, graciousness and the inclusion of others. It may depict an elderly parent or other aged relative. Alternatively, the rune depicts someone, specifically an older person, whose kindliness, wisdom and life experience will be of help to the querent.

Inverted, Hemlock suggests blindness to the foibles of others: permissiveness, overindulgence, weakness or ineffectiveness.

Contrary Hemlock **toppled** to the left, with branches up, implies intolerance, close-mindedness or stubbornness. It may point to an inability to accept mortality, thus signaling a fear of death or of growing old alone. The toppled rune may also warn the querent not to become too much of a hermit or too closed off from others, especially if lying on the right side. It is salient to remember that Hemlock likes the company of other trees. Elderly people who remain in touch with others generally experience a more rewarding old age and are less likely to suffer the depression or dementia frequently associated with growing old.

In the Talking Forest, the Hemlock rune specifically references the aging process. The wise elder learns to accept death, seeing it as the end of one aspect of life and the beginning of another. Herein lies the notion of *legacy:* the elders leave us, but we retain the wisdom, knowledge and experience they bestow on us. Elders provide continuity and are conduits to the past and to family history.

People associated with Hemlock are kindly, caring and accepting of others. They are often soft-spoken, sometimes too much so. If not careful, they can be taken advantage of by the unscrupulous. Hemlock people frequently tend to fade into the background just as the tree often does in the forest. But like the tree, they are invaluable to the community.

Rowan

Kenning: Faery, Fairy Ring

Significance: Luck, Providence

The Rowan can grow further up mountains than most other trees, thus the name mountain ash.[213] This small tree is often spotted standing alone in a field or meadow; sometimes in the strangest of places—on a barren moor or rocky crag—there as if by happenstance.

Physical Traits and Environment

The European rowan and its cousin, the North American mountain ash, are very much alike. Both are members of the genus

Sorbus within the rose family. In the Talking Forest system, the term "rowan" references both trees equally. Rowans are small, only occasionally growing to sixty feet (18 m). The bark is smooth like that of cherry and frequently a bronzy brown. The compound leaves are composed of small leaflets somewhat resembling those of the locusts, but a darker green and more pointed at the tips. Each compound leaf of the European rowan adds up to thirteen leaflets—the number of lunar months in a year. It is perhaps this more than anything else that in Europe has given this tree its magical reputation. The rowan of North America has between thirteen and seventeen leaflets, which is perhaps why the tree appears not to have had the same prominence in the "New World." Many hybrids of the species have bluish green foliage, making the little tree stand out among the grass greens of larger broad-leaved trees.

The flowers of rowan are similar to those of hawthorn: small, creamy white, subtly scented and in spring, appearing in frothy masses on the tree. Rowan is often easy to spot in winter, when the bare branches stalwartly yield heavy clusters of brilliantly coloured berries. Resembling tiny apples, the fruit is usually brilliant orange or scarlet, but there are modern hybrids of rowan that have pink or even gold coloured berries. No matter the hue, birds devour the fruit.

The berries were extensively used in folk medicine for kidney and bowel complaints, as well as to combat catarrh and sore throat. They are very high in vitamin C and are thirst-quenching as well, a trait I highly appreciate in the parching heat of Southern Ontario's August. Berries ripen from late summer to fall and any not eaten by birds may remain on the tree even into February.

The wood burns very hot and slowly, showing an affinity with the fire element.

Rowan in Folklore

From time immemorial, European rowan was believed to harbor fairies and thus was a lucky and benevolent tree. To this day rowan, along with hawthorn and elder, is the most favoured tree to stand as guardian over Europe's ancient stone circles.

In Britain, rowan was sacred to the Celtic goddess of hearth and home, called Brigantia in England and Brigid in Scotland and Ireland. The tree was believed to bring cheer as well as encouragement to those suffering from despair. Spinning wheels and spindles were made of rowan wood, perhaps because of its connection with Brigid, who was patroness of the traditional women's arts of spinning and weaving.[214] Brigid was one of the Tuatha de Danann, the ancient elvish race of Celtic Britain and Ireland. She was the patroness of the arts, healing and poetry. In addition, Brigid protected livestock, as well as mothers and small children. She was the keeper of the family flame and thus fiery rowan is sacred to her.

Rowan was also called *quickbeam;* that is, quick or live wood because it embodied spring and the quickening of life. This was in part, due to it being virtually the only tree fruiting in the depths of winter. Rowan enlivens the human spirit as well, thus its affinity with the fairies. In some parts of northern Europe, this tree was believed to have sprung from lightning strikes, and thus was sacred to Thor, the god of thunder.[215] The boughs were hung over dairies and stables to protect livestock and keep them fertile. In Wales, rowan was planted in churchyards to protect the dead. Rowan twigs in the form of a cross and tied with red ribbon protected one from spirits of the dead at Samhain.

Rowan was said to repel witches and to be the best defense against strafing magic, especially if a piece of the branch was fashioned into a looped twig, or two twigs were tied together in the form of a cross.[216] No doubt, actual witches used rowan a great deal for both religious and homeopathic purposes.

Spiritual Traits

Like Juniper, Rowan is a protector of small creatures. His fruit often stays on the bough throughout the cold months, generously providing food for our winter birds. When cut in half horizontally, the berry reveals the shape of a pentagram, a common trait amongst all of the pome fruits. Coupled with thirteen leaflets to a compound leaf, this make Rowan a very magical tree indeed, for thirteen is the moon's number. As fire is Rowan's element, the sun is his main planetary correspondence, with Mercury and of course, the moon, as secondary influences. And while Rowan is seen in some traditions as being feminine, I find the tree has a masculine energy.

Rowan's power is greatest in August, when the berries first ripen and in February, when his signature bird, the cardinal, begins his territorial "what-cheer" spring song. Candlemas or Imbolc, held on February 1st or 2nd, also belongs to Rowan and to his patron goddess Brigid. Rowan fruits are tasty and sweet, yet have a bitter aftertaste. This is a reminder that not everyone gets equal time and luck is not always with us. Sometimes the fairies play tricks on us. Karma is not simple and Brigid's spinning wheel weaves dark threads in with the light.

The Rune

As Rowan is a masculine rune, the right-handed flower spiral is larger and somewhat higher than that on the left. This shape also references the tree's tendency to have an open, layered crown. All branches end in a fruit dot to indicate the abundance of the tree. This rune resembles both the Talking Forest Bramble and Hawthorn runes. But the feminine Hawthorn's flower spiral is on the left whereas Rowan's is on the right side. Rowan's extra branch ends in a fruit dot whereas Bramble has a thorn.

Kenning: Faery, Fairy Ring
Significance: Luck, Happenstance, Psychic Defense,
Charm, Providence

Generally, good luck is simply the result of well-made decisions and actions in the past. We forget this however and put it down to simple chance. Nevertheless, there is such a thing as pure good luck, rare as it is. It is then that we wonder whether providence, the gods or the fairies, have favoured us.

Upright Rowan represents good luck in a reading: you are in the good graces of the fairies! Actually, it is more likely that actions you have carried out in the past have finally worked to your benefit or perhaps someone you have helped is now returning the favour. In any event, your luck is good now, so take advantage of the opportunity while you can.

The **inverted** rune is the same as the upright, but to a lesser degree. Perhaps nothing is working to your benefit now, but a new rowan tree is being planted. Luck may come to you soon. Alternatively, something you wish for regarding another person or an important project may soon come about.

The **toppled** or felled rune may warn of bad luck or disappointment. Only rarely does it suggest a *beguiling:* being laid under a spell or being in thrall. This is possible if **toppled to the right** with the smaller flower spiral facing upward. Here the tiny fairy flowers have enticed the querent! More likely, your bad luck is on account of you seeking the unattainable. Leprechauns do not freely give up their treasure and there is no pot of gold at the end of the rainbow! Alternatively, the rune in this position may suggest superstition or paranoia on the querent's part. People are often held back by irrationality more than anything else. "Bad luck" is also often the result of making the same mistakes over and over and not learning from them.

The rune **toppled to the left,** with the larger flower spiral up, suggests disappointment. The flower is lovely but will not last, and the sour berries may be healthy, but are not appreciated! The querent must remember that you can't always get what you want. The rune in this position frequently suggests spiritual imbalance and a need to correct it. It is pointless to climb the felled tree, but there are a few cleansing berries left to eat. Looking within may help you rebalance yourself.

People associated with Rowan are very charming and positive in their outlook on life. Rowans generally have a built-in trust in the universe. To others, they may seem to lead charmed lives. In truth, Rowans have it relatively easy and things seem to go their way only because they have learned to get along with others and are unafraid of novelty or change. They also do not dwell on failure and are able to roll with the punches when things are not in their favour.

Although they are often small in size, Rowan people are vivacious and tend to stand out from the crowd. They frequently exhibit noteworthy psychic abilities. The rowan tree's tendency to stand alone in a rocky or otherwise harsh environment is a symbol of those rare people among us, such as shamans, witches, true psychics and researchers of the paranormal who work to improve the spiritual lot of humanity. These people often have a hard path to follow. Frequently misunderstood, overshadowed by noisy charlatans, they must often stand alone against adversity. These folk must be courageous and tough, like Rowan, while being pure of heart. It is therefore prudent that they use Rowan's powers for good as "Rowan protects and gives courage and strength to those walking the path of spiritual growth and enlightenment."[217]

Gingko

Kenning: Fossil, Library

Significance: History, the Past

Ginkgo's crinkly fanlike leaves resemble waxed parchment, and indeed this museum piece tells quite a story. Although lately transplanted to North America from eastern Asia, ginkgo flourished here about seven million years ago, before the Ice Age.[218] Thus the inclusion of this non-indigenous tree into the Talking Forest system.

Physical Traits and Environment

Gingko biloba is the oldest known tree species still living, having evolved more than 200 million years ago.[219] The tree is "what some scientists believe to be the living link in the evolution of ferns to trees."[220] The only surviving member of its family, gingko predates both conifer and deciduous trees. Horticulturist Hugh Johnson states that the tree is worthy of respect simply because it has survived "the drift of continents, the rise of mountain ranges, the coming and going of aeons of reptiles and ages of ice..."[221] He suggests this resilience is why gingko is so hardy, having survived all its natural predators!

Indeed, the species is much tougher than its appearance suggests, being able to flourish in smog-ridden and polluted environments. As a result, gingko is a popular street tree in many of North America's industrial cities. So tough is gingko that six trees within the epicentre of the Hiroshima bomb blast survived the catastrophe and thrive to this day.

The gingko tree is of medium height, reaching to sixty feet (18 m). The long, slightly curving branches grow from a grey trunk that is slender in all but very elderly trees. The bifurcated leaves are a delicate jade green until mid-autumn, when they turn a charming primrose yellow. The placement of each leaf on its own tiny peg set directly on the branch recalls the larch. However, the two species are otherwise quite dissimilar. The fruit of gingko is both banal and sublime; a fleshy, apricot yellow ball encloses a hard, silvery white kernel. This in turn contains a bright yellow or jade green seed. Unfortunately, the pulpy covering has a strong vomitous smell, making it "Stinko Gingko"! The smelly fruit is toxic and if handled without gloves, can cause dermatitis. In East Asian cuisine, however, the roasted seed is considered a delicacy. The name gingko is from the

Chinese and means something like "white nut" or silver fruit," depending on your source.

Gingko in Folklore

Gingko trees were often planted outside of temples in East Asia, no doubt because of their grace and longevity. The Japanese city of Tokyo uses a stylized ginkgo leaf as its civic symbol and sumo wrestlers frequently wear a topknot called an *oicho-mage,* which is fan-shaped like a gingko leaf. The Japanese hold this tree in high regard, attributing to the plant the spirit of an old crone who watches over women and children, and especially nursing mothers.[222] This crone goddess is most likely an aspect of Kannon, a goddess of mercy and compassion, akin to the Chinese Kuan Yin. In modern-day medicine, gingko has become efficacious in the fight against diseases of memory loss, including Alzheimer's.

Taoist shamans also used the tree to "engrave their magical spells and seals on old growth gingko wood in order to communicate with the spirit world."[223]

Spiritual Traits

Ginkgo's element is air and its influence is greatest in summer and early fall—the seasons bridging spring's growth and winter's fallow. Deities are Shou, the Chinese god of longevity and the Japanese gingko crone, Kannon. Also appropriate are Cronos the

Greek god of time and Urd, the Norn who presides over the past in Norse mythology.

Another appropriate deity for this tree of two-lobed leaves is Janus, the two-faced Roman god who presided over the past and the future: beginnings and endings. Janus was often rendered as a bust with two conjoined heads facing opposite directions. Some scholars believe Janus originally represented the pairing of Jupiter, the Roman father god with his spouse, Juno. Other mythologists aver that Janus was a compendium of an archaic Indo-European *dyad* or god/goddess pairing of the sun and moon: Ianus and Iana or Dianus and Diana.

The Rune

This symmetrical rune displays a small T branch on either side of the top of the stem, referencing the bifurcated gingko leaf. Life is a journey, with divergent paths. What was done in the past is carried over to the present and echoed into the future. The two lower branches indicate a graceful tree of middling size and canopy. The whole rune indicates that the future mirrors the past.

Kenning: Fossil, Library
**Significance: Ancestry, History, the Past
and its Influences**

Comparable to the Othila rune of the Norse Futhark, the Talking Forest Gingko connotes inheritance.[224] **Upright,** Gingko suggests action from the past is now weighing on the present and will influence the future. Here and now, the querent must try to effect a positive change by learning from the past. Nearby runes should be read carefully.

Inverted Gingko speaks to the querent delving into the past to find the truth or to seek answers to chronic problems. The rune in this position may otherwise indicate someone living too much in the past, especially if toppled Maple is nearby. Inverted Gingko may also suggest past events being covered up or hidden from the querent.

Toppled Gingko reveals one who repeats the same mistakes over and over again because they do not know their history or at least, will not learn from it.

People associated with Gingko are traditionalists. They may be historians, archaeologists, or even futurists, for in order to understand the future, one must know the past. Ginkgo people, remembering their history, don't often repeat their mistakes. However, they must avoid the tendency to live in the past or see it as a golden age. Good Gingko energy realizes that understanding history clearly helps to create a vibrant present and hopeful future. Likewise, being too optimistic or pessimistic about the future may counsel visiting the past for a more holistic outlook.

Gingko comes in the middle of the sixth and final grove of the Talking Forest set. The elderly, those near the end of their lives, have lived long and seen much. Old people are a veritable storehouse of knowledge and, like Gingko, are living museums. Heed them well!

Our next rune, Yew the tree of death, is the gateway to a new life and completes the present life's history. The finality of death gives us more reasons to strive to make our lives meaningful, as well as to right the wrongs of history for those who will follow us.

Yew

Kenning: Arrow, Burial Mound
Significance: Death, Ending

Thought to be "the oldest surviving tree species in Europe,"[225] Yew is famous for its longevity. Although traditionally associated with death, the tree itself can live for thousands of years. Most other long-lived trees such as oak, pine or hemlock, rarely live more than 500 years. Botanists conclude however, that yews can live two millennia or more. One specimen in Perthshire, Scotland, is believed to be almost 9,000 years old.[226]

Physical Traits and Environment

Members of the yew species *(Taxus)* do not normally grow very tall and most are shrubs. However some, such as Pacific yew, can attain a height of seventy-five feet (23 m). Eastern or Canadian yew is native only to the eastern part of the continent. European or English yew is a very common ornamental here, often planted as a hedgerow or at the entrance to the home.

Yews will frequently copse or develop multiple trunks. The bark is reddish and stringy, resembling that of cedar and juniper. Yew needles are similar to those of fir, spruce or hemlock, but usually of a darker, denser shade of green. The "cone" however, is like that of no other tree. It is composed of an olive green seed surrounded by a pulpy scarlet coat. Called an *aril,* the fruit resembles an inverted pimento olive! The whole tree is deadly poisonous except the red part of the aril. Yew has nevertheless been very helpful in the fight against cancer. The bark and the needles contain an efficacious drug called *taxol,* which inhibits cancer cell growth.[227]

Yew in Folklore

In her excellent book *Leaves of Yggdrasil,* Freya Aswynn suggests that the Norse tree of life, the mighty Yggdrasil, was most likely a yew and not an ash tree.[228] She further states that the Eihwaz rune of the Norse Futhark literally means *Yew,* and it often suggests the act of hunting or seeking. The rune further references Uller, a proto-Norse hunting god who was often depicted as an archer. This ancient deity was believed by some to be a member of the Vanir. Others, however, assert he was far older, most likely a Saami shamanic god, predating that other sorcerer god, Odin. From prehistoric times, yew wood was employed in the making of arrows. Not surprisingly, it was sacred to Uller, whose home, called Ydalir (Yewdale), was located in a forest of yews.

It is yew's toughness and resilience that make it an excellent wood for weapons such as spears and arrows. These missiles were rendered all the more deadly by the poison in the wood. Indeed, yew wood was used to fashion bows and arrows in cultures as diverse as the Chilula of California and the Celts of Europe. The famous yew bows of the victorious English archers at the Battle of Agincourt helped change the course of European history. It is also believed that Robin Hood, the fabled English archer and outlaw, is buried under a yew tree with his sword at his head, his arrows at his feet and his mighty yew bow by his side.[229]

Due to its vigour and adaptability, its toxicity and great longevity, the Celts associated the yew tree with death and mourning, but also and especially with the soul's triumph over mortality. The Celts did not fear death, believing it "opened the door to rebirth and to the eternal life of the soul."[230]

Celtic mythology tells the tragic tale of Naoise and Deirdre. A prophecy was made asserting that Deirdre's beauty would cause men to fight over her, with war in Ireland being the eventual result. Conor MacNessa, King of Ulster, desired her but fearing the prophecy, kept her secluded from society. However, her kindly guardian secretly introduced the young woman to Naoise, a handsome young warrior of Conor's court. They fell in love and later escaped to Scotland but were found by the jealous MacNessa. Not surprisingly, all of this eventually led to war between the Ulstermen, during which Naoise was slain. Rather than marry Conor, however, Deirdre committed suicide. The lovers were buried separately and two yew trees sprouted simultaneously from the graves. Their branches intertwining, the trees flourished and became conjoined.[231] In this myth, the yew stands as a symbol of the triumph of life and love over death.

In the Mediterranean, the yew tree was sacred to Hecate, goddess of witchcraft and the Underworld. Yew was planted in graveyards and corpses were frequently buried beneath the roots of this tree. In some parts of France, it was said that the roots of yew contained the thoughts of the dead, which "the branches scatter to the winds."[232] To dream of yew portended the death of an elderly relative, and largesse from their estate would come to the dreamer.[233]

Fred Hageneder asserts that yew trees are virtually immortal. Often the inside of a very old tree is hollow, yet it can send aerial roots down from inside the trunk. Hageneder explains that the age of these hollow yews cannot be determined, as they no longer contain annual rings that can be read. Therefore, some of these trees are very likely older than the 4,000-year-old bristlecone pines of the American southwest. Hageneder concludes simply: "Yew is eternity."[234]

Spiritual Traits

With her dark needles, blood red aril and seed a sickly olive green, the poisonous Yew proclaims her link with death. The fruit represents death's inversion of life: when we live, green is all around us and red inside us. When we die, we frequently shed the blood that was given us at birth. Our flesh turns greenish and rots. Only the skeleton, like the hard yew seed, remains for a time. If Yew is the tree of death, however, she is also of life. According to various pagan and other spiritual paths, we die and return to the womb of Mother Earth in order to be reincarnated.* Yew *is* eternity.

In a triad with Birch and Elder, Yew is the crone aspect and her element is earth. Samhain, October 31st, is her time, when the veil between this and the Underworld is thinnest. Gods sacred to Yew are Uller of the yew bow, Hecate of the mysteries, Persephone and her consort Hades, rulers of the Dead in the Underworld.

The Rune

The shape of the Yew rune, with its three prongs converging from a point at the bottom, illustrates the tree's tendency to copse. Yew resembles Reed, the second rune in the set and Yew is the penultimate rune. Where Reed deals with the beginning of life, Yew deals with its end. Like Reed, Yew has three branches; these allude to the past, present and future of death. The present, central branch is the act of dying itself, of letting go. The left is the past, the former life of the deceased. The right-hand branch references the afterlife, which many religions and philosophies believe is reincarnation or alternatively, a return to the life force or Tao.

The arrow-like tip of each stem alludes to the traditional use of Yew for making arrows. The downward pointing arrow in the centre of each branch signifies the body's return to earth, while

---

* The antiquity of this belief is proven by the discovery of prehistoric burials with the body bound in fetal posture and covered in red ochre. This most likely symbolized birth blood, in the assumption that the dead would be reborn from Mother Earth.

the upward pointing one at the tip indicates the soul's journey to the afterlife. The three branches of the rune also recall the Norns and the Greek Fates: triple goddesses who mete out an individual's *wyrd* or fate. With Reed, we began the skein of the individual life. This skein is cut at Yew. The next and final rune, Elder, deals with the warp and weft, the overall design of the life lived and the patterns that repeat throughout our incarnations.

Kenning: Arrow, Burial Mound
Significance: Death, Ending, Cessation,
Silence, Transformation

Yew is the Talking Forest rune of death. However, it need not send the querent into a panic! Much like the Death card of the Tarot, which also causes much inordinate anxiety, this rune manifesting in a reading rarely means physical death. More frequently, **upright** Yew refers to the death of some aspect of the querent's life. Perhaps an old, outmoded way of thinking is in the process of coming to an end, and a new way of interacting with the world is being born.

Inverted Yew suggests stagnation or even an inability to accept loss or to mourn properly. It may also be that the querent is presently going through a "little death," the dark night of the soul, when all seems lost. This state of mind is always hard to deal with. However painful, it eventually ends, usually resulting in transformative wisdom and growth.

Contrary or **toppled** Yew also suggests the ending of something: perhaps a relationship, a loss of some sort, but not necessarily by death. It may, however, imply a loss of faith, especially if close to Larch. If adjacent to Juniper, it may represent losing faith in others, if next to Cherry, a romance gone sour or loss of idealism. Again, understand that the appearance of Yew in a reading rarely warns of actual physical death.

Yew forms a natural "hunter's triad" with the similarly shaped Juniper, protector of small animals and Sumac, the Horned God of hunter and prey. In this triad, Yew, the provider of arrow-wood, brings death and transformation to the prey animal.

People associated with Yew usually have attained inner peace with themselves and with life. They do not fear death and often work as undertakers, palliative caregivers to the terminally ill, or as grief counsellors.

Elder

Kenning: Witch, Labyrinth

Significance: Balance, Magic, Harmony

Elder is the final tree in our runic woodland: a small bush that forms thickets in meadows, hedgerows and waste spaces. Yet for all her homely appearance, from time immemorial, Elder's reputation as a mystical and prodigious healer follows her. This small tree is perhaps more associated with witchcraft than any other in European folklore.

Physical Traits and Environment

Elder *(Sambucus)* is a bush of many stems with tan coloured, usually smooth bark and branches that are hollow or contain a spongy pith. The drooping compound leaves somewhat resemble those of sumac. The cream coloured flowers grow in flat-topped clusters or *racemes* atop stems that are coloured green, fawn or magenta, depending on the species. The flowers eventually ripen into tiny red or black berries, the size of seed beads. Like the willow, the elder bush can sprout like magic from a branch that has simply been stuck into moist ground. Creeping plants such as nettle, vine, bramble and ivy enjoy the company of the elder bush, often twining among her many stems.

Elder in Folklore

This close relative of the honeysuckles was long deemed sacred, due in part to her reputation as a healer and also because the compound leaves form either five, seven or nine leaflets each. To this day, the bush continues to be revered as a healer of both physical and psychic illness and is employed extensively in holistic medicine. Elder is one of the classic "spring tonic" herbs, being a natural diuretic and diaphoretic. The mildly fusty smelling flowers can be made into an excellent heal-all tea to combat colds and flu. The berries when cooked or steeped in tea, act as a cathartic, detoxifier, vulnerary or even a midwife's aid in childbirth.[235] Elder is one of nature's best skin and beauty aids, the flowers being especially beneficial for the complexion. Author Fred Hageneder states that elder, along with linden, is one of the two "great healing trees of the temperate climate."[236]

Birds and many mammals are quite fond of the berries, being immune to the poisons therein. Traditionally, red elder tends to be best suited as food for wildlife, while black elder is used primarily for medicine.[237] The berries of either tree can be made into a healthful jam. However, they should be cooked according to instructions from a reliable source, as they are fairly poisonous eaten raw, causing vomiting and diarrhea. Cooking renders the fruit harmless to humans, bringing out their many benefits. A subtle, elegant white wine can be made from the flowers and a heady, almost black wine from the berries of black elder.

This invaluable plant's negative reputation only developed with the advent of organized Christianity in Europe. This was no doubt due in part to elder's long-standing association with goddesses, witches and herbal magic. In some parts, it was even believed that one who had been baptized as a Christian could, by anointing their eyes with juice obtained from the inner bark of elder, "see witches in any part of the world."[238] This same nosy person, however, could have saved themselves the trouble of damaging the elder bush by simply waiting patiently nearby. No doubt, before long, witches in need of replenishing their herbal supply would have simply dropped by to harvest this very useful tree!

Not surprisingly, elder's herbal treasures were also beloved of and sacred to the fairy folk. There is a delightful Danish belief that to walk under an elder bush at midnight on Midsummer's Eve would render up a vision of the Fairy King and his retinue riding off to the hunt,[239] certainly a much more stimulating event than watching some busy old crone harvesting flowers or berries!

In Denmark elder was called Hyldemoer—Elder Mother or Elder Queen—and in parts of Germany she is still known as such. She is another aspect of Holde or Hertha, who later became Mother Holly or Mother Hulda—the stern but kindly witch in the Grimm's fairy tale familiar to children of earlier generations. If her elder trees were used wisely, the goddess could help and heal, but woe betide the one who wantonly damaged or destroyed a tree. Anyone needing to take a branch from an elder or cut down a tree, first had to ask permission from Hyldemoer.[240]

Like that other sacred bush—rowan—elder was good magic to use against malevolent sorcery and ill luck.[241] In Russia, it was believed that the Elder Mother, out of compassion for humanity, drove away evil spirits–thus her great capacity in matters of physical and spiritual wellbeing.[242]

Spiritual Traits

Many of us who are adherents to pagan and Earth-based religions have a general belief in reincarnation. In the Talking Forest, Elder takes up where Yew, the rune of death and transformation, leaves off. She represents the goddess energy that creates new life out of death via reincarnation. The Milky Way, also called Hulda's Path, was the road travelled by the souls of the dead on their way back to the Source and rebirth.[243] Fred Hageneder states: "The Elder Mother carries us to the gate of death, where she soothes our fear of the unknown, and brings us gently towards the tunnel of light."[244]

Elder is the labyrinth that encompasses all aspects of existence: birth, life, death and rebirth. Her blooms are on labyrinthine stalks, the flowers of which are the ivory white of the generative fluids. Her foliage is the green of Mother Earth. The healing but also poisonous berries are lifeblood red or the black of death. So Elder encompasses all. Earth is her element and her high seasons are spring and late summer, times when the land is most fertile and great changes occur in its energy field. The rare thirteenth moon, the moon of mystery—a second full moon occurring within a calendar month—also belongs to her. Of course, the tree is sacred to Hertha or Holda, and to the triple goddesses, Persephone, Demeter and Hecate.

The Rune

Elder has place of honour as the final rune in the Talking Forest. Shaped somewhat like Ginkgo, she sports two small flower spirals on each of the forked branches at the top of the rune. Each of the two spirals below these ends in a dot, representing the fruiting qualities of this shrub. While Gingko references the past, Elder, the rune of witchcraft and magic, rules the future and thus the divinatory arts. We can often comprehend what tomorrow will bring because actions and choices in the past helped create the events of the future. The feminine Elder rune branches off on the left, indicating the bush's tendency to form sucker shoots. This reminds us that everything we do is an action that takes root and affects others, as a stem divides and creates another bush. Likewise for good or ill, actions we take today will affect our future as well as that of others.

Kenning: Witch, Labyrinth
Significance: Balance, Magic, Harmony, Completion,
Full Circle, the Future

The Talking Forest Elder has similar attributes to the World card in the Tarot deck, as well as to the mysterious Pertho rune in the Futhark. **Upright** Elder represents magic, psychic balance, the Otherworld, and completion and harmony within the universe. The upright rune suggests the querent is on the right spiritual path and should continue what they are doing. You may also experience spiritual visions or psychic phenomena. Pay close attention to any odd coincidences, premonitions, and the like that cannot be explained away, for the gods are speaking loud and clear!

Inverted Elder is a diluted version of the upright rune. In the process of developing the spiritual self, the querent is taking the path of the subconscious, culminating in the crossroads. This may be a time where cherished beliefs are questioned and answers sought on the querent's journey to seek harmony. There may be an initiation, a spiritual awakening or exploration of different religions or philosophies.

Toppled Elder only rarely means strafing or harmful magic against the querent. Much more often, it admonishes the seeker that if they are planning to raise energy to effect change on the astral plane (for that is basically what magic is), they must be very careful of motive. This is especially so if the rune **falls to the left,** with the side branch down and stuck in the mud of consequences. Magic should only be done for the benefit of all, after prudent consideration and with the consent of the recipient. Remember the three-fold law! Harm none and do what ye will.

More frequently however, contrary Elder simply indicates an imbalance in the querent's life, especially on the spiritual level. Perhaps you are not at peace with the universe or within yourself. This is most likely if the rune is **toppled to the right,** with the side shoot up. Elder is begging the querent to take that sucker and plant it in the rich, moist soil of life! Meditation, especially upon the goddess in her triple aspect, may help, for Elder is the Lady's tree. The Charge of the Goddess suggests that: "if you cannot find what you seek within yourself, you will never find it without."* Elder energy will help the seeker find the Goddess in the labyrinth within.

People associated with Elder are often involved in the work of spiritual matters. They are witches, herbalists, shamans and medicine people who see the world in its many layers. It is natural for them to regard the physical and spiritual worlds as one and the same.

Mother Elder fittingly completes our circle of trees and ends the third of our triunes of life: youth, prime and elder years. We also note that the final grove of the Talking Forest begins with a shaman and ends with a witch! The Larch rune represents the shaman on his path to the spirit world. The runes in the final grove leading up to Elder indicate ways in which this end is achieved.

---

*   Paraphrased from the poem written by Doreen Valiente.

We only reach harmony if we are well rooted in the earth (Alder), learn tolerance and kindness (Hemlock), have the blessings of the gods (Rowan), know our past (Gingko) and overcome our fear of death (Yew). Elder represents the witch, the spiritual traveller who seeks to achieve balance in the world. Never forgetting what I believe is the *true* meaning of that word's root, the witch should always seek to *bend to the will of the gods.*

In European tradition, Hawthorn, Rowan and Elder all form a magical triad. These trees were exclusively planted to guard stone circles and fairy mounds. Cutting them down or even taking branches from them was prohibited. All were afforded special protection due to their status as trees sacred to Old Gods. In the Talking Forest, these runes are the Fairy Queen Triad: Hawthorn is the tree of reverence and honour; Rowan the tree of the fairies and of the luck they bring, and Elder the tree of magic and enchantment.

SECTION III:

ARBORETUM

Methods of Divination

Runes are shorthand for the concepts or entities they represent. As such, a tree rune can stand proxy for the type of tree it embodies. In this way, the Talking Forest runes enable us to "carry the woods" with us!

You may fashion your own set of Talking Forest runes from the templates immediately preceding the endnotes in the back of this book, using wood or thick stock paper. My own personal runes are fashioned from wooden disks that are 1.5 inches in diameter. These are available from any good quality hobby store that sells wood crafting items. If inscribing the runes, I recommend using permanent ink–dark green, brown or any colour of your choice that shows up well in candlelight is fine. Double-siding the keys so that a rune never presents as blank in a layout is also a good idea. The rune on the back of the key should be identical to that on the front; that is, if you stand the key on its bottom edge, both sides should show the rune upright. Woodworkers might prefer to burn or sculpt the sigils onto the store-bought disks or onto found wooden pieces and that is an excellent endeavor. However you choose to form them, consecrating your runes before use will give them added power and vibrancy.

I chiefly use the Talking Forest for meditational purposes. For example, with each rune, I study its tree's attributes, its influences and place within the environment and the wheel of the year. In addition, I seek greater understanding of the guiding spirit or *totem* of that species. Of course, divination with the Talking Forest can be used to solve recurring issues or concerns. Following are the three methods of divination I frequently employ.

FIGURE 4

Thicket Array

© Kay Broome, 2009

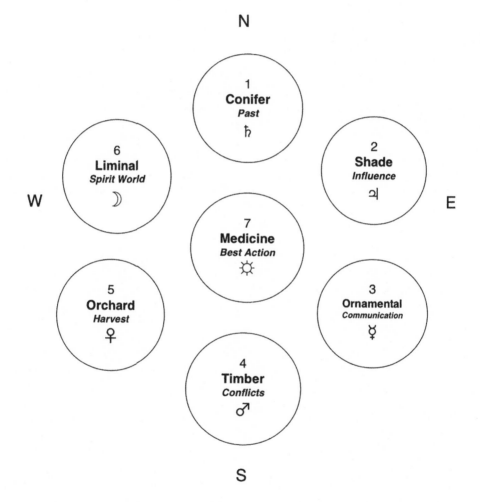

Thicket Method

The **Thicket** is the simplest and is my personal favourite. To the best of my knowledge, there is no other augury method quite like it. This is a remedial reading. It informs the reader of the tree energies best able to solve the problem which has been laid bare in the layout. For this reason and because it is a horizontal layout–a bird's eye view of the runes as seen from above–the runes can be read as upright, no matter the position in which they land.

During my experimentation with reading the Talking Forest runes, I noted two salient principles about trees in general:

1. based on their physical traits, natural habitats and the roles they have played in human history, trees can be divided into seven basic types; and
2. each type's attributes accords neatly with one of the seven planets of traditional Western occultism.

Having understood these principles, I created stations as shown in *Figure 4*, p. 313, to correspond with the seven planetary aspects.

Conifers lived on this earth for millions of years before the advent of broad-leaved trees. They retain their needles all year long, thus protecting us from the winter cold. Their seasonal metamorphoses are slower and less extreme than those of other trees. For all these reasons, conifers can be said to exhibit the immutable, timeless qualities attributed to the planet Saturn. This planet's traditional purview includes conformity, constraint and restriction. It also governs the past, as well as aspects of inheritance, agriculture and sometimes, misfortune. **Conifer** is the first station in the Thicket layout. It indicates those factors in one's life that are constant or ongoing, that cannot be changed. Here also are issues beyond our control, caused either by our former actions or by outside forces. This station occasionally signals ingrained habits or repeated behavioral patterns. The Conifer station asks: *What is the past history of the situation? What remains constant or cannot be changed? What are the ongoing concerns?*

The second station in the Thicket layout, **Shade,** corresponds to Jupiter, the planet of growth, prosperity, good fortune and material success. This station deals with law, justice and the public realm. Shade trees are large and their foliage is dense. Thus, they are often planted for privacy and to reduce noise. They regulate cold winters and hot summers and protect us from the sun's rays. Shade trees therefore assert power and status, and proclaim our command over personal property and environment. With these trees, we seek sovereignty over our lives: our careers and successes, our family and social lives. The Shade station thus indicates how we order and manipulate our lives and those of others; how we influence and interact with other people.

Although shade trees have marked influence on the amount of light and precipitation that gets through to the understory and forest floor, this factor is not consistent. For they are at the mercy of the seasons, undergoing constant changes–losing, and then again, replacing their leaves. The Shade station thus deals primarily with the present. Here we see how we cope with the changes life brings. *What are we doing currently with our lives? What are the consequences regarding our possessions and status? What are we doing to try to modify our situation and how successful are we? What could we do for others and the world around us to improve the common good?*

The third station, **Ornamental,** belongs to Mercury, the planet of communication, travel, creativity and intellect. We plant highly attractive, showy or unusual trees to express certain aspects of our personalities: our likes, lifestyles and tendencies. Just as ornamental trees are immediately noticeable to neighbours and visitors to our home, so too, this station *reveals our character, our reputation and how others perceive us. The Ornamental station illustrates how we communicate and express ourselves, how we manifest our own creativity.*

Timber trees are those whose wood is burned for fuel, or used for other things such as tools, furniture, housing and artifacts. As timber trees are damaged or destroyed by the harvest of their wood, this station implies that sacrifice may be necessary. The **Timber** station corresponds to Mars, the planet of fire, energy and strife. It indicates action needed to accomplish the best result, or to at least ameliorate the situation at hand. Timber reveals what we must do, for better or worse, to deal with our problems. This station asks: *What must we give up to achieve a better result? What can be attained or at least salvaged from the sacrifice made?*

Orchard trees are planted for food and sustenance. Not surprisingly, they belong to the realm of Venus, the planet of love, beauty, abundance and relationships. We customarily regulate and control orchard trees by pruning, row planting, hybridization and other farming practices. The **Orchard** station therefore represents matters over which we have some control. It frequently highlights our emotional bonds with those closest to us, including our children, whom we love and nurture. This station deals ultimately with fruition. Events here manifested are often the result of past decisions and actions. Orchard may also reveal what, for good or ill, is feeding the situation, as well as revealing tools that can be used to garner a desired result. Questions asked by the Orchard station are: *What is presently being harvested as a result of action taken in the past? What am I attempting to effect? What will I gain?*

Liminal trees are boundary markers. They indicate the intersection of two different environments such as river's edge, woodlot perimeter, or meadow clearing. These trees help retain watersheds and keep the soil from eroding. The **Liminal** station is governed by the moon, which influences the earth's tides, weather patterns and the reproductive cycles in plants and animals. The moon also rules the subconscious, as well as psychic, spiritual and occult matters.

The Liminal station therefore denotes cyclical changes. It seeks hidden messages and wisdom that come from both the mundane and psychic realms. This station often shows what really lies beneath a situation and asks the following questions: *What is the lay of the land? What are hidden aspects I should note? What lessons and messages from the gods should I heed?*

Many trees are used as medicine. Their sap, bark, flowers or fruit are harvested for teas, ointments and drugs to heal injury or sickness. Or their remedies may simply be used as tonics to maintain vigor and a sense of wellbeing. **Medicine** trees are ruled by the sun, whose traditional purview encompasses balance, amity, resolution and happiness. The sun also rules the conscious mind and the will, as well as governing health and recreational activities. The Medicine station asks: *What ultimately is the best possible choice, the most appropriate action to take for an auspicious outcome? What is the overall solution?*

Upon close examination of the Thicket template (*Figure 4*, p. 313), we see the Conifer station, ruled by Saturn, lying in the north. In many pagan traditions, this direction and planetary correspondence are assigned to the element of earth. Timber, allocated to fiery Mars, is placed in the south, from whence the sun shines. Both Ornamental and Shade stations are allocated to air, as are their respective planets Mercury and Jupiter. They take their stand in the east–in Western magic, the established home of the air element. Finally in the west, we find Orchard and Liminal stations, ruled by Venus and Luna respectively. Both these orbs are governed by water, the element traditionally assigned to the west. The Medicine station, ruled by the sun, is placed in the middle, to correspond to the sun's status as the centre of the solar system.

The Thicket, as a *remedial* rather than a revelatory method of divination, is most effectively used when the querent knows what the issue is, and wishes to amend it. You are not trying to find out what the future is, but simply gauging the solution to a current problem. Each rune shows how you have progressed toward the issue in all its aspects. The final Medicine station illustrates the best action that can be taken under the circumstances. This action will generally be positive or at the very least will hold forth the best outcome possible under the circumstances. The Thicket layout deals primarily with the here and now.

It goes without saying that runes will turn up on stations that do not correspond to their tree type. For example, Apple (choice, gift) is, by its nature, an orchard tree. Landing on Liminal, the rune might suggest that you will soon receive a gift from the gods. In another example, although Yew (death, ending) is actually a conifer, its placement on the centre station, would consign it as your Medicine rune. In this case, Yew is counselling that something must be sacrificed in order to create positive change. Perhaps a destructive partnership or an outmoded attitude must end in order for you to move on and evolve.

The runes or *keys* should be kept in a bag made preferably from a plant material such as silk, hemp or cotton. Alternatively, they may be kept in a wooden container with a wide enough opening to allow for ease of removal. When casting, make sure the runes are thoroughly distributed and shuffle or shake them well, so that the outcome is arbitrary. Then at random and without looking, choose seven keys, one at a time, placing each on a station in the order shown in *Figure 4*. If desired, you may think on the question at hand or recite a spell of your choosing. Or you may simply prefer to clear your mind of any thought whatsoever.

FIGURE 5

Tree Array

© Kay Broome, 2009

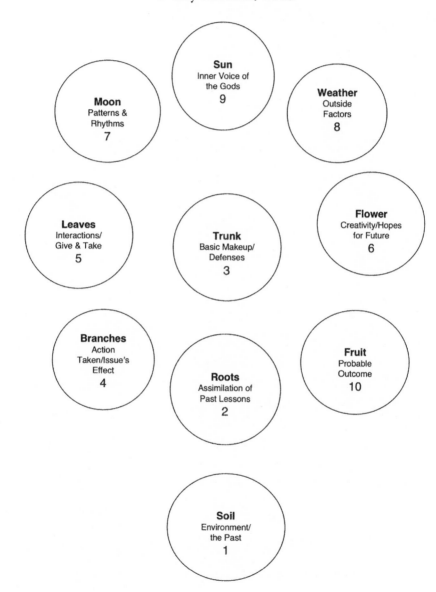

Tree Method

Of the three methods in the Talking Forest, the **Tree** layout (*Figure 5,* p. 321) is the most explicitly personal for the user. More complex than the Thicket, this layout deals primarily with the querent's personal development. There are ten stations, most of them corresponding to the parts of a tree. This layout is read vertically, as if the querent were standing in front of a tree. Therefore, the position in which each rune lands is salient to the reading, with upright generally being most auspicious and toppled, least.

This method is most suited to redressing a recurring situation or unresolved concern. Where the Thicket deals primarily with the present, the Tree layout alludes to the querent's past and actions that have led to the issue at hand. A Thicket spread seeks to examine and find a solution for a *specific* problem. The Tree layout, on the other hand, determines the querent's *ongoing* situation, while highlighting individual character traits and behavioral patterns. The stations of the Tree are devised as follows.

The type of soil in an environment will determine the species of tree growing there and how well it adapts. In like manner, the first station of the Tree layout, **Soil,** represents the ground of being, the individual's environment and background. The Soil station illustrates historical factors that have fed the situation, as well as what the querent has had to work with.

The first expression of the plant's urge to grow is the root sprouting from the seed to burrow into the soil, taking in nutrients and minerals. The second station of the Tree layout, the **Roots,** represents the querent's past, as well as any actions taken to utilize available resources. The Roots station deals with how one assimilates what they have taken in and how well they have learned from the past.

The trunk of a tree consists of three main sections: heartwood, sapwood and bark. This is the backbone of the tree. The heartwood, in the trunk's centre, is its strength and core, giving it shape and dictating the way in which the tree will grow. The sapwood surrounding it synthesizes the food and water the tree takes in. It is here too that we find the rings of a tree proclaiming its age and maturity. The bark stands out as the trunk's most prominent component. This is the protective outer layer of the tree, representing the defenses we throw up to protect ourselves, as well as steps we take to deal with issues at hand.

With all this in mind, we see that the **Trunk** station indicates strengths and weaknesses, as well as basic character. It represents the present, illustrating the effects of the past and how we are dealing with it.

More than any other part of the tree, the branches ordain the shape or silhouette and indicate how the tree deals with its environment. For example, windswept pines grow with the prevailing winds, while the low sweeping branches of fir trees can handle heavy loads of snow. A beech tree in a meadow or field has long, heavy, perpendicular branches; in a crowded forest, that same tree manifests a slender, graceful vase shape. Branches also circulate water and nutrients throughout a tree's leafy canopy. The **Branches** station therefore indicates how the issue is developing, the effect it has had on the querent and how the person is adapting.

The leaves breathe for the tree and provide nourishment through photosynthesis. Unlike the branches, which are forcibly moulded by the habitat, the leaves indicate how the tree has adapted to survive its environment. For example, conifer needles have "antifreeze" in them to deal with extreme cold; dogwood leaf veins are designed to draw rainwater toward the leaf tip. Trees give and take most obviously through their leaves: taking in carbon dioxide and presenting the world with oxygen. Their canopies have a crucial and generally positive effect on the environment: climate regulation, food and shelter for some animals, and clean air for all. The **Leaves** station illustrates those personal strengths and abilities the querent can use in order to best deal with the situation at hand. This station also indicates our effect on others and on our surroundings.

The flower, with its pollen and nectar, contains the sex organs of the plant, its ability to reproduce and create anew. It also provides food for other living creatures in the form of nectar and pollen. Flowers, with their bright colours and fragrance, frequently have an emotional as well as physical effect on humans and other animals. A tree's flowers are its expression of the life force–its artistry. This station demonstrates how the querent is working toward the final outcome, what actions they are taking to cause the issue to come to fruition. The **Flower** station further illustrates the querent's hopes and fears; how they express their feelings and how others perceive them.

Our moon controls our reproductive and growth cycles, and affects ocean tides, the amount of rainfall we receive and the development of plants. The seventh station, the **Moon,** therefore deals with cycles and patterns, and with psychic or hidden influences.

The weather can bring about frost, drought or harsh twig-snapping winds. But it also encompasses nurturing rain, pollinating breezes and the protective blanket of snow. Therefore, the eighth station, **Weather,** deals with outside forces for good or ill, that are beyond our control. It reveals people and influences working for or against the querent.

The ninth station is the **Sun.** Tree leaves actively seek out the sun to photosynthesize light into food. The Sun station represents the quest for the higher self, that which you ultimately strive for, as well as the best outcome that can be gleaned from the situation. This station suggests what your actions should be.

The last station, **Fruit,** represents the final outcome, the future; the most likely scenario that will result. Fruit is potentially a new tree. This tree may grow strong and live to a good age or it may be weakened or stunted. The final outcome depends upon various factors; in particular, the querent's actions, but also outside influences, and sometimes, sheer luck.

Stations that represent parts of the tree itself, e.g., Trunk, Leaves, and Flower, are *active* elements; that is, they are within the querent's control. Stations whose purview deals with the environment–Soil, Sun, Moon and Weather–are *passive* and thus, mostly beyond the subject's control.

FIGURE 6

Forest Array

© Kay Broome, 2009

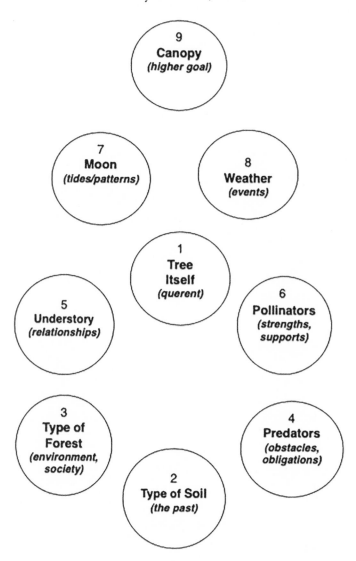

Forest Method

The third and final layout in the Talking Forest is a reading best suited to those who strive to discover their objective in life. As such, it alludes more to the future than do the other two layouts. This should be done only occasionally, say once a year, as it is a "life" reading. It borrows heavily from the principles of permaculture.

Within the convention of permaculture, there are three horizontal layers in a forest. The first, the *groundcover,* is at and just above the forest floor. This is the area where smaller woodland plants such as herbs, moss, ferns and grasses grow. In the Forest layout (*Figure 6,* p. 329) of the Talking Forest, the groundcover layer deals with the querent's *past:* origins and background, problems endured, as well as any skills and knowledge they have developed. The second layer is the *understory.* This is the area of the woodland at human eye level–where small trees, shrubs and bushes thrive. In the Forest layout, this mid-level deals with the *present* situation: what is going on at the moment and how the querent is struggling toward enlightenment. The upper layer, the *canopy,* is the summit of the woodland, where the taller trees reach for and bask in the sunlight. This layer deals with the *future:* where the querent is heading and the outcome most likely to result from their actions.

Let us begin with the first station, **the Tree.** This key is located dead centre of the middle or understory of the Forest layout and represents the querent, the person on whom the reading is centred. It deals with the basic self and the status of the individual's current development. Here, the querent is actively reaching for a higher goal, represented by the Canopy station.

The second station, **Type of Soil,** is the centre key on the forest floor or groundcover, and is directly beneath the Tree station. Here is represented the querent's childhood and past family life. Organisms growing in the soil help build a forest; likewise, our past creates what we will become.

The third station, **Type of Forest,** is on the left side of the forest floor and represents the environment in which the querent has lived. Are they struggling to survive in a desert or a taiga, or have they had the good fortune of growing within a lush rainforest or pampered garden? This station also examines the querent's maturity and asks: what has been learned from the past and what has been created from it? The third station often indicates what the querent has done with the tools they had to work with. No doubt, our environment does have an effect on us. However, some people are endowed with much, but squander it. Yet others manage to overcome adversity beyond the odds.

On the forest floor across from station 3, is the fourth station, **Predators.** Many insects and fungi attack a plant when it is young, striking root and stem, as well as leaves, thus this station's location on the bottom layer. Not all fungi or predators are harmful, however. Many interact with the trees of a forest, giving back nutrients and protection, as well as taking nourishment. For example, some caterpillars eat a tree's leaves, but the adult butterfly or moth will later help pollinate the plant. This station then, represents obstacles and obligations: things the querent must deal with that may be unpleasant or may cause difficulties. Privation can, however, help strengthen a person and build character and there is always the possibility of good coming out of adversity.

To the left of the Tree station—the querent—lies the **Understory.** This fifth station represents other trees and shrubs growing in the forest. These smaller trees often struggle to obtain air, water and light, but generally grow well in spring and fall—times of change. And while larger plants may overshadow the understory tree, blocking sunlight, they also give protection from heavy weather. This station indicates the querent's dealings with others and how they interact with them on a daily basis. It illustrates alliances and conflicts, as well as indicating family, friends and dependents.

The sixth station, to the right of the Tree, is **Pollinators.** This station represents those animals that help spread the tree's seeds. They do so by collecting pollen, consuming nectar or by eating fruit and as a result, spreading the seeds in their droppings. In addition, pollinators frequently eat organisms that prey on trees. Many of these creatures are birds, bats and flying insects, hence the station's placement in the middle layer. This station signifies the strengths and supports that the querent has at hand.

Moon, the seventh station, is on the left on the canopy, the top layer of the Forest layout. This is the first of two stations that represent outside factors and influences beyond the querent's control. These can work to aid or hinder the querent. The Moon station represents hidden and occult influences. It may also illustrate the querent's psychic and spiritual attunement.

Station number eight, **Weather,** is on the right of the canopy level. This station deals with current and future events in the mundane world that will have an effect on the querent.

The ninth and last station of the Forest layout, the **Canopy,** is at the summit and corresponds with the tall tree layer of a forest. Here the largest trees attempt to reach the sunlight in order to photosynthesize and gain nutrients and warmth. Their goal is to grow as tall and spacious as possible. The questions this final station asks are: *What does the querent ultimately seek and what is their mission in life?*

The Forest layout represents the Cosmic Tree. Read *horizontally,* the stations mimic the "Tree of Life," with the bottom three (Forest, Soil and Predators) indicating the past. The Centre (Understory, Tree and Pollinators) is the present and the top layer (Moon, Canopy and Weather) shows the future. Examined *vertically,* the stations represent the Forest as the "Tree of Knowledge." Here, the left-hand stations (Forest, Understory, Moon) represent the *environment* you have lived in and learned from. The left or distaff side pays tribute to the Goddess whose purview has traditionally been the moon, plant life and agriculture. The right-hand stations (Predators, Pollinators and Weather) represent *others,* people and groups with whom you have interacted. These stations are ruled by the Lord of animal life, whose purview also encompasses his roles as sky and weather god. The middle stations (Soil, Tree,

Canopy) represent the *individual's quest* for spiritual growth in this particular incarnation.

The Forest array is visualized from the perspective of a tree planted in the soil in the middle of a forest. Therefore, runic position is salient to the reading, with uprightness generally being most propitious and toppled least.

While the Thicket layout deals with concerns in the here and now, and the Tree array reflects on how the past is influencing the current situation, the Forest reading looks more to the future the querent seeks.

Whichever of these divination methods readers use, they can be very helpful on the personal path to a better understanding of our inner selves and the trees that share our environment.

Conclusion

We have now completed our tour and return to the edge of the woodland. I trust you have enjoyed your journey through the Talking Forest, and that these forty-two novel runes will serve as an effective tool in your quest for enlightenment and harmony. Indeed, if this book has only revealed a new and more rewarding way of interacting with the natural world and with the trees in your neighbourhood, then it will have served a noble purpose.

TALKING FOREST RUNES
1-7 Childhood
© Kay Broome, 2009

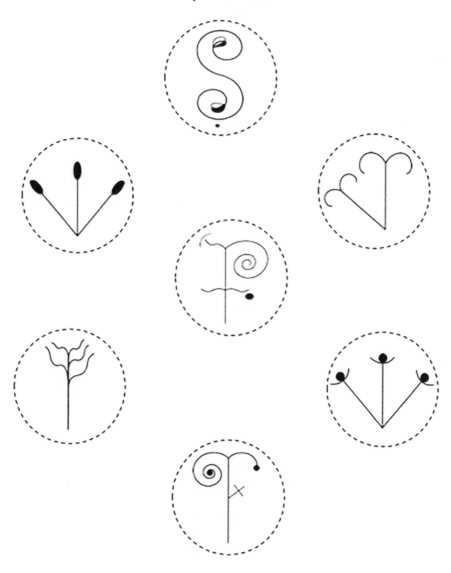

TALKING FOREST RUNES
8-14 Adolescence
© Kay Broome, 2009

TALKING FOREST RUNES
15-21 Young Adult
© Kay Broome, 2009

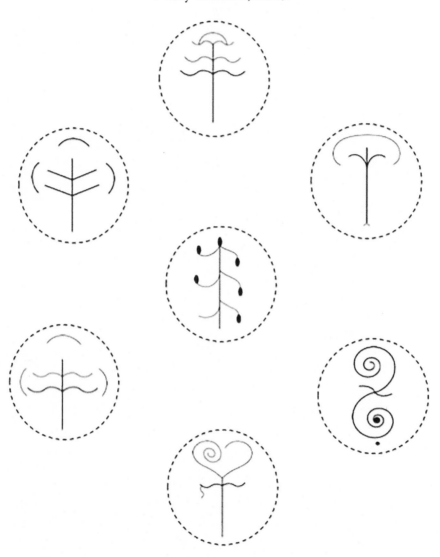

TALKING FOREST RUNES
22-28 Prime of Life
© Kay Broome, 2009

TALKING FOREST RUNES
29-35 Middle Age
© Kay Broome, 2009

TALKING FOREST RUNES
36-42 Elder Years
© Kay Broome, 2009

Endnotes

1 Fred Hageneder, *The Meaning of Trees*, (San Francisco, Chronicle Books, 2005) p. 6.

2 Freya Asswyn, *Leaves of Yggdrasil* (St. Pauls, Llewellyn, 1994) p. 36.

3 Edred Thorsson, *The Book of Ogham* (St. Paul, Llewellyn, 1994) Chapter 3.

4 Jaime Sams and David Carson, *Medicine Cards: The Discovery of Power Through the Ways of Animals* (Santa Fe, Bear & Company, 1988).

5 Fred Hageneder, *The Heritage of Trees* (Edinburgh, Floris Books, 2001) p. 71.

6 *Ivy, Chief of Trees, It is,* Hymns and Carols of Christmas, (cited March 2019), https://www.hymnsandcarolsofchristmas.com/Hymns_and_Carols/ivy_chief_of_trees_it_is.htm

7 T.F. Thiselton-Dyer, *The Folklore of Plants* (Detroit, Singing Tree Press, 1968) p. 105.

8 Ted Andrews, *Nature-Speak*, (Jackson, Tenn., Dragonhawk Publishing, 2004) p. 209.

9 Diane Wolkstein & Samuel Noah Kramer, *Inanna: Queen of Heaven and Earth* (N.Y., Harper & Row, 1983) pp. xi and 141.

10 Nathaniel Altman, *Sacred Trees* (S.F., Sierra Club Books, 1994) p. 116.

11 Christian Rätsch, *The Dictionary of Sacred and Magical Plants,* (ABC-CLIO, Santa Barbara, CA, 1992) p. 78.

12 Aswynn, *Leaves of Yggdrasil,* p. 82.

13 James Frazer, *The Golden Bough,* (abridged, MacMillan Press Ltd., London, 1978), p. 160.

14 Thorsson, *The Book of Ogham,* p. 115.

15 Rebecca Rupp, *Red Oaks & Black Birches: The Science and Lore of Trees*, (Pownal, VT, Garden Way Publishing, 1990), p. 36.

16 Raven Grimassi, *Italian Witchcraft* (Woodbury, MN, Llewellyn, 2012), p. 292.

17 R.C. Hosie, *Native Trees of Canada* (Markham, ON, Fitzhenry & Whiteside Limited, 1990), p. 120.

18 Hosie, *Native Trees of Canada*, p. 118.

19 Hageneder, *The Meaning of Trees*, p. 162.

20 Ellen Evert Hopman, *Tree Medicine, Tree Magic* (Blaine, WA, Phoenix Publishing Inc., 1991), p. 128.

21 Thorsson, *The Book of Ogham*, p. 189.

22 Edward Bach, *The Twelve Healers*, (Essex, UK, The C. W. Daniel Company Ltd., 1999), p. 10.

23 Rupp, *Red Oaks & Black Birches*, p. 195.

24 Florence Holbrook, (FCIT. (2020, July 19). *Florence Holbrook author page* (Retrieved and cited July 19, 2020) https://etc.usf.edu/lit2go/authors/123/florence-holbrook/TheBookofNatureMyths_10006785#126.

25 Sheryl Ann Karas, *The Solstice Evergreen* (Fairfield, CT, Aslan Publishing, 1991), pp. 60-68.

26 Laura C. Martin, *The Folklore of Trees & Shrubs*, (Chester, CT, The Globe Pequot Press, 1992), p. 111.

27 Alexander Porteous, *The Forest in Folklore and Mythology* (Mineola, NY, Dover Publications, Inc., 2002), p. 93.

28 Ibid, pp. 85 and 89.

29 Rupp, *Red Oaks & Black Birches*, p. 134.

30 Altman, *Sacred Trees*, pp. 61-62 and 96.

31 Thiselton-Dyer, *The Folklore of Plants*, p. 110.

32 Rupp, *Red Oaks & Black Birches*, p. 139.

33 Donald Culross Peattie, *A Natural History of North American Trees*, (New York, Houghton Mifflin Company, 2007), pp. 185 and 187.

34 Glen Blouin, *An Eclectic Guide to Trees East of the Rockies* (Toronto, ON, Boston Mills Press, 2001), p. 132.

35 Ibid, p. 132.

36 Altman, *Sacred Trees*, p. 60.

37   Hugh Johnson, *Encyclopaedia of Trees*, Hugh Johnson's Encyclopedia of Trees, (New York, Portland House, div. Dilithium Press Ltd., 1990), p. 170.

38   Jon Arno, Trees: *An Explore Your World Handbook*, (New York, Discovery Books, 2000), p. 98.

39   Hageneder, The Heritage of Trees, p. 50.

40   Ibid, pp. 122-123.

41   Altman, *Sacred Trees*, p. 175.

42   Arno, *Trees: An Explore Your World Handbook*, p. 94.

43   Porteous, *The Forest in Folklore and Mythology*, p. 63.

44   Ibid, p. 66.

45   Martin, *The Folklore of Trees & Shrubs*, p. 75.

46   Thiselton-Dyer, *The Folklore of Plants*, p. 227.

47   Rupp, *Red Oaks & Black Oaks*, p. 161.

48   Hosie, *Native Trees of Canada*, p. 216.

49   Rätsch, *The Dictionary of Sacred and Magical Plants*, p. 147.

50   Rupp, *Red Oaks & Black Birches*, p. 166.

51   Ibid, pp. 163-165.

52   John Lust, *The Herb Book*, (New York, Bantam Books, Benedict Lust Publications, 1980), p. 347.

53   Martin, The Folklore of Trees and Shrubs, p. 175

54   Ibid, p. 50.

55   Carmen Blacker, *The Catalpa Bow* (Richmond, UK, Japan Library, Imprint of Curzon Press Ltd, 1999), pp. 1-2.

56   Kim D. Coder, *Cultural Aspects of Trees: Traditions and Myths*, PDF (last cited June 2020) https://www.warnell.uga.edu/outreach/publications/individual/cultural-aspects-trees-traditions-myths p. 2.

57   Arno, *Trees: An Explore Your World Handbook*, p. 97.

58   Hosie, *Native Trees of Canada*, p. 254.

59   Hageneder, *The Meaning of Trees*, p. 19.

60   Altman, *Sacred Trees*, p. 125.

61   Martin, *The Folklore of Trees & Shrubs*, p. 199.

62   Altman, *Sacred Trees*, p. 116.

63   Hageneder, *The Heritage of Trees*, p. 123.

64 Rupp, *Red Oaks and Black Birches*, p. 50.

65 Blouin, *An Eclectic Guide to Trees East of the Rockies*, p. 49.

66 Altman, *Sacred Trees*, p. 128.

67 Hageneder, *The Meaning of Trees*, p. 23.

68 Porteous, *The Forest in Folklore and Mythology*, p. 283.

69 Diana Beresford-Kroeger, *Arboretum America: A Philosophy of the Forest*, (Ann Arbor, MI, University of Michigan Press, 2006), p. 177.

70 Ibid, p. 183.

71 Johnson, *Encyclopedia of Trees*, p. 138.

72 Culross Peattie, *A Natural History of Trees of North America*, p. 250.

73 Porteous, The Forest in Folklore and Mythology, p. 20.

74 Rupp, *Red Oaks & Black Birches*, p. 148.

75 Gayle Brandow Samuels, *Enduring Roots: Encounters with Trees, History and the American Landscape* (London, Rutgers University Press, London, 1999), pp. 113-114.

76 Marie-France Boyer, *Tree-Talk: Memories, Myths and Timeless Customs*, (London, Thames and Hudson, Ltd., 1996), p. 62.

77 Rupp, *Red Oaks & Black Birches*, p. 227.

78 Karas, *The Solstice Evergreen*, p. 23.

79 Altman, *Sacred Trees*, p. 53; Porteous, *The Forest in Folklore and Mythology*, pp. 84-85.

80 Karas, *The Solstice Evergreen*, p. 16.

81 Porteous, *The Forest in Folklore and Mythology*, p. 108, citing James Fraser from *The Golden Bough*.

82 Ibid, pp. 73-74.

83 Rupp, *Red Oaks and Black Birches*, p. 239.

84 Thorsson, *The Book of Ogham*, p. 177.

85 Beresford-Kroeger, *Arboretum America*, p. 65.

86 Rupp, *Red Oaks & Black Birches*, p. 168.

87 Johnston, *The Encyclopedia of Trees*, p. 238.

88 Jane Gifford, *The Wisdom of Trees*, (New York, Sterling Publishing Co. Inc., 2006), p. 31.

89 Porteous, *The Forest in Folklore and Mythology*, p. 93.

90 Martin, *The Folklore of Trees & Shrubs*, p. 20.

91 Thiselton-Dyer, *The Folklore of Plants*, p. 78.

92 Rupp, *Red Oaks & Black Birches*, p. 185.

93 Lust, *The Herb Book*, p. 614.

94 Ibid, p. 133.

95 Arno, *Trees: An Explore Your World Handbook*, p. 89.

96 Rupp, *Red Oaks & Black Birches*, p. 179.

97 Lust, *The Herb Book*, p. 256.

98 Altman, *Sacred Trees*, p. 67.

99 Rupp, *Red Oaks & Black Birches*, p. 180.

100 Boyer, *Tree-Talk*, p. 53.

101 Ibid, p. 59.

102 Ibid, pp. 80 and 85.

103 Ibid, p. 85 and Johnson, *Encyclopedia of Trees*, p. 151.

104 Porteous, *The Forest in Folklore and Mythology*, p. 58.

105 Rupp, *Red Oaks & Black Birches*, p. 40.

106 Porteous, *The Forest in Folklore and Mythology*, p. 249.

107 Thorsson, *The Book of Ogham*, pp. 48–49.

108 Samuels, *Enduring Roots*, p. 40.

109 Martin, The Folklore of Trees & Shrubs, p. 66.

110 Ibid, p. 14.

111 Rupp, *Red Oaks & Black Birches*, pp. 128-129.

112 Ibid, p. 125.

113 Porteous, *The Forest in Folklore and Mythology*, p. 91–92.

114 Thiselton-Dyer, *The Folklore of Plants*, p. 88.

115 Arno, Trees: An Explore Your World Handbook, p. 146.

116 Porteous, The Forest in Folkore and Mythology, citation, p. 62.

117 Hopman, *Tree Medicine, Tree Magic*, p. 29.

118 Karas, The Solstice Evergreen, p. 42.

119 Ibid, p. 42.

120 Altman, *Sacred Trees*, p. 196.

121 Karas, The Solstice Evergreen, p. 17.

122 Altman, *Sacred Trees*, p. 109.

123 Rupp, Red Oaks & Black Birches, p. 219.

124 Martin, The Folklore of Trees and Shrubs, p. 154.

125 Hosie, Native Trees of Canada, p. 50.

126 Andrews, *Nature Speak*, p. 286.

127 Arno, Trees: *An Explore Your World Handbook*, p. 118. Arno states, however, that it is only older trees that display this nasty habit.

128 Martin, *The Folklore of Trees & Shrubs*, p. 201.

129 Anne Sutton and Myron Sutton, *The Audubon Society Nature Guides: Eastern Forests*, p. 432 and Martin, *The Folklore of Trees & Shrubs*, p. 201.

130 Porteous, *The Forest in Folklore and Mythology*, pp. 289-290.

131 Ibid, p. 178.

132 Grimassi, *Italian Witchcraft*, p. 225.

133 Thiselton-Dyer, *The Folklore of Plants*, p. 107.

134 Ibid, pp. 108-9.

135 Martin, *The Folklore of Trees & Shrubs*, p. 161.

136 Boyer, *Tree-Talk*, p. 76.

137 Ibid, p. 77.

138 Beresford-Kroeger, *Arboretum America*, p. 85.

139 Martin, *The Folklore of Trees & Shrubs*, p. 52.

140 Beresford-Kroeger, *Arboretum America*, p. 154.

141 Rätsch, *The Dictionary of Sacred and Magical Plants*, p. 40.

142 Beresford-Kroeger, *Arboretum America*, p. 153.

143 Ibid, p. 154.

144 Altman, *Sacred Trees*, p. 111.

145 Porteous, *The Forest in Folklore and Mythology*, p. 62.

146 Rupp, *Red Oaks & Black Birches*, pp. 184-5. Although the idea is from a Chinese legend, the famous blue and white Willow Ware was created in 1780 by English potter, Thomas Minton.

147 Gifford, *The Wisdom of Trees*, p. 48.

148 Rupp, *Red Oaks & Black Birches*, p. 187.

149 Martin, *The Folkore of Trees and Shrubs*, p. 205.

150 Lust, *The Herb Book*, p. 402.

151 Altman, *Sacred Trees*, p. 115.

152 Ibid, pp. 64-65.

153 Ibid, pp. 73-74.

154 Ibid, p. 188.

155 Thorsson, *The Book of Ogham*, pp. 127-128. The word probably shares the same root as the Latin *salix* for willow.

156 Rupp, *Red Oaks & Black Birches*, p. 183.

157 Rätsch, *The Dictionary of Sacred and Magical Plants*, p. 177.

158 Boyer, *Tree-Talk*, p. 96

159 Sutton and Sutton, *Eastern Forests*, p. 421.

160 Rupp, *Red Oaks & Black Birches*, p. 68.

161 Hosie, *Native Trees of Canada*, p. 220.

162 Porteous, *The Forest in Folklore and Mythology*, p. 203.

163 Jacques Brosse, *Mythologie des Arbres*, (Paris, Petite Bibliothèque Payot, Librairie Plon, 1989), p. 139.

164 Ibid, p. 146.

165 Toxicity is a common theme in the cashew family. The actual nut of the tropical cashew tree is poisonous, causing blistering of the skin. The delicious "nut" we eat is, in fact, the stalk that is attached to the cashew fruit. Arno, *Trees: An Explore Your World Handbook*, p. 126.

166 Sutton and Sutton, *The Audubon Society Nature Guides: Eastern Forests*, p. 435.

167 Thiselton-Dyer, *The Folklore of Plants*, p. 318.

168 Martin, *The Folklore of Trees & Shrubs*, p. 104.

169 Grimassi, *Italian Witchcraft*, p. 292.

170 Thiselton-Dyer, *The Folklore of Plants*, p. 74.

171 Robert Graves, *The White Goddess: A historical grammar of poetic myth*, (London, UK, Faber and Faber Limited, 1977), p. 183.

172 Thiselton-Dyer, *The Folklore of Plants*, p. 183.

173 Ibid, p. 108.

174 Thorsson, *The Book of Ogham*, pp. 149-150.

175 Thiselton-Dyer, *The Folklore of Plants*, pp. 52 and 287.

176 Martin, *The Folklore of Trees & Shrubs*, p. 97.

177 Rätsch, *The Dictionary of Sacred and Magical Plants*, p. 179.

178 Rupp, *Red Oaks and Black Birches*, p. 6.

179 Ibid, p. 4.

180 Porteous, *The Forest in Folklore and Mythology*, p. 58.

181 Ibid, p. 71.

182 Frazer, *The Golden Bough* (Abridged Edition), p. 3.

183 Thiselton-Dyer, *The Folklore of Plants*, p. 31.

184 Porteous, *The Tree in Folklore and Mythology*, p. 47.

185 Thiselton-Dyer, *The Folklore of Plants*, p. 272.

186 Altman, *Sacred Trees*, p. 52.

187 Ibid, p. 170.

188 Boyer, *Tree-Talk*, pp. 39 and 42.

189 Ibid, p. 96.

190 Ibid, p. 97.

191 Samuels, *Enduring Roots*, p. 17.

192 Altman, *Sacred Trees*, pp. 173-174 and Samuels, p. 17.

193 Rupp, *Red Oaks & Black Birches*, p. 16.

194 Culross Peattie, A Natural History of North American Trees, p. 148.

195 Altman, *Sacred Trees*, pp. 183-184.

196 Porteous, The Forest in Folklore and Mythology, P. 54.

197 Ibid, p. 54.

198 Hosie, *Native Trees of Canada*, p. 168.

199 Gifford, *The Wisdom of Trees*, p. 40.

200 Martin, *The Folklore of Trees & Shrubs*, p. 4.

201 Gifford, *The Wisdom of Trees*, p. 42

202 Thorsson, *The Book of Ogham*, pp. 124-125.

203 Gifford, *The Wisdom of Trees*, p. 44.

204 Ibid, p. 46.

205 C. Frank Brockman, *Trees of North America: A Guide to Field Identification*, (Racine, WI, Golden Press NY, 1979), p. 42.

206 Martin, *The Folklore of Trees & Shrubs*, p. 101.

207 Arno, *Trees: An Explore Your World Handbook*, p. 145.

208 Robert Shetterly, Courage, Commonsense, and the World Before Us: Some Thoughts for High School Seniors, from Common Dreams website, June 17, 2009. https://www.commondreams.org/views/2009/06/17/courage-commonsense-and-world-us

209 Beresford-Kroeger, *Arboretum America*, p. 169.

210 Ibid, p. 172.

211 Martin, *The Folklore of Trees & Shrubs*, p. 101.

212 Coder, Cultural Aspects of Trees, p. 2.

213 Gifford, *The Wisdom of Trees*, pps. 18 & 24.

214 Ibid, p. 20.

215 Thiselton-Dyer, *The Folklore of Plants*, p. 43.

216 Porteous, *The Forest in Folklore and Mythology*, p. 86.

217 Gifford, *The Wisdom of Trees*, p. 24.

218 Arno, *Trees: An Explore Your World Handbook*, p. 95.

219 Laura C. Martin states that they date from the Paleozoic, between 225 to 280 million years ago: *The Folklore of Trees & Shrubs*, p. 88.

220 "Ginkgo: the Tree That Lived With Dinosaurs," Wood Species Guide from Wood Magazine, cited October 7, 2006. https://www.woodmagazine.com/materials-guide/lumber/wood-species-2/ginkgo

221 Johnson, *The Encyclopedia of Trees*, p. 68.

222 Altman, *Sacred Trees*, p. 62.

223 "Gingko", Classical Chinese Medicine, quoting Li Shizhen's revision of Li Dongyuan's work, cited April 17, 2015. https://classicalchinesemedicine.org/ginkgo-cultural-background-and-medicinal-usage-in-china/

224 Aswynn, *Leaves of Yggdrasil*, pp. 99-101.

225 Altman, *Sacred Trees*, p. 168. It should be noted here that gingko, a far older tree, became extinct in Europe during the last Ice Age.

226 Gifford, *The Wisdom of Trees*, p. 136

227 Altman, *Sacred Trees*, p. 158.

228 Aswynn, *Leaves of Yggdrasil*, pp. 62-66.

229 Boyer, *Tree-Talk*, p. 22.

230 Gifford, *The Wisdom of Trees*, p. 139.

231 Frank Delaney, *The Celts* (London, UK, BBC Publications, Hodder and Stoughton, 1986), pp. 153-7.

232 Boyer, *Tree-Talk*, p. 22.

233 Thiselton-Dyer, *The Folklore of Plants*, p. 110.

234 Fred Hageneder, *The Spirit of Trees: Science, Symbiosis and Inspiration*, (Edinburgh, UK, Floris Books, 2006), p. 233.

235 Lust, *The Herb Book*, pp. 178-180.

236 Hageneder, *The Spirit of Trees*, p. 189.

237 Beresford-Kroeger, *Arboretum America*, pp. 136-137.

238 Thiselton-Dyer, *The Folklore of Plants*, p. 63.

239 Ibid, p. 85.

240 Porteous, *The Forest in Folklore and Mythology*, p. 90.

241 Hopman, *Tree Medicine Tree Magic*, p. 153.

242 Porteous, *The Forest in Folklore and Mythology*, p. 86.

243 "Myths and Legends of Black Elderberry," In the Garden of Paghat The Rat Girl, cited September 29, 2006. http://www.paghat.com/elderberrymyths.html

244 Hageneder, *The Spirit of Trees*, p. 193.

Acknowledgements

For reviewing my book proposal and offering support: Catherine Starr and Jackie from U of T pagans, Marc and Betty Belanger, Rhonda Teitel-Payne and Janet Patterson.

For patiently sitting for readings: Janet P. again, my sisters Julie and Karen, Amy Jutras, Rachel & Siobhan Meyer, Gaye Wignall, and the late Marie Swidrok.

To Lynna Landstreet for the idea of creating my own oracle system and to Gaye again, who saw the trunk of a tree in my runes and thus laid bare a hidden mystery.

To author Ken McGoogan for his engaging course on non-fiction writing; to the other students in his class: thank you all for your courage in revealing and laying bare your inner demons and desires; and for being unflinchingly honest yet compassionate in criticism. All the best to you in your future endeavours!

To Richard Dionne for his excellent editing skills, his support and insight, and his many helpful tips on getting published. To David Gryfe for recommending Richard in the first place. To Aaron Davis for his charming book cover design; to Danielle Smith-Boldt for her patience and guidance and her elegant and skillful design work. Last but not least, to the folks at Reedsy for their frequent assistance.

Bibliography

Folklore & Mythology

Altman, Nathanial, *Sacred Trees,* San Francisco, Sierra Club Books, 1994

Boyer, Marie-France, *Tree-Talk: Memories, Myths and Timeless Customs,* transl. by Muriel Zagha, London, Thames and Hudson Ltd., 1996

Brosse, Jacques, *Mythologie des Arbres,* Paris, Petite Bibliothèque Payot, Librairie Plon, 1989

Graves, Robert, *The White Goddess: A historical grammar of poetic myth,* London, Faber and Faber Limited, 1977 (orig. publ. 1961)

Karas, Sheryl Ann, *The Solstice Evergreen: The History, Folklore and Origins of the Christmas Tree,* Fairfield, CT, USA, Aslan Publishing, 1991

Marshall, Sybil, *English Folk Tales,* Illustrated with wood engravings by John Lawrence, London, Phoenix, a division of Orion Books, Ltd., 1996

Matthews, John, *Classic Celtic Fairy Tales,* Illustrated by Ian Daniels, London, Blandford, A Cassell Imprint, 1997

Matthews, John and Caitlin Matthews, *The Aquarian Guide to British & Irish Mythology,* Illustrated by Chesca Potter, Chatham, UK, The Aquarian Press, 1988

Porteous, Alexander, *The Forest in Folklore and Mythology,* Mineola, NY, Dover Publications, Inc., 2002 (orig. publ. 1928)

Thiselton-Dyer, T.F., *The Folklore of Plants,* Detroit, Singing Tree Press, 1968 (orig. publ. 1889)

Wolkstein, Diane and Samuel Noah Kramer, *Inanna, Queen of Heaven and Earth: Her Stories and Hymns from Sumer,* New York, Harper & Row, Publishers, 1983

Wicca & Paganism

Andrews, Ted, *Nature-Speak: Signs, Omens & Messages in Nature,* Jackson, TN, USA, Dragonhawk Publishing, 2004

Gifford, Jane, *The Wisdom of Trees,* photographs by Jane Gifford, New York, Sterling Publishing Co. Inc., 2006

Grimassi, Raven, *Italian Witchcraft: The Old Religion of Southern Europe,* Woodbury, MN, USA Llewellyn Publications, 2012

Hageneder, Fred, *The Heritage of Trees: History, Culture and Wisdom,* Edinburgh, Floris Books, 2001

———, *The Meaning of Trees,* San Francisco, Chronicle Books, LLC, 2005

———, *The Spirit of Trees: Science, Symbiosis and Inspiration,* Edinburgh, Floris Books, 2006

Hopman, Ellen Evert, *Tree Medicine Tree Magic,* Illustrations by Diana Green, Blaine, WA, USA, Phoenix Publishing, Inc., 1991

Runelore & Divination

Aswynn, Freya, *Leaves of Yggdrasil: A Synthesis of Runes, Gods, Magic, Feminine Mysteries and Folklore,* St. Paul, MN, USA, Llewellyn Publications, 1994

Gray, Eden, *The Tarot Revealed,* New York, Signet Books, New American Library, 1969

Sams, Jamie and David Carson, *Medicine Cards: The Discovery of Power Through the Ways of Animals,* Illustrated by Angela C. Werneke, Santa Fe, NM, USA, Bear & Company 1988

Thorsson, Edred, *The Book of Ogham, The Celtic Tree Oracle,* Illustrated by Anne Marie Hoppe, St. Paul, MN, USA, Llewellyn Publications, 1994

Fiction, Fairy Tales and Children's Stories

East, Helen and Eric Maddern, *Spirit of the Forest: Tree Tales from Around the World,* Illustrated by Alan Marks, London, Frances Lincoln Limited, 2002

Hardy, Thomas, *The Woodlanders,* London, Everyman Publ., J.M. Dent, 1994

Holbrook, Florence, (FCIT. Florence Holbrook author page, Lit2Go, (July 19, 2020) https://etc.usf.edu/lit2go/authors/123/florence-holbrook/TheBookofNatureMyths_10006785#126

Jakubans, Andris, *A Son's Return,* from: *The Storyteller: Short Stories from around the world–Reflections in Fiction,* edited by James Barry and Joseph Griffin, Scarborough, Nelson Canada, A Division of Thomson Canada Limited, 1992

Singh, Rina, *A Forest of Stories: Magical Tree Tales from Around the World,* illustrated by Helen Cann, Cambridge, MA, USA, Barefoot Books, 2003

Anthropology & Sociology

Blacker, Carmen, *The Catalpa Bow,* Richmond, UK, Japan Library, Imprint of Curzon Press Ltd, 1999, pp. 1-2, e-book

Campbell, Joseph, *The Masks of God: Primitive Mythology,* New York, Penguin Books, Arcana, 1991

Coder, Kim D., *Cultural Aspects of Trees: Traditions and Myths,* pdf publication, Warnell School of Forest Resources, University of Georgia, November 1996, http://warnell.forestry.uga.edu/service/library/index.php3?docID=129&docHistory[]=2

Delaney, Frank, *The Celts,* London, BBC Publications, Hodder and Stoughton, 1986

Eliade, Mircea, *Shamanism: Archaic techniques of ecstasy,* London, UK, Penguin Books, Arcana, 1989

Frazer, J.G., *The Golden Bough: A Study in Magic and Religion,* (Abridged Edition), London, The MacMillan Press Ltd., 1978 (orig. publ. 1922)

Jans, Nick, *The Grizzly Maze: Timothy Treadwell's Fatal Obsession with Alaskan Bears,* New York, Plume, Penguin Group, 2006

Krakauer, Jon, *Into the Wild,* New York, Anchor Books, A Division of Random House, 1997

Martin, Laura C., *The Folklore of Trees & Shrubs,* Illustrations by Muro Magellan, Chester, CT, USA, The Globe Pequot Press, 1992

Rival, Laura, ed., *The Social Life of Trees: Anthropological Perspectives on Tree Symbolism,* Oxford, UK, Berg, an imprint of Oxford International Publishers Ltd., 1998

Rupp, Rebecca, *Red Oaks & Black Birches: The Science and Lore of Trees,* Pownal, VT, USA, A Garden Way Publishing Book, Storey Communications, Inc., 1990

Samuels, Gayle Brandow, *Enduring Roots: Encounters with Trees, History and the American Landscape,* London, Rutgers University Press, 1999

Vaillant, John, *The Golden Spruce: A True Story of Myth, Madness and Greed,* Toronto, Vintage Canada, Random House, 2005

Botany & Tree Guides

Arno, Jon, *Trees: An Explore Your World Handbook,* New York, Discovery Books, Random House, 2000

Beresford-Kroeger, Diana, *Arboretum America: A Philosophy of the Forest,* Ann Arbor, MI, USA, The University of Michigan Press, 2006

Blouin, Glen, *An Eclectic Guide to Trees East of the Rockies,* Toronto, Boston Mills Press, an affiliate of Stoddard Publishing Co. Limited, 2001

Brockman, C. Frank, *Trees of North America: A Guide to Field Identification,* illustrated by Rebecca Merrilees, Racine, WI, USA, Golden Press New York, Western Publishing Company, Inc., 1979

Culross Peattie, Donald, *A Natural History of North American Trees,* Illustrated by Paul Landacre, New York, Houghton Mifflin Company, 2007 (orig. publ. 1948)

Eastman, John, Illustrated by Amelia Hansen, *The Book of Forest and Thicket: Trees, Shrubs and Wildflowers of Eastern North America,* Harrisburg, PA, USA, Stackpole Books, 1992

———, *The Book of Swamp and Bog: Trees, Shrubs and Wildflowers of Eastern Freshwater Wetlands,* Mechanicsburg, PA, USA, Stackpole Books, 1995

———, *The Book of Field and Roadside: Open-Country Weeds, Trees and Wildflowers of Eastern North America,* Mechanicsburg, PA, USA, Stackpole Books, 2003

Hosie, R.C., *Native Trees of Canada* (Eighth Edition), Markham, ON, CA, Fitzhenry & Whiteside Limited in cooperation with the Canadian Forestry Service (Environment Canada), 1990

Johnson, Hugh, *Hugh Johnson's Encyclopedia of Trees,* New York, Portland House, a division of Dilithium Press, Ltd., Crown Publishers, Inc., 1990

Sutton, Anne and Myron Sutton, *The Audubon Society Nature Guides: Eastern Forests,* New York, Alfred A. Knopf, 1992

Wohlleben, Peter, *The Hidden Life of Trees, What they Feel, How They Communicate: Discoveries from a Secret World,* Vancouver, Translated by Jane Billinghurst, David Suzuki Institute, Greystone Books, 2015

Herbal Guides and Gardening

Bach, Edward, *The Twelve Healers and Other Remedies,* Essex, UK, The C. W. Daniel Company Ltd., 1999 (orig. publ. 1933)

Kloss, Jethro, *The Original Back to Eden,* New York, Benedict Lust Publications, NY, 1971

Lust, John, *The Herb Book,* Bantam Books, Benedict Lust Publications, New York, 1980

Rätsch, Christian, *The Dictionary of Sacred and Magical Plants,* Translated by John Baker, ABC-CLIO, Santa Barbara, CA, USA, 1992

Tallamy, Douglas W., *Bringing Nature Home: How You Can Sustain Wildlife with Native Plants,* Portland, OR, USA, Timber Press, Inc., 2007

Websites Cited within Book

A Note on Citations

I have taken the liberty of eliminating some citations from Wikipedia and other sources in this book, as the information taken from them are common knowledge to be found in various other places, such as scientific or folkloric studies. The chapter to which citation refers is noted in brackets in front of the reference.

(Ivy) Hymns and Carols of Christmas ("Ivy, Chief of Trees, It Is", Hymns and Carols of Christmas, (cited March 2019) https://www.hymnsandcarolsofchristmas.com/Hymns_and_Carols/ivy_chief_of_trees_it_is.htm

(Birch) Museum of Archeology South Tyrol, "The Iceman's Equipment", Museum of Archeology South Tyrol, (last cited July 13, 2020) https://www.iceman.it/en/equipment/

(Locust) Wood Database: Fluorescence: A Secret Weapon in Wood Indentification by Eric Meier, The Wood Database, (last cited May, 2019), https://www.wood-database.com/wood-articles/fluorescence-a-secret-weapon-in-wood-identification

(Locust) Wood Magazine: "Black Locust", Wood Magazine.com, (cited July 27, 2006) https://www.woodmagazine.com/materials-guide/lumber/wood-species-1/black-locust

(Sycamore) BBC News: *The Disease killing Europe's plane trees*, Gerry Haddon & Rob Hugh-Jones, October 19, 2011, (cited April 11, 2015) https://www.bbc.com/news/magazine-15305048

(Hemlock) Common Dreams: Robert Shetterly, *Courage, Commonsense, and the World Before Us: Some Thoughts for High School Seniors,* Address given at George Stevens Academy in Blue Hill, Maine, June 14th, 2009, from Common Dreams website, (posted June 17, 2009, Article cited June 20, 2009) https://www.commondreams.org/views/2009/06/17/courage-commonsense-and-world-us

(Gingko) Wood Magazine: "Ginkgo: the Tree That Lived With Dinosaurs", Wood Species Guide from Wood Magazine, (cited October 7, 2006), https://www.woodmagazine.com/materials-guide/lumber/wood-species-2/ginkgo

(Gingko) Classical Chinese Medicine "Gingko: Cultural Background and Medicinal Usage in China" by Subhuti Dharmandanda and Heiner Fruehof, Classical Chinese Medicine, (cited April 17, 2015), https://classicalchinesemedicine.org/ginkgo-cultural-background-and-medicinal-usage-in-china/

(Elder) In the Garden of Paghat the Rat Girl: "Myths and Legends of the Holly Tree", In the Garden of Paghat The Rat Girl, owner: Paghat the Ratgirl, (cited September 29, 2006) http://www.paghat.com/hollymythology.html

_____, "Myths and Legends of Black Elderberry", In the Garden of Paghat The Rat Girl, (cited September 29, 2006), http://www.paghat.com/elderberrymyths.html

Other Websites and Online Articles

Manning, Richard, "The Oil We Eat: Following the Food Chain Back to Iraq". Harpers Magazine, February 2004, Via Resilience.org: https://www.resilience.org/stories/2004-05-23/oil-we-eat-following-food-chain-back-iraq/

About the Author

The Author, Kay Broome, grew up on a farm in Southern Ontario. She has lived in Toronto most of her life as well as some years in Winnipeg and Vancouver. This is her first book. For queries, the author may be reached at the following website:

www.talkingforestrunes.com